Brother Men Who Fly

Brother Men Who Fly

A World War II Gunner's Personal Quest

– by –

Benedict Yedlin
With
Alexander M. Jeffers

Publisher:
Liberator Crew Productions
1000 Herrontown Road
Princeton, New Jersey 08540-2830

ISBN 0–9675333–1–7

For the members of my crew, who flew combat missions on *The Buzzer* during the spring and summer of 1944.

Pilot	Norman C. "Buck" Rogers
Co-Pilot	Bobbie Bennett*
Bombardier	George W. "Baldy" Hinds, Jr.
Navigator	James E. "Shorty" Carlson*
Engineer/Top Turret	Phillip L. Rizan*
Radio Operator/Waist Gun	Rudy (NMI) Acosta
Nose Turret	Robert M. Simons
Waist Gun	Dean A. Girton*
Tail Turret	Jack M. Cox

*deceased

To the best of my knowledge this book reflects the latest information available to me as of March 2002.

Benedict Yedlin

Dedication

On total reflection, I am struck by the paradox of the situation represented here. Whereas we had lost far too many fine men flying in combat operations, here is a case where we had lost sixteen kindred souls, most of whom had also flown combat missions, and some of whom had successfully completed tours of duty, in a circumstance where they were only at risk due to the hazards of flight compounded by the fickle effects of weather. They were far from the threat of enemy fighters, flak or formation flying and long missions over hostile territory. But, I am convinced that *The Buzzer* and its occupants, just like all of the other casualties, were certainly true heroes, lost in a wartime theater of operations where they would not have been except for the conflict, making the ultimate sacrifice for their country and freedom.

The fate of those that we lost could have befallen any of us, but as it happened, fate chose other of our comrades. It is understandable in these circumstances to wonder "why them and not me." It is easy to think "there but for the grace . . ." So this accounting is a labor-of-love done with humility as a tribute to the unfortunate sixteen and all others that we lost. It is something that simply has to be recorded for posterity.

Harold A. Strack
Brig. General, USAF (Ret.)

Crew and Passengers of *The Buzzer* on December 9, 1944

1st Lt. Ellis Arieff

1st Lt. Francis G. Baldwin, Jr.

T/Sgt. Ralph G. Ballou

2nd Lt. John T. Boswell

1st Lt. Joseph Brehun

2nd Lt. Julian L. Caldwell

1st Lt. Fowler C. Doyle

S/Sgt. Alex Eckerling

T/Sgt. Donald A. Erickson

S/Sgt. Albert Ganim

T/Sgt. Joe L. Gettys, Jr.

1st Lt. Roy L. Groeger

2nd Lt. Albert E. Marple

1st Lt. William G. Stevens

S/Sgt. Manuel Suarez

Pfc. Paul F. Watson

"The Buzzer" B-24H-10, s/n 41-29307

Crashed 12/09/44 MACR 10576

CREW	RANK	ASN	POSITION	BURIED	CREW AFFILIATION	MISSION
Caldwell, Julian L.	2nd Lt.	0-674556	Pilot	Lodge, SC—private	Caldwell	Ferry flight crew
Boswell, John T.	2nd Lt.	0-714632	Co-Pilot	Jefferson Barracks National Cemetery	Caldwell	Ferry flight crew
Marple, Albert E.	2nd Lt.	0-2061112	Navigator	Sicily, Rome Military Cemetery	Caldwell	Ferry flight crew
Suarez, Manuel (NMI)	S/Sgt.	32886654	Flight Engineer	Long Island National Cemetery	Caldwell	Ferry flight crew
Ganim, Albert (NMI)	S/Sgt.	15119342	Radio Operator	Jefferson Barracks National Cemetery	Caldwell	Ferry flight crew
Stevens, William G.	1st Lt.	0-672706	Pilot	Jefferson Barracks National Cemetery	Stevens	instructor pilot ?
Baldwin, Francis G., Jr	1st Lt.	0-828910	Co-Pilot	Sicily, Rome Military Cemetery	Charnes	Gift for son, born 11/30/44
Arieff, Ellis (NMI)	1st Lt.	0-560560	Bombardier	Philadelphia, PA—private	Mealey (O'Malley)	Flying time?
Watson, Paul F.	Pfc.	39274212	Headquarters	Jefferson Barracks National Cemetery	None – adm.	Ride
Davie, Fowler C.	1st Lt.	0-711158	Co-Pilot	Lexington, KY—private	Bache	Home
Brehun, Joseph (NMI)	1st Lt.	0-718229	Navigator	Jefferson Barracks National Cemetery	Aldrich	Home
Groeger, Roy L.	1st Lt.	0-703408	Bombardier	Jefferson Barracks National Cemetery	Underwood	Home
Erickson, Donald A.	T/Sgt.	39408284	Flight Engineer	Sicily, Rome Military Cemetery	Bache	Home
Gettys, Joe L., Jr.	T/Sgt.	17096828	Radio Operator	Jefferson Barracks National Cemetery	Bache	Home
Ballou, Ralph G.	T/Sgt.	17067509	Nose Gunner	Cedar Rapids, IA—private	Bache	Home
Esterling, Alex (NMI)	S/Sgt.	32622991	Waist Gunner	Jefferson Barracks National Cemetery	Bache	Home

About The Author

Benedict Yedlin was born in Brooklyn and attended Abraham Lincoln High School and Brooklyn College. When the U.S. entered World War II, he left college to join the Army Corps of Engineers and served as a photographic mapping technician before transferring to the Army Air Corps. Trained as a gunner and stationed in southern Italy, he flew most of his 50 combat missions in a B-24 named *The Buzzer.*

After the war he completed his college degree, married, and joined his father's business, building single family houses in New Jersey. Charles, the youngest of his children, joined him in the business and expanded into a full fledged building, development, general contracting and property management company called The Yedlin Company, located in Princeton, New Jersey. In the 1990s, Mr. Yedlin turned over its operation to Charles, and devoted his time to other interests, memoir writing, video production, traveling and bicycling.

He is a member of the 449th Bomb Group Association, the 15th Air Force Association, the International B-24 Liberator Club. In addition, he organized the Princeton area office of Cancer Care and serves on its board. He produced a video, *B-24 Bomber Crew,* about his crew's reminiscences of their experiences in World War II. This was broadcast on The History Channel and New Jersey Network.

In addition to his son, Ben has two daughters, Jane Yedlin of Cranston, Rhode Island and Nancy Yedlin of New Haven, Connecticut. Jane is the author of several English as a Second Language textbooks and a doctoral candidate in language and literacy at Harvard Graduate School of Education. Nancy holds a Masters degree in Public Health from Yale University and is currently an independent consultant. Ben has six grandchildren. His second wife of 21 years, Nancy M. Yedlin, died in 1989.

About The Writer

Alexander M. Jeffers has worked in journalism and public relations. He has written feature stories for local newspapers in Britain and America. Among these was a long article based on a tour of the Commonwealth War Graves Commission headquarters. His late father was wounded in late 1944, while serving in reconnaissance in the Netherlands with Britain's 52nd (Lowland) Division.

Mr. Jeffers has a B.A. in English from England's Lancaster University, and a J.D. from the State University of New York at Buffalo. A spec "Murphy Brown" episode won him selection to Martha Greenhouse's TIP-East television writing workshop. He is currently writing an unserious guide to newspapers, law and politics, and a screenplay. He lives in Rocky Hill, New Jersey, with his wife and daughter.

Contents

Preface

It was a particularly sad twist in war's fortunes when *The Buzzer*, a B-24 Liberator bomber, crashed in December 1944. All sixteen men aboard lost their lives. Most of them had survived aerial combat over Hitler's Europe. Seven had completed their fifty-mission tours and were headed home. They died on what should have been a ninety-minute passenger flight, far from enemy action, on a plane that had flown dozens of combat missions without a turn-back for mechanical problems. I had flown many of my missions on that same plane.

This book is the story of those men, and of my own training and combat experience on *The Buzzer* and other planes. I did not know the sixteen men, but we were from the same base and the same unit. We had many of the same experiences in joining the forces, going through training, travelling overseas, and entering combat. This is also, very much, the story of these men's backgrounds, friends, and above all, families.

In thanking people who made this book possible, I must give those families special recognition. Fifty years after the crash, I managed to contact families of fifteen of the sixteen men. After fifty years, the memories they shared with me still carried a terrible emotional weight. I cannot thank them enough for the letters, memorabilia, official documents, and hospitality they offered me.

I began research on *The Buzzer* crash in 1992. I undertook the project with the purpose of producing a book that would be a tribute to the men who perished and to their families, deceased and still living.

It was a sad act of fate that a combat veteran aircraft would end its days at the bottom of a mountain ravine, and that sixteen men would lose their lives in such a tragic manner. When I visited the Sicily-Rome U.S. Military Cemetery where three of the men in this book are buried, I was struck by the thousands of crosses and Stars of David, each bearing the name, rank, unit, home state and date of death of an American who died in the Mediterranean Theater of war. Members of our crew survived the war. We were the fortunate ones.

Acknowledgments

Specifically, I wish to thank:

Sylvia Fisher, Lt. Ellis Arieff's widow, and his cousin, Herbert Weinman;
Francis and Susan Baldwin, son and daughter-in-law of Lt. Francis G. Baldwin, as well as Polly Dupree and Louise Walker, friends of the family, William Baldwin Jr., his nephew, and Alvin E. Charnes, his pilot.
Earl O. Ballou, brother of T/Sgt.Ralph G. Ballou, his sister, Audrey Morehead, and his widow, Lorraine Fowler;
Rita Shander and Marie Brehun-Wagner, sisters of Lt. Joseph Brehun, and Francis Brehun, his brother;
May C. Reid, sister of Lt. Julian Caldwell, and his brother, Mendel Caldwell;
David and Betty Doyle, brother and sister-in-law of Lt. Fowler C. Doyle, his late wife, Mitchell Stamper, and Larry David Doyle, his son;
Arnie Eckerling, cousin of S/Sgt. Alex Eckerling;
Evelyn Dunlop, sister of T/Sgt. Donald A. Erickson;
George Ganim, brother of S/Sgt. Albert Ganim;
Gene Gettys, brother of T/Sgt. Joe L. Gettys Jr.;
Ralph G. Tamm, high school classmate of Lt. Roy L. Groeger; Sam Taylor, crewmate;
Bernice G. Quamme, sister of Lt. Albert E. Marple;
Viola Madden, sister of Lt. William G. Stevens;
Frank Suarez, brother of S/Sgt. Manuel Suarez, and Frank Suarez Jr., his nephew.

William Watson, brother of Pfc. Paul F. Watson; and William Zartman, an armorer in the 719th Squadron.

I am grateful to Linda Abrams, who located Frank Suarez and Bernice Quamme, and to Karen Alderson, who found members of the Ballou, Baldwin and Stevens families.

Dick Downey, secretary of the 449th Bomb Group Association and newsletter editor, was especially helpful in putting me in touch with members of the Group who might shed additional light on *The Buzzer,* its crew and passengers. They include Dick Asbury, Walter Hannah, Larry Hamblen, Phil Jensen, Preston Kiel, Michael O'Malley, Tom Skinas, Tom Sommers and the late John Vest, all former members of 719th Squadron who were at Grottaglie at the time. They provided helpful information, as did Norman "Buck" Rogers, Bob Simons and Rudy Acosta and Jack Cox of my own crew, and Bart Peluso, our ground crew chief.

Barbara Johnson provided the first draft of *The Lost Bomber: A WWII Gunner's Personal Quest* known as "a missing air crew report." She went through many loose leaf books of archival material related to the crash and the men who died. This was a monumental task.

Through their card-by-card search of names and burial sites of the 449th Bomb Group members who had been killed, the Graves Registration Department and the Veterans Administration provided one of the first clues as to what might have happened to *The Buzzer.* I am grateful to former New Jersey Senators Bill Bradley and Frank Lautenberg for intervening to expedite the release of information I was seeking from official sources. I also owe thanks to former Senator and Secretary of the Treasury—and fellow 449th veteran-Lloyd Bentsen.

Thanks also to Essie Roberts of the Archives Branch, Department of the Air Force, Air Force Historical Research Agency at Maxwell Air Force Base, Alabama for microfilmed records of official documents related to missions flown by the 449th in 1944, and to the American Battle Monuments Commission for grave location of Donald A.

Erickson, Albert E. Marple and Franklin G. Baldwin, Jr. in the Sicily-Rome American Cemetery and Memorial.

For information on Amelia Rufolo Clemente, the woman who notified the authorities after *The Buzzer* was found, I appreciate the help given me by Judge Nicholas Clemente and the late Angelina Sgarrino Setaro, her cousins in New York City.

I owe special thanks to Josy Giaquinto for her translation and interpretation of correspondence and telephone calls to and from Italy and her continuing involvement and contributions to my project. I am also grateful to Doina Popescu who translated and interpreted for me on four visits to Ploesti, Romania, and also served in that capacity on my second trip to Italy in October, 1996.

Roy Grisham did extensive and tedious copy editing and produced the index.

My friends, Paula and William McGuire, gave valuable advice during the initial stage of this project. William's late brother, Robert, was founder of the International B-24 Liberator Club. He was a Navy photographer on a Navy B-24.

Susan Mauro's word processing skills and her ability to decipher my handwritten letters were equally invaluable, as well as her patience and availability.

Marie Landolfi, who is employed in Yedlin Company's office in Princeton, deserves special mention for her painstaking work making editorial corrections in the manuscript.

Mildred Forrell and Vivian Greenberg were my sounding boards on many issues relating to the investigation.

My daughter, Jane Yedlin, gave a great deal of time and thought to my project, not withstanding her own heavy schedule as a doctoral Candidate at Harvard. Jane was a source of encouragement and gave helpful advice on writing. Thanks also to my daughter, Nancy, and son, Charlie, for their time-consuming support and advice during my recent illness.

I wish to acknowledge the role of my very dear friend Antonia Flint, who accompanied me on my first visit to Italy in May, 1996, and shared with me the emotion of visiting the towns of Oliveto Citra and Senerchia where *The Buzzer* crashed, meeting residents who had first or second-hand knowledge of the crash, and seeing for the first time parts of the airplane which had been retrieved and used in new ways on farms in the area. It was Toni's enthusiasm that inspired me to continue my work. She was from the very beginning a staunch companion.

In Italy, many people in Salerno and Avellino provinces assisted me as translators, interpreters, guides, hosts and sources of information who were willing to be interviewed. They are too numerous to list here, but their contributions helped fill in missing details of the story. Still, I must single out at this time the help I received from the Acquaviva family of Oliveto Citra.

B-24 Liberator experts Allan Blue and Roger Criplever offered their knowledge generously. So did Hal Strack, on issues of navigation and life in Grottaglie.

The volumes of the *History of the 449th Bomb Group,* by Damon Turner and members of the 449th Bomb Group Association (449th Bomb Group Association and Norfield Publishing, of Panama City, Florida) were a great help to me in writing this story. Books 1 and 2, *Tucson to Grottaglie* and *And This Is Our Story* were published in 1985, as one volume. Book 3, *Grottaglie, and Home* was published in 1989, and Book 4, *Maximum Effort,* in 2000.

D. William Sheperd, who worked with Richard Downey and others compiling and editing those volumes, has also published *Of Men and Wings: The First 100 Missions of the 449th Bombardment Group (January 1944 - July 1944)* (1996, Norfield Publishing, Panama City, Florida), based on the wartime diary of Charles A. Sheperd of the 718th Squadron.

I also found these volumes useful: *Aerial Gunners: The Unknown Aces of World War II,* by Charles A. Watry and Duane L. Hall; California Aero Press, Carlsbad, CA, 1986; *The Army Air Forces in World War II,* Vol. III, by W.F. Craven and J.L. Cate; University of Chicago Press, Chicago, IL, 1951; *The B-24 Liberator,* by Allan G. Blue; Charles Scribner's Sons, New York, NY; *Goodbye Liberty Belle: A Son's Search for His Father's War,* J.I. Merritt; Wright State University Press, 1994; *Into the Guns of Ploesti,* by Leroy W. Newby; Motorbooks International, Osceola, WI, 1991; *Log of the Liberators,* by Steve Birdsall; Doubleday and Company, Inc., Garden City, NY, 1973; *The Official Guide to the Army Air Forces,* Pocket Books, New York, 1944; *Ploesti Raiders,* by Myles O'Neill; Adams Press, Chicago, IL, 1993; *Randall Jarrell Selected Poems,* Edited by William H. Pritchard; The Noonday Press, 1991; *The Soldier Consolidated B-24 Liberator,* by Paul Perkins and Michelle Crean; Howell Press, Charlottesville, VA, 1994; and *Wings of Morning,* by Thomas Childers; Addison-Wesley Publishing Company, 1995.

December 9, 1944

When you say that the Second World War occurred in the first half of the twentieth century, it sounds like that was a long time ago. But just a few years ago, Mrs. Lorraine Fowler was on a tour of Italy. She realized she was not far from where her late husband's B-24 had crashed in 1944. She told the tour operator, and the bus made a short detour to the mountain village of Oliveto Citra, in the province of Salerno. Even though she knew her husband, Ralph Ballou, was buried back here in the States, she recalls, "I kept looking at the faces of the people in the town. I kept thinking that somehow all the news we got might have been a mistake, that I might see him."

The same thing happened to Joseph Brehun's sister, Rita. May Caldwell once briefly thought her brother Julian had appeared in her church one Sunday morning, decades after the war.

For these women, and many people like them, myself included, the war was not long ago at all.

My name is Benedict Yedlin. I flew fifty missions over Europe in B-24 bombers during World War II. I was a ball-turret gunner. The ball turret was suspended on the underside of the plane, between the bomb bay and the waist. I actually flew thirty-six sorties, or bombing flights. A number of them were considered hazardous enough to count double toward my required fifty missions.

My unit was the 719th Squadron, 449th Bomb Group, 47th Wing of the Fifteenth Air Force of the U.S. Army Air

Forces. We were based at a former Axis airfield at Grottaglie, near Taranto in southern Italy.

Most of my missions were flown in one plane, a B-24 "H" model, serial number 41-29307, christened *The Buzzer.* Many years after the war, I learned that my old plane, which had been credited with seventy-seven combat missions without one turn back for mechanical problems, had crashed on a non-combat, passenger flight in Italy late in 1944, several months after I had finished my missions and come back to the U.S.

All the crew and passengers, sixteen men, including fifteen combat veterans and seven who had survived their fifty-mission tours, were killed. Those seven were on their way to Naples to board a ship back to the States, in hopes of spending the Christmas holidays at home. One survived the crash by several days but died before any help reached him.

One of the passengers had a five-day-old son. Another had a several-months-old child he would never see. All had families. One of those families had lost a son in Germany just the week before. None of the sixteen got to hear about VE Day, or VJ Day, or the first moon landing, or the Genome Project. They missed the construction of the Berlin Wall, and its destruction. They missed grandchildren. These were young men, as young as I was; most of them missed most of their twenties.

The crew of *The Buzzer* that day consisted of 2nd Lt. Julian L. Caldwell, pilot, from Lodge, South Carolina; 2nd Lt. John J. Boswell, co-pilot, from Cleveland, Ohio; 2nd Lt. Albert E. Marple, navigator, from Burien, Washington; S/Sgt. Manuel Suarez, flight engineer, from New York City; and S/Sgt. Albert Ganim, radioman, from Cincinnati.

The passengers were 1st Lt. William G. Stevens, from Chicago; 1st Lt. Francis G. Baldwin, from Cincinnati; 1st Lt. Ellis Arieff, from Philadelphia; Pfc. Paul F. Watson, from Los Angeles; 1st Lt. Fowler C. Doyle, from Lexington, Kentucky; 1st Lt. Joseph Brehun, from New Salem, Pennsylvania; 1st Lt. Roy L. Groeger, from Chicago; T/Sgt. Donald A. Erickson, from Turlock, California; T/Sgt. Joe L. Gettys, from Harlan,

Iowa; T/Sgt. Ralph G. Ballou, from Cedar Rapids, Iowa; and S/Sgt. Alex H. Eckerling, from Bronx, New York.

✈ ✈ ✈ ✈ ✈

Flying our bombers hundreds of miles over enemy-held territory, against fighters and flak, was extremely hazardous. More men finished their missions and went home than were killed, wounded or captured, but casualty rates were high. To finish your missions was a goal that could seem impossibly far away. There were days like the 449th's mission on May 12, 1944, to bomb Porto San Stefano, when forty-two planes from the 449th got over the target, and none were lost. But there were days like April 4th, when seven out of twenty-eight 449th planes went down. As you can imagine, men made all sorts of calculations about loss rates and numbers of missions they had to fly.

The twenty-five-mission tour was established in 1943 when loss rates among the Eighth Air Force operating out of England ran at about four percent. When the Fifteenth Air Force started bombing targets in Germany, Austria, Italy, and Romania, loss rates were lower, so tours were upped to 50 missions. Then it turned out that some missions were a lot more dangerous than others, like Vienna, or Ploesti, where I went six times. Men who flew these higher-loss missions were given double credit.

Of the seven fifty-mission men who died on *The Buzzer*, five were from one crew, that of 1st Lt. William Bache. One was from 1st Lt. Ray Aldrich's crew, and one was from 1st Lt. Robert Underwood's. Bache, who lost so many crew members in the crash was from New Orleans, where he had worked on the levees. He had stayed behind on the day of the flight to complete paperwork involved in his promotion to captain.

The Buzzer was retired from combat, and its guns were removed. It was used as a ferry plane and an "air discipline plane," helping guide bombers into formation after takeoff and intercepting them on return to assist as necessary in getting back to the base. Norman "Pop" Blomgren, a 719th pilot and Hal Strack often flew "air discipline" missions, many times in *The Buzzer,* other B-24's and even a B-25. Hal flew as copilot, even though he was a navigator and it really was not legal for him to do so.

On the day of the crash, Aldrich had taken off on a bombing mission, but it was scratched by bad weather to the north. He urged Caldwell, pilot of *The Buzzer,* and his own navigator, Joseph Brehun, not to fly. First Lt. John Vest, Aldrich's co-pilot and a "weather buff" had the same advice.

Because of the predicted bad weather, *The Buzzer* was supposed to avoid the direct route to Pomigliano airfield, near Naples, and instead take a safer, longer route. This alternate route would have taken *The Buzzer* to the southwest, through a break in the Apennines at the Cassano Pass, to the west coast of Italy, then up the coast to the Naples area. The direct route, which passed over mountainous territory, was a distance of about 146 miles, 64 miles shorter than the safer alternative route.

At 11:12 AM, on Saturday, December 9, 1944, *The Buzzer* took off.

At 6:22 PM, Pomigliano asked Grottaglie for the plane's whereabouts.

At 8:05, Grottaglie sent a correction to *The Buzzer's* serial number, which had not been correctly reported in its departure message.

Just after midnight on December 10, Grottaglie asked Pomigliano if there was any news about *The Buzzer.* There was none. The plane was reported missing. Four inches of snow fell on southern Italy that night. At first, some fellow airmen at Grottaglie thought the plane had put down somewhere near Naples until the storm lifted. News of the "Missing" report hit many fellow flyers hard. On Friday night, there had been a party in the Officer's Club for the men returning home.

Sunday morning brought more bad weather, but planes took off from Grottaglie to search for the missing

Liberator. Aldrich went up twice, and Bache flew searches for three days.

At 6:35 on Sunday evening, Regional Flying Control at Pomigliano announced that it had made a wide sweep of coastal areas where the plane might have landed or crashed. It had avoided an overland search because of the bad weather. On Monday, six B-24s from Grottaglie searched over a wide area. Two of them flew along the direct route. One airman thought he saw a plane in a deep ravine, but could not find it again because of the snow.

The weather on Tuesday, Wednesday and Thursday continued to be adverse. The Regional Flight Control at Pomigliano announced no results from further searches and called off its flights. On Friday, December 15th, a week after the disappearance of *The Buzzer* and, as the bad weather continued, a Grottaglie-based B-24 searched for an additional three hours.

Major Jonathan Knox, of the Grottaglie-based 449th Bomb Group, said that day: "Further search of the area north of the 40th Parallel will be conducted on the first day that weather permits. The search will not be abandoned by the Group until complete coverage of the area has been made."

On December 16th, the names of those aboard were sent from the 449th headquarters to the commander of the 47th Wing. The names of the sixteen missing men were sent to Fifteenth Air Force headquarters on December 21st and to the headquarters of the Army Air Force on December 30th. Then the telegrams went out to the next of kin.

✈ ✈ ✈ ✈ ✈

Although my time at Grottaglie overlapped with the tours of some of the men who died on *The Buzzer*, I hadn't known any of them. Still, I knew their military experiences, which, from training to base life to missions, had been very much like mine. We had not only been at the same base, but had been on some of the same missions in different planes, bombing the same targets.

For some reason, their luck had been much worse. I wanted to find out, if I could, why. I had a strong feeling of "There but for the grace . . ."

✈ ✈ ✈ ✈ ✈

The MACR, or Missing Air Crew Report 10572, dated 12 December 1944, notes the takeoff time, names of crew and passengers, and ranks, serial numbers, position, and next of kin; mother, father, wife and home address.

The first volume of the history of the 449th Bomb Group, *And This Is Our Story, Tucson to Grottaglie,* by S-2 Officer Damon Turner, reported the common story that *The Buzzer* was lost in the Bay of Naples. Apparently some airplane wreckage caught by a fishing net in the 1970s was thought to be from my old plane (later volumes have updated the facts).

Then, an article by unit historian Richard Downey in the winter 1992 edition of the 449th newsletter *Late Pass* ("Late Pass" was the Grottaglie control tower call sign) was illustrated with a group burial marker in the Jefferson Barracks National Cemetery at St. Louis listing the names of eight men who died on *The Buzzer:* Boswell, Brehun, Eckerling, Ganim, Gettys, Groeger, Stevens and Watson. There was also a listing for Manuel Suarez, buried at Long Island National Cemetery, Farmingdale, New York.

I telephoned Jefferson National Barracks Cemetery and asked if the men's remains were actually interred there, or if this was a memorial grave marker. The man I reached checked his records and told me the men's remains were there.

I was shocked. Supposedly, *The Buzzer* had crashed into the sea. I checked with the Kirtland AFB archive of noncombat Air Force accidents, which holds more than 300,000 reports, and there was nothing on *The Buzzer.* Obviously I had some work to do.

War Comes To New Jersey

Who am I, and how did I get involved in this - traveling the country to meet people who'd lost a loved one many years before? How did I go from college to Italy, from helping bomb Romania in 1944, to helping that country's young children in the 1990s?

I was born in Brooklyn in 1922. My family - mother, father, sister, and I lived in a two-story, two-family house in the Seagate section of Coney Island. I went to school there - Public School 188, Boody Junior High, and Abraham Lincoln High School. I graduated from Lincoln on January 28, 1939. I went to Brooklyn College and majored in geology.

In September of that year, when war broke out in Europe, President Roosevelt appealed to the Axis and the Allies to declare there would be no bombing of civilian targets.

I enlisted in the U.S. Army on September 15, 1942, a week before my twentieth birthday. I was a college senior, one semester short of graduation. Our country had been in the three-year-old war for three seasons.

My father, Robert, was cited for bravery in the First World War. He was a litter-bearer in the 29th Division and was decorated for carrying wounded men under heavy fire. We never talked about our respective war experiences; I'm not sure why. But he did collect every newspaper article he could find about air combat action in my theater of war. My parents put a blue star in the window, indicating a son in the service.

7

Fords, New Jersey, where I then lived, was a community heavily involved in the war effort. The nearby Raritan Arsenal, where I had worked and where my mother worked, was operating around the clock, as were many nearby defense-related plants. The local newspaper, the weekly *Fords Beacon,* carried casualty lists from the Army, Navy, Marines, Coast Guard and Merchant Marine—killed, wounded, or missing.

There was a guy working at the Arsenal when I was there who walked with a limp from a wound he'd received at Pearl Harbor. He was very much treated as a returned hero, and many of us were in awe of him. The idea of coming back to civilian life a war hero was another incentive for young people like myself to join up.

My mother Sybil had been working in a hat shop in Perth Amboy. But, because she had a background in art, when she went to work at the Arsenal, she was assigned to "opaqueing"—blocking out portions of picture diagrams to focus attention on relevant detail. She may even have done the work for the illustrations in my .50-caliber machine-gun manual.

When I joined up, I had a strange feeling of relief. My life was now in the hands of the U.S. Army. From here on, there were few decisions for me to make. I enjoyed that feeling!

I was inducted at Fort Dix, New Jersey. My parents gave me a lift down there. It was the day the carrier U.S.S. *Wasp* was torpedoed by a Japanese submarine. Since I had been a geology major, it seemed right that I'd work on maps. I'd enjoyed that as a student; I collected maps; all maps were my hobby. Actually, I enlisted with the understanding and the supporting documents that I would be sent to Fort Belvoir, Virginia, where the Corps of Engineers was based.

As I hoped, after a short stay at Fort Dix, I was shipped to Fort Belvoir, about eighteen miles from Washington, D.C., to join the Co-B 30th Engineer Battalion (TOPO).

Since I was joining a special engineers outfit, I didn't have to go through a lot of the arduous boot camp basic training you see in the movies—obstacle courses and so on.

But there was drill, and there were loud 4 a.m. wake-ups. There was also policing—removal of cigarette butts, gum wrappers, and all other trash from a given area. The noncoms would shout "I want to see only assholes and elbows!' Everybody had to do this at some point. It wasn't a punishment; sometimes it just had to be done.

Pretty quickly, things went wrong with my work. I turned out to have a vision problem that made me unable to "fuse the dots" on the aerial photographs projected by the multiplex machine, a skill needed to make contour maps from the photos. This was a skill I could not do without in my chosen Army career.

I started getting all kinds of menial jobs. I hadn't joined up for that. Of course, even at the best of times, base life involved a lot of mopping and policing and cleaning, but now I had no prospect of following a real career in the military. I learned somehow that the only way out of this unit was a transfer to aerial gunnery or the paratroops.

Gunnery sounded more glamorous than being a paratrooper, so I put in a request. I never really considered the possibility that if I'd just settled for what I was doing around the base, I might have seen out the war bored, but far from any potentially lethal hostilities. My father was in the Great War, I was going to be in this one—so it wasn't a question.

While I awaited the outcome of my request for a transfer, I was put on "detached" service and helped the stoker in the barracks. I was second in command of feeding fuel to the coal-fired boiler. Thus began several depressing weeks of listening to the main fireman read me his girlfriend's erotic letters.

Some of the letters were pretty explicit. Because he wasn't much with words, he asked me to reply to them. I was such a nice kid that I'm sure I didn't reply exactly in kind. I never figured out how any female could find the fireman interesting.

Finally, I got my transfer to aerial gunnery school at Tyndall Field, near Panama City in the Florida Panhandle. I was in the Army Air Corps.

It was a busy place, training a group of Free French air cadets as well as Americans. Most of my fellow gunners were aviation buffs, including a lot of washed- out flying cadets. My class yearbook from gunnery training even had "A Gunner's Vow," an official poem that started out: "I wished to be a pilot, / and you along with me, / But if we all were pilots, / Where would the Air Force be?" My T-5 insignia, Technician Fifth Grade - equivalent to a corporal - gained in the Engineers was unusual, so I was nicknamed "T-5."

Our instructors were fliers who might have had a lot of flying experience but didn't necessarily have combat experience. I think the gunner training was improvised, in a way - no one started out knowing how to train us. But I think the training we got was good.

I turned out to be pretty handy with a rifle and a shotgun. We did some skeet shooting and riding around in a truck shooting at targets. We trained in a chamber where enemy fighters were projected on a wall. We studied a surprisingly complex set of rules for getting enemy fighters in our sights.

I learned, like everyone else, to take apart and reassemble a machine gun blindfolded. I wrote home about it, and the version that reached our street through my grandmother had me field-stripping and rebuilding the whole airplane blindfolded.

Dealing with the gun was work enough. The .50 calibre guns on our bombers could shoot eight hundred rounds a minute. The bullets left the barrel at more than 2,900 feet per second, and could penetrate even the engine of an attacking fighter. The guns weighed sixty-five pounds, and the waist gunners on bombers had to manhandle theirs against the slipstream of an open waist window.

I had one singularly gratifying experience while I was at Tyndall. I was on a pass and went into nearby Dothan, Alabama and stopped at a diner. The waitress saw I was a lefty - a southpaw and served my coffee accordingly. Apart from my late wife, Nancy, that's about the only time that ever happened.

Ten Men And A Plane

The next stop was Salt Lake City, Utah. There I met the men I would fly with, across the Atlantic and into combat. As I recall, we enlisted men—the gunners, radioman and flight engineer all met on a railroad platform. Robert M. "Bob" Simons, still a good friend, was there with Jean, his wife. He had grown up on the South Side of Chicago, in an area that was then more rural small town than city neighborhood.

His father and uncles had been in the First World War, and, he later told me, he'd grown up with the idea that there'd be another war and that he would be in it.

We enlisted men pretty much all became friends, the officers—pilot, co-pilot, navigator, and bombardier—soon joined us.

Our pilot, Norman C. "Buck" Rogers, was a newspaper photographer from Belleville, a small city in Illinois. At the time, he seemed rigid and accordingly was not well liked by the crew. His father had been in the military, and was stationed at a nearby Army airfield in Illinois. He said his community was heavily German-American, but completely united in support-ing the U.S. against their ancestral homeland.

When the war broke out, Rogers told me later, his fa-ther had recently died, and he wanted to enlist, rather than be drafted, so his father wouldn't spin in his grave. Rogers also told me that he started out wanting to fly P-38 fight-ers, but he was told he couldn't fly B-24's because he was too small, or light, and his pride was piqued.

11

There were official weight limits for airmen—we were supposed to be between 105 and 200 pounds, but pilots were supposed to be at least 114 pounds. Flying a bomber really did require physical strength.

When he first learned to fly, Rogers said once, he was told by the instructor to learn to feel how the plane was flying. Their trainer had a tachometer and an altimeter, but no air speed indicator. He was told that's how Lindbergh learned to fly.

According to Rogers, he hurt his tailbone playing football during training and literally learned to "feel it" when the plane was skidding or not flying as smoothly as it should.

Co-pilot Bobbie C. Bennett, from Ohio, was a more easygoing fellow, who seemed more on the crew's side of things. George W. "Baldy" Hinds, bombardier, was a self-described womanizer from Texas. Our navigator was James E. "Shorty" Carlson, from a very small mining company town of about 800 in Minnesota.

He was a mechanic's helper, and had tried to enlist in the Marines, who rejected him for flat feet. He says it was ridiculous because his four friends all got into the Marines, and he walked further than any of them on hunting or fishing trips, but he was glad he didn't end up a Leatherneck.

The other enlisted men were Philip L. Rizan, Jack M. Cox, Dean A. Girton, and Rudy Acosta. Phil Rizan, our flight engineer, was another Texan, and waist gunner Dean Girton was another Ohio native. Jack Cox, who was to be our tail gunner, was from Kingsport, a city of about 13,000 in east Tennessee, but considered himself a city boy. He had always wanted to fly.

Rudy Acosta and I were the two NMI's, which is Army officialese for No Middle Initial. He was a Mexican from Los Angeles and had been at the Las Vegas Gunnery School. We hit it off from the start and have remained to this day close friends despite the distance of our homes. He's still "Cabron," Spanish for "buck" or "billygoat," and I'm still "Benny." Maybe it was big city backgrounds that formed the bond. More likely it's that we were both minority guys—Rudy a Mexican and I a Jew.

Rudy recalls that on the day he shipped out to Salt Lake City to meet the rest of us in his crew, he was awakened at 4:30 in the morning and told to get packed and get ready. It was Thanksgiving Day.

He was actually our third Texan, born in El Paso. His father worked for the Southern Pacific Railroad. He moved to Los Angeles when he was twelve. He remembers going barefoot to school, but not thinking it was a big deal. At times he and his brothers and sisters would be bundled up with coats and take the train to northern California to work as fruit pickers, for $1.90 a ton. Eventually he became a machinist.

He told me that he'd tried and tried to enlist in the Navy and other branches of the service, but wanted to avoid the Army. But he was told that once he'd registered, he had to wait until he was drafted.

As our radioman, Rudy would be stationed just back of the flight deck, near the navigator and top turret gunner. He was in charge of the first-aid equipment. He was also, of course, one of the waist gunners, along with Dean Girton.

I think Rudy and I were the only two guys in the crew who weren't would-be pilots or at least some kind of aviation bug. I remember once taking pictures of a plane that ditched off Coney Island, but that was about it.

Like other differences, this was easily overcome, and in general the friendships that formed as our group of ten grew into a crew were one of the real pluses of my Army experience.

There were others. I was to live for three years away from father, mother, sister, and grandparents; the Army became a kind of mother and father to me. My basic needs were taken care of. It was a secure environment - at least, until I started flying in bombers in training and combat.

Until I joined the Army, the farthest from home I had ventured was a trip to Washington, D.C. in my 1937 Chevy with some guys from college. In the Army, even before going overseas in March 1944, I'd been stationed in Virginia, Florida, Utah, and California.

I had Army buddies from almost every one of the 48 states, men who talked and thought differently and had different values from mine. But we trained side by side, shared barracks and mess halls.

I discovered in the Army that not everyone loved FDR as I did. I remember Bob Simons getting his *Chicago Tribune* delivered, and seeing bitter anti-Roosevelt cartoons in it. This was in the days when the paper was run by Colonel McCormick, the idiosyncratic isolationist and rabid hater of the New Deal and American involvement overseas.

The men on my crew seemed to work together as a unit despite our different backgrounds. In the Army, Rudy Acosta was very aware of being a Mexican-American pretty much on his own, and Jack Cox has said people sometimes judged him to be on the dumb side, despite his 132 I.Q., because they thought he talked "funny," being from Tennessee.

Within the crew, though, things worked. Rudy says he was so busy thinking of his Army time as an adventure that he wasn't conscious of who was of what ethnicity.

When I think of my crew and the unit we formed and what we went through and the things many of us still share, I can't help thinking of the men who died on *The Buzzer*. Five men from one crew who were flying the plane, seven men from another crew who had finished their missions, and four other men travelling for different reasons that day . . . it brings home yet again the extremities of fortune.

For a lot of us, Army life was, in some ways, an improvement on civilian life. When we were still training Stateside and got passes to leave base and go into town, Los Angeles or Pensacola or Salt Lake City, we were welcomed and treated as heroes even though none of us had done anything heroic so far. We could spend money; at that stage we were making a good $50 a month. To be part of the all-out national war effort was good for my self-esteem, and I sensed a growing confidence. For me, these were exciting and heady times. Later, the money got better. In early 1944, a staff sergeant made $96 a month, and a technical sergeant $114 a month, including flight pay. A first lieutenant made $2,000 a year, a colonel made $4,000, and generals, including four-star ones, made $8,000.

Our immediate task was air unit training, training as a crew. This stage was a ninety-day course, consisting of three overlapping phases. As the 1944 Army Air Forces Official Guide describes the phases, there was work on individual skills, learning teamwork, learning techniques and equipment, with the aid of films, technical manuals, posters, and practice models; then formation flying; then training in more battle-like conditions, including long-distance bombing missions, in formation, day or night. These flights could range pretty widely over the continental U.S.

The newly formed crew took a train ride, to Wendover Field, Utah. Most of our long-distance travel was by train; and, as you can imagine, they were crowded. We would try to sleep sitting up as the trains chugged along all night. I enjoyed it, though, at least during the daylight hours. I was seeing the country and it was a thrill.

This trip, however, didn't take us to a very promising destination. Wendover Field was right out on the famous Utah salt flats. It was not a great setting for a rich social life. Luckily, we weren't there long. We were supposed to be there for operations training but were shipped out instead. We were told the weather and visibility conditions were bad and too many planes were crashing. After the war I found out they moved us because the crews who were eventually to carry A-bombs were going to train there.

Then it was on to operational training at March Field, near Riverside, California. The base dated to 1918 and was one of the first Army airfields. Its alumni included big air war names like H.H. "Hap" Arnold, Commanding General of the Army Air Corps, Carl Spaatz, who commanded our air forces in Europe, and Ira Eaker, leader of the Allied Mediterranean theater air forces. The names didn't mean much to me at the time.

As we approached the siding, the train slowed, and some of us jumped off and grabbed ripe oranges off trees in the groves bordering the tracks. What an experience!

March Field was close enough to Los Angeles to hitch rides there. Rudy Acosta invited us all to his family home for dinner. I remember being very attracted to one of his sisters.

Operational training meant training as a crew. We were supposed already to have our separate skills; now we had to learn to use them as part of a team. I have heard that some crews cross-trained—gunners got some instruction on navigating, bombardiers learned to fly, and so on. I just got more gunnery training.

It was my first time in a B-24 Liberator. The models we trained on were D's. They had no nose turrets, and I don't recall them having ball turrets—the turrets became standard only on later models—but we practiced firing what guns there were at targets towed by other planes. It was tricky because the tow planes tended to keep a very safe distance from amateur marksmen like us.

We practiced bombing runs on Muroc Dry Lake, where Charles Yeager later broke the sound barrier. For one practice, a huge outline of a battleship was built on the ground. The pilots also got training in formation flying—a crucial skill for both mission success and crew survival.

At March Field, we really sweated over mechanical problems. There were accidents in training, some because crews were inexperienced and some because of mechanical failure. We would be somewhere around the base and hear a sudden loud explosion and look over and see a big mass of black smoke. One problem could kill the ten men on a plane, and it seemed to happen a lot.

The pilot of *The Buzzer* when it crashed, Julian Caldwell, had complained before going overseas that he was more at risk from student pilots during his stint as a Stateside instructor than he would be from the enemy over Europe. It is easy to see why he felt that way at the time.

After March Field, we got on another troop train and were shipped to Hamilton Field, close to San Rafael, Port of Embarkation, outside San Francisco. Since we were so close to the Pacific, we figured that we'd be fighting Japan, based on an island somewhere in the South Pacific.

We got our plane at Hamilton Field. Because of nearby Mount Shasta, it got christened *Shasta Shack*. Then our orders arrived. We didn't know our final destination, but we started flying east in stages.

.

Liberators

When we got to March Field, the planes we trained on were B-24 Liberators; so we knew we'd be flying in one, for better or for worse.

There were many variations on the B-24 Liberator during the war. By 1944, there were more than fifty. The "J"'s were the most numerous. *The Buzzer* was an "H". The Consolidated B-24 Liberators were not only built at Consolidated's Fort Worth plant—like *The Buzzer,* but also by Ford, at Willow Run (changed to "Will It Run?" by some aircrews) and by North American.

The Liberators became the most produced plane in America. More than 18,000 were built, more even than any fighter. They were four-engine aircraft, with a "Davis Wing" whose aerodynamics and eighteen wing-embedded fuel tanks helped extend their range to almost three thousand miles. They could carry up to four and a half tons of bombs.

An engineer called David Davis had already developed his extra-efficient wing when the Army Air Corps was looking for a new heavy bomber design. The new wing design was subjected to several subsequent wind-tunnel tests after its first one, because engineers couldn't believe how good the results were. Consolidated Vultee tested the XB-24 at the end of 1939. The story goes that extra length was added to the fuselage to improve its stubby appearance.

The B-24 continued to attract unattractive unofficial names: the "Flying Boxcar," or the "Whistling Outhouse," or the "Flying Prostitute" (it had no visible means of support).

The wings were mounted high on the fuselage to make possible the greatest storage capacity for bombs. The bombs were stored in a two-section bomb bay. A catwalk extended through the bomb bay, which a crew member sometimes had to walk across when the bay was open . . . not something everyone liked to do. The earliest models had only a few machine gun posts, but experience quickly changed that; the more the better, it was realized.

B-24's played a vital role in strategic and tactical bombing campaigns in both Europe and the Pacific. They were even important in antisubmarine warfare. France ordered 175 early-model B-24's but capitulated to the Germans in 1940 so quickly that the planes could not be delivered. Britain bought most of these planes; after modification in Scotland, they were put to work hunting submarines.

Used this way by the R.A.F., Liberators were important in winning the Battle of the Atlantic; their long range shrank the "Air Gap" in convoy defense. This was the stretch of Atlantic between the range limits of convoy escort planes based in North America and those in Europe. Instead of bombs, these sub-hunters carried depth charges and "Leigh lights," five-million candlepower searchlights used against U-boats running on the surface.

In late 1941, two Liberators were rigged as spy planes to fly over Japanese forces in the Pacific. One of them was destroyed on the ground at Pearl Harbor. Eventually, in their role fighting in the Pacific, B-24's destroyed a great many Japanese planes on the ground in raids on island airfields. Liberators also did transport work. Averill Harriman's mission to Moscow in 1941 used them, and Winston Churchill's regular transport, the *Commando,* was a B-24.

A variant of the B-24 that was used in the Pacific was the SB-24. These planes were equipped with radar that let them bomb Japanese ships despite cloud cover. In China, Liberators of the Tenth Air Force dropped supplies to forces fighting the Japanese. A B-24 wreck recently turned up in a mountainous region of southern China. As with *The Buzzer,* the find stirred many emotions among the families of the men who were lost.

The original design had no tail turret—that was added after a wise French request. And I don't know where I'd have ended up, if I'd shipped over earlier than I did, because the first few months that B-24s flew in Europe, they had no ball turrets, and suffered for it. The "H" was the first series to have a nose gun turret.

One of the many variants of Liberators was used in Project Anvil, also called Operation Aphrodite, an experimental program of unpiloted "flying bombs." These were bombers packed with explosives and flown by a crew part way over the English Channel to their target. Then, after the crew bailed out, they were handed over to radio control. They were supposed to become part of Operation Crossbow, the major air campaign against German V1 and V2 sites in Western Europe, or to be used against German submarine pens on the Atlantic.

A premature explosion of one of these planes killed Joseph Kennedy Jr., elder brother of John F. Kennedy, in 1944. Kennedy had volunteered for the project after piloting Navy PB4Y-1's on antisubmarine duty in the waters off Great Britain.

The many improvements and variations on Liberators did not slow down production. At the different plants where Liberators were made, they were sometimes put together by assembling kits made elsewhere; as the war went on, the production process grew more and more efficient and mechanized. In 1943, it took 40,000 manhours to build a Liberator; two years later, it took only 8,000.

The Ford plant at Willow Run had an unusual "L" shape. This was not "L" for Liberator; as the story goes, it was the result of Henry Ford's command that the gigantic plant not extend out of its Republican-held district into a Democratic-controlled district.

There has always been rivalry between admirers of the B-17 Flying Fortress and those of us who flew on Liberators. The B-17 had debuted in 1934; the original B-24 design came in response to a call in 1939 for a new bomber that could outperform the Fortress. Nevertheless, in 1942, H.H.

"Hap" Arnold, commanding general of the Army Air Forces, said: "We find ourselves faced with what may be a real and acute problem in psychology and in leadership." He was talking about the runaway public relations success of the B-17, to the undeserved detriment of the Liberator.

At one point, Jimmy Doolittle wanted his Eighth Air Force to be all-B-17. The Eighth was always looking for ways to lighten the B-24, including eliminating the ball turret. Weight at 500 pounds and wind resistance created drag.

A famous anecdote about the rivalry concerns a B-24 crew eastbound over the Atlantic, who saw a B-17 ahead of them, at a lower altitude. The B-24 dove and increased throttle until it was gaining fast on the B-17, then leveled off, cut and "feathered" two props, and zoomed by the Fortress crew, who must have been impressed to be passed by a Liberator running on only two engines.

I am informed by Liberator expert Roger Criplever that the name "Liberator" resulted from a contest at Consolidated. The winner was submitted anonymously by Dorothy Fleet, wife of Major Reuben Fleet, who created "Consolidated" out of a merger of two previous companies. She wrote later that she, her husband, and their children's English governess had been speaking of the plane's purpose in the larger scheme of things, as a "liberator" of conquered nations, despite the immediate destructiveness of its operations.

Liberators had wingspans of 110 feet. Their length varied from model to model, but it was usually around 67 feet. Fully loaded, they weighed more than thirty tons. Their engines were Pratt & Whitney. Their top speed was about 300 mph, but the typical cruising speed was closer to 200 mph.

They could climb almost five miles high, but getting to bombing height over target took awhile; a heavily laden Liberator required about six minutes to rise one thousand feet. The standard overloading of Liberators on duty, crammed with bombs, fuel, and ammunition, meant that their operational performance was not exactly the same as their potential in ideal conditions.

✈ ✈ ✈ ✈ ✈

When I recently went to Italy to try to find people who knew something about *The Buzzer* crash, and was told the plane hit a mountain only meters short of the peak, I couldn't help wondering if the mountain was sighted but simply could not be avoided.

The Buzzer was a B-24H with the serial number 41–29307, from Consolidated Fort Worth—or, technically, Convair Fort Worth. Early in 1943, Vultee bought Consolidated and the new entity was called Convair, for Consolidated Vultee Aircraft Corporation.

It was one of 738 built by Consolidated or its corporate relatives at Fort Worth; Douglas and Ford produced hundreds. All the H's had nose turrets. The engines were first run November 10, 1943. It was officially inspected the next day and given a test flight the day after that. Air Corps inspection and acceptance were on November 14, and the plane was delivered November 16. Then came modification for the Army Air Corps at a center operated by Bechtel-McCone-Parsons in Birmingham, Alabama.

From Chatham AAF, Savannah, Georgia, *The Buzzer* was flown overseas and arrived at Grottaglie on February 4, 1944, a couple of months ahead of me. It was painted a dull desert drab, which was a sort of camouflage. The plane was built just before the decision was made to dispense with camouflage paint and send the bombers into combat with their silvery metal aluminum skin showing. I've seen several reasons put forward for this change: a saving of more than seventy pounds in paint weight; less paint reduced skin friction; an improvement in fighter cover made camouflage unnecessary; and German radar, which made camouflage pointless. The first set of metallic-finish bombers made quite a sensation when they first appeared. Later models of the Js, which were manufactured starting in late 1943, had exhaust-heated de-icing equipment.

Four Continents
And An Ocean

Flying across the United States was an adventure without equal. Rudy Acosta remembers seeing his first P-51 Mustang at Sky Harbor, Phoenix, our first stop. Then a dust storm kept us on the ground for several days at Midland, Texas. Finally we proceeded to Memphis, Tennessee, where we were grounded by more stormy weather. Rudy recalls that we tried once or twice to climb over the storm clouds but we simply couldn't—they must have been well over 30,000 feet high. We bought a lot of whisky in Memphis.

We were held up by storms again for a while at Morrison Field, near Jacksonville, Florida, and eventually flew on to West Palm Beach, our last stop in the U.S. At one stage we were flying across Florida swamps at 200 feet, and some of the guys were playing poker and drinking, until Rogers called back to them to stop the game.

Rudy Acosta remembers our navigator, Shorty Carlson, pointing out the crossing of a small road and a railroad track on the map, and saying "If we keep our heading we should pass over this in thirty seconds." We did! Rudy was impressed that Shorty could do that AND play poker.

Of course we now assumed we were going to be flying in Europe, but most of us guessed we'd be going to England, where the Eighth Air Force was based. Just as most movies and publicity about U.S. bombers in Europe focused on B-17 Flying Fortresses rather than B-24 Liberators, most people were much more aware of the England-based Eighth than the Italy-based Fifteenth. It's still true.

The Fifteenth Air Force had been set up to use recently Allied-controlled airfields in Italy to bomb targets in central, southern and eastern Europe that the Eighth Air Force couldn't reach. It officially went into action in November 1943. Ploesti, Romania would be its biggest target, followed by synthetic oil plants—part of the same strategy.

Anyway after we left Florida and the U.S. behind, the sealed orders were opened and we found out we were going to Italy.

Next stop was Trinidad, where I bought a local paper and sent it home. Now I was really getting to some exotic locales! Then it was across the mouth of the Amazon and the Equator to Belem, Brazil, and another leg to Fortaleza, Brazil.

For some reason it was customary for aircrews passing through Brazil to buy leather boots there. We followed the tradition. I know guys who still have theirs. We were also offered what a pedlar said was a shrunken human head, but nobody wanted it.

Then we flew across the Atlantic to Rufisque, near Dakar, in French West Africa, which is now Senegal. Looking at a map of the world, the leg from Brazil to Senegal is just one portion of the long haul from Florida to Grottaglie. But it was a hazardous one. It was known that planes sometimes had fuel and navigation problems and had to ditch in the Atlantic, so we were told to keep an eye out for any of our aircraft in the water.

We found out they weren't kidding about those risks; *Shasta Shack* nearly became one of those planes. Rudy Acosta recently reminded me of some of the details of the trip. Twelve bombers took off at ten-minute intervals. Our plane was carrying extra supplies for the base in Europe—blankets, game equipment, and rations. Rudy, as our radio operator, was supposed to call in to our airfield in Brazil every half-hour. He did—until he lost contact.

Many hours later, when we were about halfway across, and Rudy had been trying and trying to raise our base, he decided to try calling our destination in West Africa. It worked. But by the time we got close to where the coast of Africa should be, we were very low on gas. Finally one of us saw some faint white movement far ahead. It was surf!

We found the Dakar airfield, and landed, startled by the noise our landing gear made on the Army Corps of Engineers special metal-mesh runway, and as we rolled to a stop two engines just shut off. We were flat out of gas.

Jack Cox told me he thought our plane made it over when a number ditched because we had a good crew, a good plane, and a great navigator.

Again in Senegal we had the feeling of being in an exotic new world. I remember the Senegalese soldiers in their uniforms being a novel sight. The next day we flew on to Marrakesh, Morocco, over the Sahara Desert and the Atlas Mountains. Down in the Sahara we could see river-valley patterns. In Marrakesh, Rogers remembers hearing the sounds of bells on donkeys, and the muezzin's prayer calls.

In the winter of 1943–44, a B-24 flown by Captain David Councill, the Squadron Commander of the squadron we were joining, the 719th, crashed into a peak in the Atlas Range. Fourteen men were killed, the first to die in an airplane out of the 449th Bomb Group. It was strangely like the fate of *The Buzzer* on an Italian mountaintop a year later.

Djeda in Tunisia was the next stop, and then it was finally across the Mediterranean to Italy. We made a short stop at our 47th Wing Headquarters in Manduria, where the 450th Bomb Group was also based. We weren't there long enough to get off the plane before we took off for our new "home"—Grottaglie. Our trip had taken eighty hours of flying time, spread out over seventeen days.

The Place Of Many Caves

At the start of the war, on September 1, 1939, the Army Air Force was using sixty-nine air bases. It had two hundred bases by December 7, 1941. Two years later, at the end of 1943, there were 1,400, with 800 of them overseas. One was at Grottaglie, home of the four squadrons that made up the 449th Bomb Group, which was part of the 47th Wing of the Fifteenth Air Force.

Grottaglie was, and is, famous for pottery. It is a small city in the province of Taranto, in the Apulia region of southeastern Italy. *Grottaglie* means many caves, and the same local limestone geology that makes it a pottery region provides many grottoes and caves.

Signs have been discovered of Bronze Age settlements there. In the Tenth Century A.D. local people used the caves to hide from Saracen invaders. Even more recently, there was talk during the 1999 Balkan War of using the airfield as a substitute for Bari and Brindisi, which were closed to civilian traffic during the NATO campaign against Slobodan Milosevic.

When the airfield was still in Axis hands, not long before the 449th moved in, it had been heavily bombed and strafed by Allied planes based in North Africa. I remember being particularly impressed by the burned-out ruins of a dirigible hangar, former home of the dirigible *Roma*.

Grottaglie had been an Italian dirigible base before the Germans started using it. Its former name was Marcelio

Arlotta Aerodrome. It was built as a dirigible and biplane base in 1915–16, during the First World War.

Just days after the Germans fled the area, the field was visited by an official party, including the future British Prime Minister Harold Macmillan and U.S. Army General Maxwell Taylor. They were sent to make contact with Italian government officials, thought to be nearby.

The runway was dirt. As at all bases, an effort was made to scatter the parking places of the planes, against air attacks.

The 449th had been born as a unit in May 1943, less than a year before we joined it. It was based at Davis-Monthan Army Air Field, in Arizona, Alamagordo Army Air Field, in New Mexico, and Bruning Army Air Field, in Nebraska, before transferring overseas in November 1943.

A unit citation received by the 449th for its bombing campaign in the spring and summer of 1944 notes that the unit "was ordered to occupy an airdrome not released as operational by the Corps of Engineers." Accounts of early days for the 449th at Grottaglie make it clear that a combination of bomb destruction and foul winter weather, with the attendant mud, made operations difficult and life uncomfortable in the early months of 1944. Men had to travel for a hot bath, and would gladly go by road to the nearby port of Taranto.

✈ ✈ ✈ ✈ ✈

Some places had it worse. In March 1944, near Naples, Mt. Vesuvius erupted and sixty planes were destroyed on the ground. Wind carried the ash all the way to Grottaglie.

The bomb group had been busy. The 449th flew its first mission on January 8, 1944, against an airfield at Mostar, Yugoslavia. It was the first of 254. The last mission was against an ammo dump at Casarsa, Italy, on April 26, 1945. As I've said, my missions were in the spring and summer of 1944; those of the men who died on *The Buzzer* were in the summer and autumn of that year.

Among many other early 1944 actions, a successful bomber attack on an Axis reconnaissance base at Perugia helped the January Anzio landing. Later, heavy bombers from the 449th helped preserve the tenuous Anzio beachhead by bombing a road the Germans were using to bring up reinforcements. More invasion support was given by a big raid by units including the 449th on enemy fighter bases near the Austrian border.

This raid involved what A.F. Simpson, in volume 3 of W.F. Craven and J. L. Cate's *The Army Air Forces in World War II,* calls "one of the cleverer tricks of the air war." A large force of B-17s and B-24s, including the 449th, with their usual fighter cover, headed for the target at normal altitude, visible on enemy radar.

Naturally, Axis fighters were scrambled to meet the threat. But a force of our P-47s set out later than our bombers, staying low and over the sea, climbing high only after they passed our bombers and were near the target, fifteen minutes ahead of the Liberators and Fortresses.

This meant they caught the Axis fighters as they were either taking off or getting into formation, and were able to ambush them. Not only did our P-47s destroy several dozen enemy fighters, with two losses, but our bombers then came in with next to no resistance and dropped fragmentation bombs on the airfields. Overall, about 140 enemy planes were claimed. Our forces lost six bombers and three fighters.

Bombers from the 449th also took part in "Big Week" raids on the Messerschmitt factory at Regensburg on February 22, 1944, and on the ball-bearing factory at Steyr, Austria, the next day.

My crew arrived at a bad time. It was April 5, 1944. The 719th squadron—the squadron we were joining, one of four in the 449th Bomb Group—had sustained its heaviest losses thus far in the war the day before, in its first raid on Bucharest, Romania. Seven out of twenty-nine planes were lost from the 449th, and five of those losses were from the 719th. The 719th had put up nine planes that day. Anyone who was in the 449th Group knows what "4/4/44" means.

It turned out that, of the seventy-one men aboard the seven downed 449th planes that day, thirty-seven were killed in action and thirty-four were captured. All seven crews suffered at least two deaths; one plane lost all ten men.

The 449th had been part of a large Fifteenth Air Force attack on the railroad marshaling yards at Bucharest. Weather problems led to a "recall" of the bomber force, which was not received by the 449th and led to the planes of the 449th attacking without other groups and without fighter escort. All of the enemy fighters were able to concentrate on the single group, attacking long before and after the bomb run, which was completed successfully. Although bomber losses were high, a large number of enemy fighters also were lost. It was a real "shoot out". One of the two Presidential Unit Citations awarded the 449th resulted from that day's action.

Of course we didn't know anything about losses in general when we were on our way over. After we landed, a truck picked us up and took us with our gear to the tent area. We passed several tents with M.P.s stationed in front of them and then realized what losses the 719th Squadron had sustained the day before. Lt. Rogers was met by the squadron commander, who told him officially about the losses of the previous day.

Bart Peluso, our ground crew chief, remembers that when my crew arrived, he thought we were a bunch of kids. Well, we were; but he was the same age, about twenty-one. Of course, he was married and a father, so he seemed a more mature figure.

It was dismal seeing those empty tents, with guards around them. Another big raid, this one to Ploesti, was going on that day, April 5. It was the first of twenty-four Ploesti raids the Fifteenth Air Force and R.A.F. 205 Group would make. The 449th eventually took part in eleven of these. That April 5th outing included 146 B-24s and 90 B-17s from the Fifteenth. We thought, "If this is typical—Holy Shit!"

Suddenly the sense of elation and adventure we had experienced flying to Italy disappeared, and dismay took over. I wondered about our chances of survival with losses like those of the day before. The fate of the downed crews-seventy-one men—was not known. How many were killed, wounded, taken prisoner? Airmen had a higher chance of ending up in enemy hands than ground troops.

There was also the possibility of bailing out successfully and being killed by civilians on the ground. I heard a story later about a crewman found with an ax in his head.

✈ ✈ ✈ ✈ ✈

I wondered what would happen to me, a Jew, if I parachuted into enemy territory. My dogtags had an "H" for Hebrew. It turned out that about half of the men shot down survived bailout and captivity and returned home. But we didn't know that at the time.

We enlisted men found a tent in the enlisted men's section, in an almond grove, and the officers found a tent in theirs. We had six-man tents. The sections were separate. In the tent Buck Rogers shared with Bobbie Bennett, Baldy Hinds, and Shorty Carlson, there was no floor; so the four men set about making floors from pieces of wood. Each made his section of the tent a little higher than that of the other officers, so Rogers could later claim that he ended up living in the base's only four-story tent.

There were separate officers clubs, messes—everything. Buck tells me that the Officers Club "was a room about 10 feet by 10 feet, where we could drink a little beer and some whiskey." We were only together as a crew when we flew or went to a rest camp.

The crappers were distinctive. They were planks, set on oil drums, with holes cut in them, right out in the open air. It got to be perfectly natural to be sitting there while people from town, mostly women, would come by to barter eggs or deliver laundry.

The living conditions didn't make such a terrible impression on me. Because of the time of year we were there, we didn't have to cope with mud. The men who died in *The*

Buzzer had to endure late-year bad weather that I missed; but when I was there, the weather was good and progress had been made in devising decent living conditions.

✈ ✈ ✈ ✈ ✈

In general, the fact that we shared the discomforts made it easier. It would have been worse if I'd been alone. But I was part of a crew, with real camaraderie. The ability to bitch helped preserve our spirits. I even have photos of myself smiling!

We had to sleep under mosquito netting. Malaria was a concern; we took an atabrine pill every day to ward it off. We heard rumors of men suffering from atabrine dermatitis, but I don't recall this being a problem any more than its less reliably reported side effects—impotence and insanity.

In the Apulia region there are reportedly some pretty fancy local dishes, including a fish soup with lobsters, mussels, and sometimes sea scorpion; spaghetti with sea urchins; and spaghetti with squid (including the ink-bags and gonads).

I say "reportedly" because we were on Army rations, which were far less imaginative. To be honest, as far as food goes, again, I had no real complaints. We could get powdered scrambled eggs, or French toast, for breakfast, and typical Army food at other meals. I remember a staple was creamed chipped beef on toast—A.K.A. "S.O. S."(shit on a shingle). On missions, we ate snacks rather than meals, even though we were sometimes aloft for most of a day. I also remember a little round can of cheese being especially prized. As Lt. Rogers remembers, "There were no in-flight lunches."

But as everywhere else in the service, food was important. As you'll see, complaints about it show up even in official post-mission debriefing forms.

Buck Rogers recalls how we enjoyed visiting the nearby port of Taranto once our Navy arrived, bringing good shipboard food. They were good about giving us airmen a meal when we visited. Lt. Rogers thought our regular food was "terrible." "I had dinner aboard the *Arkansas,* it was exquisite," he said.

Rudy Acosta reminded me that we started out with an advantage, as far as food was concerned: "When we first got there, we had the rations to give to the group, along with baseball equipment and so on. But it was never requested, so we kept it."

But the food at the base? According to Rudy: "Breakfast was mush. Cream of wheat with lumps, oatmeal in lumps, powdered milk with lumps. Scrambled eggs made into a big omelet. It was jaw exercise."

Into Combat

Sometimes crews went on missions several days in a row, and sometimes the bomb group as a whole would "stand down" for several days at a time. Weather, availability of functioning planes, and a desire to give crews rest between missions, when possible, were all factors.

On April 7, the 449th struck a marshaling yard at Mestre, Italy, and went out again April 12 to bomb the heavily defended Messerschmitt assembly plant at Wiener-Neustadt, south of Vienna.

For this mission, our plane, the *Shasta Shack*, was needed before we were ready to fly. It was taken over by another crew, whose pilot was 2nd Lt. Kenneth V. Heinbuch, and was shot down on its first sortie. According to a witness's report, the plane was attacked by enemy aircraft striking from "two o'clock high." 'Number 2 engine caught on fire, and ship went into a spin. Three chutes were seen."

✈ ✈ ✈ ✈ ✈

We felt like we'd lost "our plane," but we were glad we weren't on that mission. We didn't know then the fate of the crew; but after the war we found out that everyone bailed out and became a P.O.W.

The 449th attacked Vecses Airport, Budapest, on April 13th. They were part of a 3,000-plane Allied effort, against a variety of targets that day, involving bombers from the Fifteenth and the Eighth. It was Rudy's first mission. At first, new crews were split up at first, so we could all go on a few missions with more experienced men before going out together as a crew.

The 449th went to attack the infamous marshaling yards at Bucharest on the 15th. That would have been my first mission, but it was a "non-eff," short for "non-effective," meaning my plane had to return to base. Then came my first mission: marshaling yards at Brasov, Romania on April 16th.

Like many missions flown by the Fifteenth Air Force, this one was intended to support the Soviet advance into Romania. I, of course, knew nothing of this, and didn't really have a strong idea from day to day what grand strategy a given mission was designed to further, except that I knew a trip to Ploesti was about oil.

On the Brasov mission, I was a replacement ball turret gunner on a crew that was flying its last mission. The plane was piloted by Lt. Leonard Waine. I remember when I was still in the waist, watching antiaircraft flak go off, and not thinking much of it, even thinking it was kind of pretty. It was puffs of black smoke, and I could hear a "WHOMP!" sound. But I could see these veterans flinch at it.

In time, I learned to flinch. Jack Cox has said that when we started out, we didn't have enough experience to be afraid. Every mission after the one on April 16th, I just held my breath, hoping to hell that we would not get hit. There was no defense. We could only sweat it out, and hope.

We weren't supposed to break out of our large formation because we'd be more vulnerable to fighters if we did. We'd also weaken the whole formation's fighter-defense abilities.

In addition, we released our bombs by watching when the lead plane dropped its. Accuracy in hitting the target depended on a tight formation. But that made it very rough when the antiaircraft gunners found your range and speed early. In Joseph Heller's memoir, *Now and Then,* he talks about the Germans sending planes up to match altitude and speed with big bomber groups and radioing the details to the flak batteries below.

Rudy Acosta said once that he felt "invincible" in combat; he had his machine gun and there were nine more like it on the plane; a fighter was heavily outgunned. Of course, this leaves flak out of the equation. Once, a piece of flak shrapnel hit his gun mount and ricocheted several times around the inside of the plane before hitting his elbow and falling to the deck, spent.

Buck Rogers says that flak was dangerous about sixty feet around a shellburst, and was more dangerous below you than above. Rudy says a close burst sounded like a nearby lightning strike.

Another problem with flying close to other planes, beside the obvious and very real danger of collision, was the increased risk of being accidentally bombed from above by one of your own planes. A number of airmen lost their lives this way, and my crew once saw another plane's bombs go right by us.

Buck Rogers saw a horrific incident on one of his first missions, on April 13th. A group of planes was late arriving over target and lower than they should have been, and a squadron above them let go with fragmentation bombs. One landed square on a plane flown by Warren Rustad, a friend of Rogers, someone he'd trained with. The plane disintegrated. There were no survivors.

Rogers says that, a few days earlier, his friend had told him he wasn't going to make it, and Rogers had tried to cheer him up. He says these accidents were not uncommon, but not surprising, given how inexperienced most of the pilots were.

On my first mission, fighters were the main concern. There were probably more attacks than on any other mission I was on. What a way to start. I tried to do my part to ward them off. I certainly fired the guns, but I've no idea if I hit anything.

I'd never trained in a powered ball turret. I think it was my first time in one. My hands went on the controls that moved the turret around and I fired by pushbutton. There was a special optical sight, the Sperry K-4, used in the turrets and not the waist guns, which was supposed to improve your chances of hitting an attacking enemy plane by computing wind deflection and other factors.

I'm sure this veteran crew, on its last mission, would have preferred to have a more experienced ball turret gunner guarding the ship's underside. Three planes from our group went down that day, and a Liberator from another group shot down a P-51 Mustang it had mistaken for a Messerschmitt 109.

Fighter attacks on our bombers were "coordinated and very aggressive," according to the official Special Narrative Report on the mission. The attacks concentrated on stragglers: "The main direction of attack was from the rear, but varying all around the clock, with the exception of the nose. They would come in line astern at 6 o'clock high, firing cannon, machine guns, and rockets. Large red flashes were seen."

As Rudy Acosta puts it, we arrived at the height of the air war, before the strength of the Luftwaffe's fighter force had been broken. "When you fire at a fighter, and you see the guns on his wings firing at you, you know you're playing for keeps; you know you're in real combat."

Bob Simons adds that, "in combat, one was so busy trying to do the job and get the bad guy. Fear wasn't present; there just wasn't time, at least near the target."

The report notes an enemy fighter tactic of attacking through vapor trails, making them hard to see until they were very close and they closed to within seventy-five yards before peeling off. They seemed to be well-armored, too; the report notes that observers reported seeing tracer fire bounce off them.

Jack Cox told me "he would fire off tracers at enemy fighters as soon as he saw them, and that sometimes this put them off, but that sometimes they'd just bore in on you."

Rudy Acosta had a particularly rough time going to Brasov April 16, on another plane, on what was his third mission: "I had my heated suit on, it was sixty below without wind chill. My gloves shorted and started burning. I was

being stung all over. I finally disconnected them. My hands
started to freeze.

There were twenty-eight fighters that day approaching Brasov. There were lots of clouds that
day, huge cumulus clouds. When the ME-109s attacked I had one hand in my crotch trying to keep
warm and one to shoot with. Then I would switch
to warm the other hand up.
I saw the face of an ME-109 pilot right below
me right before our ball-turret gunner blew him
up. We bombers shot down eight out of the twenty-
eight fighters that day . . . we were lucky we
weren't shot down."

I don't remember being sure I ever shot down a fighter,
whether German or Romanian. I know Bob Simons was sure
he shot down a Romanian fighter; but many times, as he
said, many guns on a number of bombers shot at the fighters, many fighters went down, and credit was hard to assign.
Rudy's story continues: "After the attack I kept both
hands in my crotch. One finger is still awry. At the base,
when we turned our equipment in, I handed over the suit
and said "Shove this!" They gave me a new suit, the latest,
with silk gloves. It was pretty nice."
Rudy was lucky in a way; more bomber crewmen were
disabled for duty by frostbite than by wounds. At forty
below, a typical temperature when we flew near our ceiling,
frostbite could set in within minutes.
Not only cold, but sheer altitude was potentially deadly.
Everyone had to go on oxygen above 10,000 feet. Men sometimes died on missions from faulty oxygen supplies. In addition to big bottles of oxygen stowed all around the plane,
one of which, from *The Buzzer,* is now in my house, there
were little portable bottles you could carry with you, if you
had to move from one part of the plane to another. Our intercom microphones were built into our oxygen masks.

I still have a copy of the *New York Times* front page for Monday, April 17, 1944, which includes coverage of the mission that day, my first combat mission. The headline puts our efforts in strategic context: "Russians Hammer Sevastapol, Seize Yalta In Flanking Drive; Allies Bomb Rail Lines To Front."

Other news that day included a deadly tornado in South Carolina and a forecast by supporters that New York's Governor Thomas E. Dewey would win the Republican nomination on the first ballot.

A small item in that day's paper notes the amazing production rate at Ford's Willow Run plant, where B-24 Liberators were coming off the line at a rate of one an hour.

There is another item relating to the air war. Pacific air ace Richard Bong, who had shot down twenty Japanese planes, was not allowed to receive a case of Scotch or champagne as a reward. First World War ace Eddie Rickenbacker had promised the prize, but General MacArthur nixed it, saying it was "inappropriate."

Anyway, it was decided that our Brasov mission counted for two credits, so it was good to have the mission over with.

Who gets to be ball turret gunner on a B-24? The position is not exactly sought after. If the plane is in trouble and the bailout bell rings, the ball-turret gunner is in about the worst position, stuck in a ball that has to be raised so he can escape. Then your chute has to be handy—the turret was too small to wear a chute inside.

I couldn't remember how I got the job, so I asked my former crewmates. Bob Simons said it was probably because I could fit into the turret. Buck Rogers wrote to answer my question: "You volunteered for the ball turret. I can see you now, smiling a little and saying 'I will get in the ball turret.'" He said he thought my fellow enlisted men had decided who went where before we met the officers. Some people say ball gunners were always chosen for their lack of height, but I was five feet eleven in those days, so I don't think that was the real factor.

Another fear was that any damage to the ball turret mechanism could prevent it from being moved into just the right position to be raised back into the plane. I remember being mortally afraid of that happening. Also, the B-24, unlike the B-17 Flying Fortress, couldn't land with the turret down.

I vividly remember seeing other bombers, B-24s and B-17s, hit by flak and going to earth in a spin or careening crazily, and I always wondered if their ball turret gunners would get out.

Rudy and I used to practice getting me out in a hurry. As left waist gunner, he was in the best spot. I used to tell Rudy that if our plane was hit and the bailout alarm was sounded, if he didn't help me out of the turret I'd fire my machine gun at him as he parachuted out. Happily for both of us, the plane didn't go down, and Rudy did not have to help, and I didn't shoot Rudy, and we've remained close buddies for more than fifty-five years.

At least I wasn't claustrophobic. I actually found the turret fairly snug and comfortable. My blue coverall-style electric suit always worked, and I was never bothered by the cold. Rudy Acosta, who wasn't as lucky with his suit, remembers that if you blew your nose, the mucus would turn to ice. And, if your goggles got foggy, your eyelashes could ice up.

Luckily, I wasn't in the turret for the duration of a mission, which could last more than eight hours. It was lowered only when we got close enough to enemy-held territory that there was a risk of fighter attack. Of course, I'd come back into the plane once we were close enough to Grottaglie. I had no other duties than shooting at fighters. When we were not under attack, I would doze, talk, or listen to music on Armed Forces Radio. I liked swing. Naturally, the pleasure in lying in the turret and relaxing occurred only on our way home from a target.

In the early days of the B-24, there had been attempts to use remote-fired guns to guard the undersides; but the need for manned turrets was soon realized. They were built for the D-series B-24s. The entire unit moved with the gunner when he changed his aim. In my turret, I could rotate completely around, and could shoot anywhere up to 90 degrees of elevation—apart from where a special device stopped me from accidentally shooting my own plane. Some ball turrets were equipped with instruments to show the gunner his position in case he became dizzy or disoriented, as the plane maneuvered and he spun his turret. Sometimes I did become a little disoriented; although I don't remember this being a serious problem.

In theory, the ball turret could be ditched when a limping plane needed to get rid of every possible bit of weight. At more than 500 pounds, the turret was a heavy assembly. If the situation called for flak jackets, guns, and ammo to be jettisoned, ditching a ball turret would significantly help.

Allan Blue, author of *The B-24 Liberator,* responded to an e-mail query about it this way: "It was a very common practice to jettison equipment from returning aircraft with mechanical problems. The bottom of the English Channel, for example, must look like a junkyard.

> The ball was very heavy, of course, and dropping it might make the difference between a safe return and a big splash. I'm not sure this was provided for in the original design, but eventually there *was* a provision for its quick release.
>
> I have read interrogation reports where crews describe using the "Crash Axe"—-standard equipment on every B-24-to get rid of the turret. The whole unit . . . was suspended by a single rod attached to the roof of the plane (the hydraulic retraction cylinder). This, in turn, was attached to the middle of the "hanger assembly" which was shaped like a sawhorse, with each of its four legs attached to a point on the ring around the top of the ball.
>
> I have examined the drawings for this and, if I were asked to design a "quick release" system, I would provide a special tool which would release the "sawhorse" from the retraction cylinder and thus let the turret drop . . .

It goes without saying that, the gunner would have gotten out of the turret first! I don't think I ever seriously thought of the possibility of the turret falling out accidentally . . . which is probably just as well.

Ideally, crews were given a day off between missions; but my second mission was the day after my first. On April 17, I went to Sofia, Bulgaria. I was with my regular crew this time. Marshaling yards were again the target. We had a ship called *Lady Lightnin'*. Our plane blew #2 engine " . . . almost out of the nacelle" according to a crewmate. At the start of the bomb run; we had to abort the mission. No planes from the 449th were lost on that day's mission.

Then it was twelve days until my third sortie—to bomb submarine pens at Toulon, France. In the meantime, other crews from the 449th had been on missions to marshaling yards at Treviso, Italy, (on the 20th), the Schwechat aircraft factory in Vienna (the 23rd), a marshaling yard at Ploesti (the 24th), and a seaplane base at Orbetello, Italy (the 28th).

✈ ✈ ✈ ✈ ✈

Once we started flying on raids, our feelings about the risks varied with the targets. We went to briefings at 4:00 or 5:00 a.m., when we learned where we were going that day. Usually, if it was somewhere in Germany, Romania or Austria—at which we'd think: "Shit!"

Rudy Acosta remembers a few details of our daily routine on bomb days: "We wore fatigues in the morning. We checked our shoes for spiders. We washed and walked over to the gear supply. We'd tell them who we were and what group and get our chute and harness and Mae West life preserver, and a helmet and oxygen gear. We also turned in our personal stuff." This included wallets and anything that would identify [to the enemy] who we were and where we were from, beyond the information on our dogtags. Bombardiers always picked up their bomb sights before every mission, and handed them over for safe keeping after returning.

After breakfast, we'd ride out to our plane on a truck and lie around on the ground by the plane, using our chest pack parachutes as pillows, waiting for the go-ahead green flare. The parachutes were pretty comfortable as pillows. I'd be hoping the mission would be scratched. But I'd also be hoping to get one more mission out of the way. As a rule, though, we didn't talk about wishes like that. Once we got the go-ahead, things happened fast. Planes took off at thirty-second intervals before flying a circular holding pattern while joining preceding aircraft getting into formation.

Another look at a mission from the pilot's point of view was sent to me by Rogers. It was one of the Ploesti missions, but not our first one; this one was quieter than that.

A TYPICAL MISSION

0400:   Awakened by Ops Officer. Get dressed, go wake up crew.

0410:   To mess hall, have cup of coffee, and a couple of cigarettes, joke nervously with other crew members.

0425:   Walk to Group Ops. See target on large briefing wall map. PLOESTI—Shit!

0455:   Walk back to Squadron Area, take a crap, have more coffee.

0530:   Pick up chute, go to plane, still making nervous jokes, all of the crew is joining in, including ground people, we're all in this together.

0545:   Start engines, taxi out.

0600:   Take off, find place in formation.

0645:   Over enemy skies, gunners check guns.

0700:   Climbing through 10,000 feet, everyone on oxygen, and check in.

0945:   Starting bomb run, damn, flak is heavy.

1000:   Bombs away, get the hell out of here, crew is calling out fighters and bombers going down. I don't see this, busy flying "off" the other airplanes.

1020: Start to descend, good, crew and ship okay, let's go home.

1040: Below 10,000, take off mask, have a cigarette and some K-ration chocolate. Go take a pee.

1245: Over the Adriatic, now can relax a bit. Almost home.

1315: Over the base, waiting turn to get in the pattern and land.

1335: Land, taxi home, shut engine. Joking all around, crew chief glad, so are we.

1350: Debrief, get a shot of whiskey, put up chute.

1420: Hit the sack, still nothing to eat. Not hungry.

1700: Awake from nap, starved, go to mess hall, have Vienna sausage, not appetizing but filling, make jokes about bombing the sausage factory next time we go to Vienna.

Rudy Acosta adds:

Coming back from missions, we were told not to throw shell casings overboard to lighten the load, in case they hurt other planes. We still threw them. We'd land, taxi, and park the ship near the hangars, then get out and sit on a box with Red Cross coffee and doughnuts. The G-2 officer would debrief us, asking about results, fighters, losses, chutes . . . then we'd turn in our equipment and go to the chow tent. Then to the medic's tent for a double shot of whiskey in a tin cup.' Sometimes these whiskeys were saved up.

When we set out to bomb Toulon on April 29, my plane was one of 573 bombers, the most sent to one target in that theater of war up to then. The load dropped, 1,312 tons, was also a record. The next day, other bombers from the 449th were in action against a marshaling yard at Alessandria, Italy. Then no one from the 449th went out until May 5, which was a bad one.

Cinco De Mayo

Our crew's first trip to Ploesti was May 5, 1944. Thanks to Rudy Acosta, I knew that May 5—Cinco de Mayo—was a big holiday for Mexico and Mexicans. It celebrates the victory of General Zaragosa and a Mexican army over invading French forces and their Mexican allies.

Some Cinco de Mayo! It turned out to be another two-credit mission, which I think we earned.

Ploesti is less than forty miles north of Bucharest, at the edge of the Carpathian Mountains. In addition to fighter cover and a smokescreen, the thirty square miles of the Ploesti refineries were defended by 250 heavy flak guns, 88s or larger, and 430 mobile flak guns of 20mm to 37mm. Fifty thousand Germans took part in the defense, in addition to many Romanians.

The smokescreen was specially set up so that the thousands of smoke generators took the best advantage of the prevailing winds. It took about half an hour for a good cover to be generated—if the winds cooperated. German radar and spotters in Yugoslavia gave the defenders time to start the screen, scramble their fighters, and evacuate the refineries. There was also a fake Ploesti built by the Germans about ten miles away, in the hope of luring bombers; but this was more of a concern for the British, who bombed at night.

I have descriptions from several of my crewmates of how the May 5 mission appeared to them; so I want to describe this mission in some detail, not only to give an idea of what others were like, but to show what sort of experiences our counterparts who ended up dying in the December 9th *Buzzer* crash had been through. I have the official briefing notes. ("RR" stands for railroad.)

TARGET

1. As has been brought out in the briefing of the past two days, your target affects RR communications and oil production. In addition to temporarily disrupting all RR traffic to the Southern Russian front, this attack will result in the destruction of refinery sidings, tank cars, pumping stations, refineries, and supplies of oil vitally needed by the German war machine. The importance of this target is indicated by the fact that this is the third day in succession that it has been given to us.

2. We attack this target at 1400 Baker along with the 450th Group with us in the lead. A good feature of today's attack is that we are the first group of the Air Force over PLOESTI, so we shall probably have the best chance of hitting the target on the nose and perhaps before the smokescreen becomes so effective and before smoke from the hits of other groups is added to the effects of the smoke screen. The 304th Wing hits PLOESTI 10 minutes after us, followed by the 55th Wing 10 minutes later, and the 5th Wing 10 minutes after that. There will be 14 groups in all over PLOESTI in the space of 30 minutes. At the same time, other groups will be attacking TURNU SEVERIN and PODGORICA to further spread and confuse the enemy defenses.

3. One group of fighters will provide penetration escort. There will be fighters flying on each side of your formation to attack and drive away any enemy "stool pigeons." Two groups of fighters will provide target cover and two more will escort you on withdrawal from target.

A.   TARGET DETAILS

1. Your target lies in the Southeast section of the city of PLOESTI, and consists of RR trackage and the Standard Oil Refinery. Any spillage of bombs in this area will result in important damage as the Speranza oil refinery is just beyond the Standard refinery and on the other side of the M/Y [marshaling yards] is the Concordia Municipal Factory.
2. You can anticipate a very effective smokescreen, so let us pick out as many checkpoints as possible and have their relation to your aiming point well memorized. Thus, if only one shows up through the smokescreen, you can line your sights up on that one . . .

Then, as usual, the briefing covered a detailed list of landmarks and aiming points, just in case any were visible through the smoke.

We were technically after a marshaling yard that time, not the refineries, although historians of the war report that different planners had different priorities, and that many didn't mind if attacks on marshaling yards, which happened to be next to refineries, did plenty of damage to the oil industry.

In any case, the railroad yards were full of tank cars headed for the front farther east in Romania, so our bomb damage was spectacular.

Our plane that day was the *Salty Dog*. As things turned out, we got pretty badly shot up by flak. A lot of our plane's hydraulics lines, so vital to control of the aircraft, were severed and the landing was tricky.

I have a copy of the official Special Narrative Report on the mission and how it turned out for the 449th in general. As an example of one day's mission, it's interesting to compare the official *briefing* with the official *report,* and with my own crew's memories. The official report starts like this:

Forty B-24's took off at 1010–1039 hours to bomb PLOESTI M/Y. Two returned early, jettisoning 5 tons in the

Adriatic. Thirty-eight dropped 78 tons of 500 lb (.1 and .01) GP bombs* on target at 1357 hours from 18,300–21,000 feet. 32 returned at 1704–1821 hours. Four lost, 1 missing, and 1 at friendly field.

The report goes on to describe rendezvous with other bombers, rendezvous with fighters, and the departure of our fighters. "Conflicting reports were received on fighter cover at target. Most crews report no fighter cover but a few report P-51's 8,000 feet above formation but they did not attempt to drive off E/F's".**

Buck Rogers remembers that day. I should add that a "box" was two or more flights, and a flight was four to eight planes:

When to my surprise and shock, the alternate box broke up, each plane finding some one to tag on to, we were already getting anti-aircraft fire. I kicked [our plane] in the tail to get closer to some of the home folks. I latched on to a Mickey [radar plane] and by now the flak is getting pretty heavy. I know we are being hurt, for I hear the shells detonating, and I feel the ship being pushed by the concussion. After an eternity I see the Mickey finally drop his bombs. Before I could tell Baldy to let'em go, he had. We rally to the left still with the Mickey.

In the turn Bob the co-pilot punches me (whenever he punched me I knew there was something bad wrong), this time hard and points to number three engine. "On fire" says he. "Feather," says I, and feather he did.

"Feathering" the engine meant to fix the propeller of a dead engine "edge-on" to the wind, so it would cause minimum drag, and not "freewheel". Free-spinning props could start friction fires.

Rogers goes on:

Suddenly we find ourselves in amongst a whole bunch of B-24s. They had rallied to the right

---

*A GP bomb was a general-purpose bomb.
**E/F's were enemy fighters.

but at this point who cares. Now I hear "fighters at twelve o'clock" and sure enough there were two [ME] 109s looking at us.

One of them turned, fired four rockets which went right over our head, [he] then made his pass. I tell you it's damned tough to fly formation and keep your eye on an incoming fighter whose fifties*** are winking at you in a most unfriendly fashion. As he passed overhead I knew Bob [Simons] in the nose and Phil [Rizan] in the top turret were putting shells in him. The other fighter decided he wanted no part of us, broke it off and went home.

Because we are descending I can pretty well stay with the formation, whoever they were, I don't know. I ask for a check on everybody, no one hurt, thank God. When we get low enough to get off of oxygen, Rizan makes a survey, then informs me that among other things we have eight hydraulic lines cut and things will be nip and tuck on landing. I believe that at that time he passed a helmet around so that every one could pee in it thereby giving us some extra fluid for the hydraulic system. And now I observe the rest of the folks we are traveling with are starting to leave us. Once again we are alone.

Somewhere in Yugoslavia we pick up some flak. There are six guns down there, put there just for aggravation. But we alter our course every couple of seconds or so and soon we are over the Adriatic.

Since we were not on a bomb run, there was no reason not to avoid the flak here. "As we approach the base," Rogers continues:

Phil tells me we can get the gear down, about twenty degrees of flaps, and one application of brakes. The landing was good and as we approached

***.50 caliber machine guns

the end of the runway I felt the brakes getting mushy. I ground looped it then shut the remaining engines down. The aircraft drifted back on the edge of the runway and stopped. We all got out of the aircraft quite pleased with our efforts. Capt. Hicks, my old friend, started to give me hell for not completely clearing the runway. I told him if he could do better then he could have the god-damned job. Later we became close friends and to-gether helped the new guys coming over. END OF SAGA. Time 7:50 hours. In summary, "The wind blew, the crap flew and there was no-one around to talk to.

Much later, Rogers added a memory about the fighter attacks that day. "I remember watching a 109 making a head-on pass on the run to Ploesti on May 5th. Most of the time they made their passes from the tail-closure wasn't as fast and they could get a better shot."

I recently asked some of my crewmates which mission was our worst, and Rogers replied: "Worst is a bad adjective here, scary is better, and the mission was to Ploesti on 5 May."

A particular job of number three engine on a B-24 was to push the hydraulic system; so, a problem with number three was an extra nuisance, to put it mildly. Hydraulics ran the plane's landing gear, bomb bay doors, turrets, and wing flaps.

Bob Simons, our nose gunner, reported the same mis-sion this way: "On the way to the target we ran into an area of very accurate flak near Bor, [Yugoslavia] and picked up some holes but no damage. Flak over the target area was very intense, accurate and heavy."

The official report echoes Bob's report of the flak. In this phrase, we heard so much of, it was "intense, accurate and heavy." In fact, on mission report forms our pilot had to fill in, the section on flak just needed an underline on the right word—intense, moderate, or slight—for flak, both heavy and light.

Bob's account continues:

While we were on our bomb run, a mix of German and Romanian fighters came at us through their own flak firing 20mm, 13mm, 79mm ammo, rockets and air-to- air bombs. From the nose I had a good shot at an ME 109 that came in at 12- o'clock level, and the tail gunner reported he was on fire when coming out of his pass.

Upon leaving the target area we were pretty badly shot up and struggling behind the rest of our formation. Our return route once again took us over Bor [where] we picked up some additional damage. We returned to base, landing low on fuel, but worse, the entire hydraulic system had been shot out, leaving us without flaps or brakes. We tied parachutes to the gun posts in the waist and threw them to stop the ship on touchdown.

It was a bad situation we were in for awhile, because the German fighters would look especially for stragglers and damaged ships. Even a healthy ship on its own was an easier target for them, without the massed firepower of all the guns in a group of bombers.

On May 5, 1944 a group of four bombers that fell behind the formation "was attacked viciously by 15 to 20" enemy fighters, according to the Special Narrative Report. That report details fighter attacks as close as twenty-five yards, rocket attacks by FW-190s, and three cases of enemy planes dropping "large bombs" from five thousand feet above the formation.

Rudy Acosta recalls that day: "It was uneventful until we reached the I.P. [initial point]. Then all hell breaks loose. God, I can still see a B-24 blow up like a giant ball of fire. 'Are we ever going to get the hell out of here! It's like a lot longer over this target than the previous times."

To Rudy, our plane seemed to fly over the target twice; but, he later realized we had flown over two heavily defended targets, the first one that had been bombed only days before.

Rudy continues:

By the time we are out of flak range we are flying by ourselves'. We pick up a bomber here and another one there. Six of us flying by ourselves. Fighters jump us. First attack I see one bomber go down with a wing on fire. I count six chutes before I get busy again firing at fighters coming low at 7 o'clock. Second pass of fighters, another bomber going down on fire - too busy to look for bailouts. It seems like forever before we get to Danube River and Yugo. At least if we bail out now we will be in partisan country.

We get to the Adriatic Sea and feel better, except we gripe about how the hydraulic lines have been torn apart by flak. "Damn, look at the size of the hole on our right wing, you can crawl through it."

Over the base now, Rizan has to crank gear down by hand. We check yellow lock markers to see that landing gear is down and locked - it's OK, we hope. Rizan, and I can't recall who else, were trying to plug hydraulic lines with rags as we land and have barely enough fluid to brake at the end of the runway and get off a little bit to one side. We all jump off and the truck picks us up and takes us to debriefing.

Later that night, we go to see the damage to the ship. I remember I started to count the holes in our ship. A few hundred holes later I gave up. It takes six weeks to repair the ship. We inherit *The Buzzer*. Good old *Buzzer*, it got us through the rest of the tour!

At one point, Bob Simons also had his hand around a hydraulic line, trying to stop the leak, and the red fluid was spraying all over him. He looked like he'd been wounded, at least to me. Of course I am partly color-blind.

Missions were written up in detail. Planners wanted to know where flak came from, what tactics the fighters used, any signs of new factory construction or rail traffic- anything. There was even a form for reporting seeing other bombers get hit, called the Enemy Evasion Aid Report, which listed the type of airplane, date, time, place of take-off, target, place of trouble (like "over target") and nature of trouble, (for instance "hit by fighters").

The example I have in front of me now, reporting one of the losses of that day, also lists the ten men aboard, their names, ranks, serial numbers, and position in the plane. This one has the typical set-up: pilot, co-pilot, navigator, bombardier, nose gunner, top gunner, ball-turret gunner, tail gunner, and right and left waist gunners. Just like on my plane. But in this case, the plane didn't come back. The final item on the report is Witness' Statements: "A/C #13 (42–50307) hit by 8 fighters over the target and burst into flames. No chutes were seen. Position of crash was 45 00 N–24 55 E. Witness: Lt. Fee's Crew: 717th Sq." These reports were given to escape intelligence services, whose job it was to try to coordinate a safe return if any crew survived a crash and evaded capture.

Of course, when a ship went down, there was much more administrative detail, including the assignment of personnel to take custody of the lost airmen's belongings. These were usually held for a period in case the airmen returned, which did happen often enough. Planes made forced landings at friendly but distant airfields and returned after repairs, as we did once on Corsica. If a crewman escaped capture and was hidden by partisans and returned after being MIA, he had to deal with missing belongings. This happened to Ellis Arieff, one of the men who was to die on *The Buzzer.*

Of the four 449th losses that day, one was blamed on flak: "8 chutes seen to open," and three from fighters: "16 chutes seen to open."

Beyond the losses, the report tallies damage, casualties, and victories over enemy fighters. The damage tally was eleven damaged by flak, four of them severely; and one severely damaged by fighters. Two men were killed by fighter attack, and one seriously hurt by flak. In addition, four "slight" casualties were reported, two each from fighters and flak.

It was a regular practice at bomber base hospitals to warm up blood plasma for use when a flight of bombers were expected back from a raid. A plane with wounded aboard could fire a red flare, get landing priority, and be met by ambulance teams.

Under victories "(claim sheets being submitted)," five Messerschmitt ME-109s and five FW-190s are reported destroyed, with two more ME-109s listed as probables.

Further pages of the report detail which gun positions are claiming credit for the victories, and recount the last time the missing plane was seen: it was hit and left formation just before the formation reached Ploesti.

Each crew had to provide many details of its mission. Ours included details of rounds fired (900) and bombing results observed: "Huge fire seen and smoke rising to 10,000!"

Under "observations," our form reads:
   1 B-24 Ship exploded before hitting ground. 1404. No chutes seen. Another B-24 seen to go down at same time. #4 engine seen on fire. 2 chutes seen. 1 chute seen at 6:30 o'clock several miles behind.
   1 B-24 seen going down with white smoke trailing. No chutes seen. Time was 1404.

Accounts like this were looked at alongside similar ones from other planes. Often reports varied as to how many chutes were seen.

Under RESULTS, the official report says, "Because of effective smoke screen, results were difficult to observe. Some hits were reported in target area from visual observation and smoke and flame were reported. Smoke and cloud coverage over target prohibit plotting of bomb bursts on bomb strike photos."

Our 449th planes were among about 500 put in the air by the Fifteenth Air Force that day. More than a hundred enemy fighters rose to meet us.

The raid was written up in the May 6 *New York Times:* "Bombers Pound France, Balkans." There is also a story that day by the *Times,* famous military correspondent, Drew Middleton, on the vast collection of aerial reconnaissance photos the Allies were building up for the invasion that was expected sometime that year. Of course, now we know that D-Day was just a month away.

Mission After Mission After Mission

Several of us, including myself, remember a mission when we were so badly damaged, and isolated from other planes, that we stood little chance of surviving further attack.

I remember this happening, but I'm not sure which mission it was. We were separated from our group on several missions. I should mention that, in addition to the difficulties a ball turret gunner had bailing out, most of us had had no parachute training. We were, however, given instruction on the *theory* of bailing out. One piece of advice was to wait a long time before opening the chute-assuming that we weren't already at low altitude. This would accomplish two things: take us away from enemy fire, and get us down where the air was both warmer and richer in oxygen. Supposedly, some crews had bail-out oxygen bottles to use if they had to fall from 25,000 feet down to around 10,000 feet, where the air was breathable. I don't remember.

A good delay would also prevent us, with luck, from getting entangled in and dragged down with our plane's wreckage or having our chutes catch fire. Both did happen.

In addition, a delay cut your forward speed, which would lessen the jolt when the chute opened. Hanging from the chute, we were supposed to face the direction we were going, if possible, land with bent legs, and try to run forward while gathering up the shrouds to help get the wind out of the chute. Landing in trees or in water had its own special techniques.

Anyway, if we had to bail out, it would be our first jump, in conditions far from ideal but with plenty of incentive.

We had the next day, May 6, off. Some 449th units attacked Brasov's marshaling yards. On May 7, our target was the marshaling yards at Bucharest; but we had to turn back less than two hours after takeoff, because of engine problems. We could not reach altitude and were falling behind the formation, which you can't afford to do as you get close to enemy fighter territory.

May 10th brought more 449th attacks on the Wiener-Neustadt aircraft factory in Austria. About seven hundred planes from all units took off that day, and about three hundred turned back for one reason or another; twenty-eight were lost in combat.

On May 12, we joined the entire Fifteenth Air Force in attacks on German targets in Italy. As the briefing plan put it, "The entire Air Force is flying double sorties against selected objectives in ITALY in support of an all-out effort by the ground forces to break the present stalemate on the ITALIAN Front." This day's work aimed to destroy German headquarters and disrupt their communications, destroy port facilities where the enemy were being resupplied, cut rail links through the Appenines, and wreck marshaling yards.

My Mission Record for the 449th doesn't show an outing on May 12th, but I have not only briefing forms, showing a mission was planned, but debriefing forms and reports showing that one was flown.

The men going to bomb German headquarters had a tough assignment. The briefing paper described one target like this: "Monte Scratte-Tunneled into the side of a mountain, near an old and unused quarry is the general headquarters of Marshall KESSELRING, Commander of all Axis forces in ITALY. There are nine entrances into the tunnels, opening onto a road which winds along the side of the mountain . . ."

Our unit attacked the Port of San Stephano, where our group dropped some bombs on target and some in the water. Flak was "MAH"- medium, accurate, heavy.

One weapon against the German ground defenses was "window," or chaff, little strips of foil dumped out of the plane to try to confuse enemy radar. It was first used by the RAF's Bomber Command in the deadly firestorm raids on Hamburg in 1943.

Instructions for its use on one of our missions read: "Four cartons of window in each ship. Start dispensing four minutes before I.P. and increase rate of dispensing to 12 units every 30 sec in actual flak area." On our ship, the chaff dispenser was whoever had a free hand in the ship's waist. Usually it was Rudy Acosta and his fellow waist gunner Dean Girton. If we were under attack by fighters, there were no free hands; so chaff would generally be used against flak radar. Also, usually, when there was flak, there were no fighters very close. Anyway, when we got into a hot situation, there was no question of dispensing the stuff at a measured rate. It was cast overboard as fast as possible, in bigger and bigger clumps.

On May 13th, marshaling yards were again the goal on my next trip out, this time at Piacenza, in northern Italy. The mission was part of a vast Fifteenth Air Force effort to give tactical support to the Allied spring offensive in Italy.

Other 449th units were in action three times before my next outing, on the 19th. On May 14th, 449th bombers struck marshalling yards at Vicenza, Italy. On May 17th bombers went after the harbor at Orbetello, and the next day bombed a marshaling yard at Belgrade. Strange to think that we were bombing the same city again, fifty-five years later. May 18th was also the day Monte Cassino finally fell.

Oil was the goal on my next mission on May 19th, this time a storage facility at La Spezia, Italy. Ground support for the Italian campaign continued with my next flight, a May 22nd attempt against a railroad junction at Guilianova.

On the 23rd, other 449th units targeted troop concentrations at Grottaferrara. My next was a two-credit mission on May 10th my first to Wiener-Neustadt. The briefing for a mission to Ploesti on May 31st notes that successful attacks on Wiener-Neustadt's aircraft factories had raised oil to top priority.

The next day, May 25, we took part in a big attack on another oil storage facility, this one at Porto Marghera, Italy. Our third mission in three days was to bomb a railroad bridge in Var, France, in an effort to cut off supplies to the German forces in Italy. This was the time of the Anzio breakout. Var was just outside Nice, on the French Riviera.

Then I was done until June 2nd. However, other elements of the 449th were having their turns, against the St. Charles marshaling yard in Marseilles on May 27th, against Wollersdorf Airdrome at Wiener-Neustadt on the 29th, and against an aircraft factory in Ebreichsdorf, Austria, on the 30th.

It was usual for crews well into their tours to be given a visit to rest camp. I think we went about this time. Some of the men who died on *The Buzzer* had their rest camp on the Isle of Capri. My crew went to Cesarea Terme, on the heel of the boot of Italy. It was nice, with hot springs and so on. It was about the only thing officers and enlisted men did together as a crew, apart from bomb Axis targets.

It was a three - or four - day break, on the Adriatic coast opposite Albania. Rudy Acosta recalls:

There were high bluffs and caves and people fishing, "There was a movie screen and sulfur baths. The first night we used the saved-up whiskey [whiskey saved from the tots given after missions]. No chasers. We were on the third floor of this beautiful hotel. I blacked out. We went to town. I came to twice. Once in a theater where I threw up. My friends held me up. The second time I was on the ground, in gravel. Rizan says he was carrying me but he dropped me. He'd been drinking too.

Then at the hotel they got a stretcher to carry me upstairs but Rizan dumped me down and watched me roll down the stairs. I was very bruised. I had a sore head the next day. We had a quiet day. The second night Phil Rizan got drunk and walked around on this ledge twenty or thirty feet up. Phil was laughing. The third day we went sailing and saw the big caves.

My crew didn't fly on that May 31st Ploesti mission, whose briefing mentioned Wiener-Neustadt, but; a closer picture of a crew's day-to-day concerns can be seen in that mission's Deficiencies and Suggestions Report, where mechanical or planning problems plaguing each crew were aired. These items are selected from the forms of a number of aircraft:

All glass on ship should be washed.

Sight in nose turret double image.
Link chute in right gun tail turret jams.
Right waists one of spade rests loose. Needs special tool.

Flak in #3 cowling.

Tail turret booster went out.
Camera man's heated plug was out.

#2 voltage regulator out.
Bolts and nuts holding felt in nose turret loose.

Engineer cranked landing gear down, practically every mission.
Interphone out.

Had to pull excessive power on climb.
Load good today.

#3 prop gov. out and had to be replaced twice before T/O.

Bomb wouldn't release, cocking lever bent.

#3 and #4 tachometer out over target.
Fuel and oil pressure gauges stuck.

Tail turret need front skirt or apron on flak suit, wouldn't issue it to him.
Heated suits out, one on fire.
Ball turret right gun out (ten minutes.)
Left hand bomb bay doors difficult to open.

No A-5.
No interphone.

No damn good for any lead such a group.
Bombsight bad.

No tape, sulfa tablets or iodine in First Aid Kit.
Went over target with ball and tail turrets out, caused by improper maintenance.

Tail turret gun inoperative.
Jones cord on top turret inoperative, shorting out mike switch.
Right nose gun inoperative.
Guns dirty second day in a row.
One sustenance kit short.

Aerial shot out.
Remote reading compass shot out.
Nose turret out completely.
A-5 went out.
"B" section extremely straggled and fly all over sky.
Conveyor belt sprung, left waist ammunition hangs.
Flimsy on route was ambiguous.

Turned in fighter as destroyed last time and it was given to "B" section, they were in "C" section which was the one shot at by whole section.
Why turn in fighters destroyed if credit given to someone else.

Nose turret, opening in plexiglass.
Charging handle in tail turret needs fixing.

Nose turret door will not open from inside.
Ball turret earphone junction box fell apart.
Not enough time between awakening and start engines.

#4 engine out by flak.
Electrical system shot out.
No instruments, radio, compasses.
Threw out waist guns, flak suits and ammunition preparing to ditch.

Wing man #27 and 71 flew excellent formation.

#1, 2 and 4 generators out, inverter for instrument and radio only electric equipment used.

Some don't want "K" rations, some do.

"Look[ed] like enemy knew we were coming, that smokescreen was 100% effective."
Hole caused by lead plane in this box cleaning up brass and links after test fire, put big hole (2" in diameter) in top turret.

This is what some of the bomb crews had to deal with that day when it came to enemy fighters, according to that mission's Special Narrative Report, Section IV A, on Fighters:

15 Me 109s and FW 190s observed over target area at 1004 [10:04 AM] at 20,000 [ft]. An Me 109 attacked this formation over island of VIS at 9,000 [ft] from 1240 to 1255 hours, he made 5 passes from 6 o'clock high, 9 o'clock high and 12 o'clock high. 1 Ju 88 [Junker] attacked this formation at target from 7 to 8 o'clock level then went down. 1 Ju 88 came from nose on dive from 1 o'clock to 6 o'clock at target. 1 FW 190 attacked this formation at 1004 hours 20,000 feet just after target, it was reported that he slid across, came up at right wing then dropped behind. He had yellow nose, wide yellow band around fuselage; painted

brown. At the target FW 190s were attacking stragglers. Just after target 1 Me 110 came in from left, closed to 800 yards and went down on left side. At the target FW 190s were firing 20mm cannon. 10 minutes after target 1008 hours at 20,000 [ft] an FW 190 came in at 4 o'clock, closed to 500 yards and peeled off at 6 o'clock low. 4 to 5 Me 110s fired rockets into formation just after target at 20,000 [ft].

And, of course, there was "intense, accurate, heavy" flak, too.

Most of the 719th squadron had a stand-down on June 2nd, but we were one of ten ships and four crews that joined the 449th on a two-credit trip to marshaling yards at Simeria, Romania. The log for that day shows that we took off at 5:43 in the morning and landed at 12:43 pm. We fired fifty rounds. Results: "Hit to left of target-C section did not hit tgt. . . . Was hit by another gp. Ahead of us" This mission must have been a lot more pleasant than most in one respect—on the line for flak, there is a nice fat "0."

That was the first of four missions in five days. On June 4th, the day Rome fell, we went to bomb docks at Savona, Italy. The next day we attacked marshaling yards at Bologna. We were one of eleven 719th planes that day, and our squadron had no injuries.

Although our missions were all over southern Europe, my memory focuses most on those two-credit Ploesti days and similar tough rides to Vienna. Many of the missions we flew in northern Italy were part of an effort to tactically support Allied ground forces by denying retreating German forces needed access to escape routes and supplies. Thus, we bombed harbors in enemy hands, train yards, bridges . . . anything that would make the loss of Italy more of a blow to the Germans.

D-Day . . . Over Ploesti

It's very easy for me to recall what I was doing while Normandy was invaded on June 6, 1944. It was the day of our crew's second mission to Ploesti, my sixteenth mission overall. It was another two-credit trip. Our target was the Romano Americana Refinery. It was an important one. As the briefing said,

> The Wing Commander requests that attention of all crews be directed to the fact that groups of this Wing have been selected to hit the one remaining important oil target in PLOESTI . . . capacity of the PLOESTI refineries has been reduced approximately 90% in the series of attacks by the 15th Air Force which commenced on 5 April and continued through 31 May.
>
> The refining capacity of 9,225,000 tons which existed on 5 April is now between 900,000 and 1,500,000 tons. The Romano American Refinery had an active capacity of 1,000,000 tons on 5 April, and it is still relatively undamaged, its capacity being currently estimated at 900,000 - almost the entire remaining productive capacity at PLOESTI.

The Intelligence Annex to the operations orders said, ". . . the destruction of the remaining active capacity at PLOESTI will create a critical situation for the entire Axis war effort and make possible further important inroads through attacks in Austria, Hungary, Yugoslavia and Italy.

We didn't know about the Normandy landings right away. We were doing our part to stop Hitler by cutting off his chief source of oil. At briefings, the intelligence officers kept saying each mission to Ploesti was the last. *The Buzzer* was one of thirty-nine 449th B-24s on that day's raid.

Some have said we held off bombing refineries with connections to American oil companies. When I visited Romania in the 1990's, I learned that a reservoir of pro-American feeling in Ploesti dated from oil business investment and contacts dating back to the nineteenth century. Nevertheless, the Romano-Americana was our goal that day. We certainly knew to expect plenty of flak. As the briefing dryly noted, "Photo recce to May 5 reveals the presence of 194 heavy guns in the PLOESTI Area . . . "

As the attack on Ploesti unfolded, I had a fine view from my ball turret, as I watched the corrugated metal bomb bay doors slide open and saw the ten five-hundred-pound bombs plunge from the plane, which lurched upward as it lost the weight. I watched the cluster of bombs dive earthward and then as always at Ploesti, lost them in smoke.

I remember that on other missions, if there wasn't an undercast I could watch the bombs all the way down till they exploded on the ground. In my six missions to Ploesti, however, I never saw the city or the refineries or the railyards, thanks to the smokescreen.

I could tell that the bombs were causing some damage, though, because huge pillars of black smoke were rising up through the white smoke of the defensive screen. And our forces had been hurt too. The flak had been "IAH"—Intense, Accurate and Heavy.

As we left the area, Lt. Rogers took the plane down from our five-mile-high bombing altitude to about nine thousand feet. We could take off our oxygen masks, which by now were wet with saliva.

Whenever we reached the Adriatic, I would position the turret for "Exit," guns pointing down then I would open the hatch and climb up into the waist. The final maneuver was to retract the turret into its well in the fuselage.

Early in combat our crew learned that if the ball turret was pointed toward the front of the plane, and a crew member used the "fore relief tube," urine would spray all over my safety glass window, where it would freeze quickly and completely obscure my vision.

This didn't matter on the way home; but if it happened on the way out, it was a serious problem, because there was no way to clean it up. The turret would be useless, the use of its two .50 calibre machine guns would be lost, and the plane's underside would be blind and undefended. So, my deal with the crew in the forward compartment - pilot, copilot, navigator, bombardier, nose gunner, and flight engineer - was that, if they had to use the tube they would let me know via intercom, and I would turn the turret aft with a flick of the control handle.

On this particular day, I was still in the turret as we flew homeward west over Yugoslavia's Dinaric Alps, with the blue Adriatic in sight. I was facing aft, listening to Armed Forces Radio, and wondering about the fates of the men who had been shot down on the mission. Did they get out of the plane and parachute safely to earth?

As I've said, at the time, we had no information on what happened to our men. As for the people on the ground where our bombs were landing, I had no concern. As far as I was concerned, they were all Nazis and enemies.

While listening to music, and speculating in a comfortable, almost supine position, I noted drops of liquid leaking through my hatch door. My first thought was that it was hydraulic fluid. Many of the systems on the B-24 were operated by hydraulics, including brakes and flaps. Loss of fluid could cause serious landing problems. It had already happened to us on the May 5th raid. So, my first thought was that the hydraulic lines in the bomb bay had been damaged by flak.

I was in a panic but not yet ready to notify the pilot. Being partially color-blind, I wanted to check further. Removing a glove, I applied a finger to the liquid still leaking in and touched it to my lips. It tasted salty. Then I realized it was not hydraulic fluid. I screamed on the intercom: "Who in hell is taking a piss? It's leaking into my turret!" Somehow it had not sprayed all over, but was just seeping.

I was greeted by raucous calls of denial and amusement. It had to be someone in the forward part of the plane. Baldy Hinds finally owned up. To say the least, I wasn't happy. But I was still glad it was not hydraulic fluid.

As always, Ploesti's smokescreen made bomb damage assessment difficult. The June 6th strike assessment for the 449th logged thirty to forty bomb bursts in open fields, one and a half to two miles from target; twenty bursts in open fields, two and a half miles from target; fifty to sixty bursts in open fields and riverbed four to five miles from target; and ten bursts near a small village six miles from the target.

And yet . . . as the "Remarks" section of that report says, "Although the smokescreen is very effective, intense black smoke building up through it after the first section's bombing indicates that oil installations of some sort were hit."

Despite the heavy flak that day, no ships were lost. Two planes were damaged by flak near Belgrade, on the way to the target, and had to return to base. Another returned when its engine failed, and another returned because of a sick man aboard.

As usual, there was no hanging back when it came to "Deficiencies and Suggestions" from various planes:

Nose turret doors stick. On return at 15,000, speed was too slow to make formation flying easy.

Hydraulic leak in brake cylinder. #3 & #4 generator out. Sight gauges out.

No tools. Supercharger went out, crew chief had no tools to repair it with.
Radio compass works off and on. 2 superchargers, 1 &3, 1 on and off, 3 out complete.

Route miserable. Foolish to go over Belgrade. [Group] leader made right turn which carried us into flak that could easily be seen.

Very low air speed going to target. Ships in rear had hard time staying in formation. Oxygen outlets, flight deck and nose turret, either leaking or freeze at altitude.

Oxygen in ball leaked somewhere. Interphone out in ball turret. Ear phone in camera hatch out. Bomb sight toggle switch froze, hard to salvo.
Lost power #3 over target. Gas or oil leak out of #4. Latches on waist window worn out. Too much load for long trip.

Turned into flak over target and into Belgrade. Third straight day, low element of B unit has been in trail of attack unit A and too close, in prop wash and makes for poor formation.

Basters [sic]-Why in hell did we go over Belgrade? Why on oxygen for 41/2 hours? Why in hell over target on way back at 155 indicated?

Fruit for breakfast.

Twice now both switches put in wrong in ball turret. Why go over Belgrade? That was rough!

Oxygen seems to run low-check pilot's system for possible leak. The altimeter in nose (which we never use) could be taken out to give us more room. "Extra curricular flak areas should not be crossed.

Left wing will have to be changed. Returned because of flak damage.
Lead went over Belgrade. Wing leadership *very* poor. Group lead poor.

Right waist mike switch jammed. Right waist suit did not work. Why go over Belgrade?

Leadership over Belgrade—Shame!

Interphone garbled. Sperry ball elevation gears seemed frozen. Pilot and co-pilot seats cannot be moved by one man—would be difficult situation in emergency. Why over Belgrade?

Ball turret would not fire. Booster on tail turret jammed.

Heated clothing poor, freeze or burn!

Lost one engine over I.P., squared away at target, had to return unescorted and on 3 engines all the way. Called fighter and could not get escort - really sweated it out.

Piss poor ship. Do not care to split up crew—they trained together and wish to fly together.

Want whiskey as before when can drink at leisure - for whole crew. When go all way up to target, can't see why don't go over it.

Lead poor over Belgrade. No K rations. Heated suit burned, blisters leg.

Too much noise in barracks at night, especially engineering barracks.

Poor mission in every way.

#4 turbo shot up by fighters. #1 engine riddled by fighters, and #2 engine oil system shot up. Rough mission— came back on wing, 2 engines and prayer.

Other 449th crews hit oil installations at Porto Marghera, Italy on June 9. Trieste was my next mission, on

June 10. We struck oil storage and refineries. I was back with my regular crew. There was black and red flak - it often came in different colors. The weather at target was cloudy; our plane dropped some bombs on target, but some may have gone into the water. The report for the group says, "Visual observation reported exceptionally large fire was started in target area."

Our own complaint on this mission was: "Formations dropping bombs through our formation. [B-24s] came from different [headings]." Luckily, there were no casualties from this, or any on the whole mission for that matter, even though four planes had minor flak damage.

In addition, on our ship's Interrogation Report, under "evaluation of fighter escort," the word "None" is underlined many times. In fairness, the unit's Narrative Report for the mission says that while no specific rendezvous was made with fighters, "friendly fighters were seen in the target area."

The incident of the other formation dropping bombs through our formation featured in the Deficiencies and Suggestions report. One plane said the "friendly" bombs fell just fifteen feet back of the tail. According to the official report, twenty bombs were dropped through the formation, and vapor trails were seen above.

As usual, the complaints ranged in seriousness from "Bomb rack, #3 in left rear, hung [up]. Emergency release failed to release" to, "Want better food, green powdered eggs no fucking buona."

In case you think the feedback was all negative, that day rated a "Good deal today" from one pilot and, "All in all nice job of bombing today" from another.

Mission after mission after mission . . . there was no one big end-of-the-movie fight that settled things for the strategic bombers—just several long years of relentless, industrial process. But, of course, each day could be hugely dramatic-or-tragic for the individuals involved.

A tour seemed like a very long time, full of many missions, even to men who, like myself, came over to serve for just a few months. Even one mission could be a long time.

Damaged planes sometimes managed to land somewhere short of base. Some came down in neutral Switzerland, and the crews were interned. Some came down at other bases in Italy. Often, planes returning over Yugoslavia landed at the small airstrip on the Partisan-held island of Vis on the Yugoslav coast. The Partisans there and in many parts of the Balkans were supplied by airdrops by Allied planes, including some based at Grottaglie. A few times, we thought we would have to ditch, and might meet the British who ran a marine rescue service in the Adriatic.

We did get into so much trouble on one mission that we had to make an unscheduled stop. In this case, it was not in the Adriatic but west of Italy, on Corsica.

"Before the target, we lost an engine," Rudy Acosta recalls. We were struggling, and having trouble with another engine. We got one string of bombs off. By that time, we had only two engines working. We knew we couldn't get back to base than a third engine started acting up. We headed to our airfield at Corsica.

We buzzed the field and set off a red flare and landed. A Jeep full of officers pulled up. They were angry we'd landed with a red flare when we had no injuries. When they found out we had no radio it was OK.

We had to "overnight" there while our plane was fixed. Rudy remembers: "They told us we'd be bombed that night. Our tent was next to an antiaircraft gun. They gave us a pick and shovel, but the ground was hard rock. I dug a six-inch deep trench. That's enough, unless it's a direct hit, and if it's a direct hit, it doesn't matter. There was no raid, and we left the next day. We'd been declared MIA already - our tents were guarded [to prevent theft].

It was a reminder of the haunting sight of guarded tents that had greeted us when we arrived at Grottaglie. This time, though, we were soon back to reclaim our tents.

On June 11, we had another two-credit job - the oil refinery at Constanta, Romania - all the way over to the Black Sea coast. I was to visit Constanta again five decades later, on a very different mission.

The overall aim of our mission in 1944 was to slow down the Germans as much as possible by attacking their supply of oil. The idea was that crude oil no longer being refined at Ploesti was coming to this site by pipeline, then being shipped by barge up the Danube to refineries in Yugoslavia, Hungary, and Austria. Another part of this strategy was mining the Danube by RAF bombers.

The day of our mission, thirty-nine planes took off for Constanta, and two returned early. Thirty-six returned after bombing the target; one was missing. The mission report notes that good bombing results were claimed by the bombers, and that photographs back up claims of many hits on oil storage tanks and nearby marshaling yards. The report also acknowledged misses that landed in residential areas or open fields.

Some Deficiencies and Suggestions:
Left waist gunner oxygen box shot out.
Right waist gun hit.

Tail turret electrical system, interphone shot out.

One plane had an engine shot out by flak. One reports ominously, "Tail turret completely out."

Neighborhood
And Neighbors

We didn't meet many of the local people of Grottaglie. There were the women who sold eggs; but, socially, the local women wouldn't go near us, except for the prostitutes. We in the Fifteenth weren't like the Eighth Air Force guys in England, who could get local girlfriends.

Rudy Acosta recalled to me one attempt we made to get acquainted with some local women. One day, our crewmate, Phil Rizan, took us into Grottaglie. We knocked on this door, and Phil said, "You know me." According to Rudy, "The guy screamed 'Niente!' and we heard a police whistle. We ran. It was pitch black, and we didn't know the town.

> We came to a dead end. It was a wall with a wooden door in it. We went in. I took out my Zippo and lit it. It smelled bad in there. We realized it was the back of the public toilet, and that we were at the downhill end of it, and it had been raining. We ended up running back to our base. It was a nightmare.

Our ground crew chief, Bart Peluso from Brooklyn, did get to know more local people, but he was based there a good while. Bart's father had worked in the New York fruit markets. He remembered being amazed that his father had worked during the Depression, when so many didn't. Bart grew up, like many of my crewmates, intoxicated by flying. When he was a child he took the twenty-five cents he'd saved up from selling The *New York Post* and bought a pair of silver wings to pin on. He recalled these being a big hit at his school. He joined up not for adventure, but because, like myself and my other crewmates, he knew Hitler had to be stopped. He wanted to stop him, and get home to his wife and child.

My crewmates and I, like so many, were only there a very short time, from April 5 to early August, 1944. To be honest, we were more focused on getting it over with and going home than on establishing a local social life. This went for other men at the base, too; we didn't get to know the British, or even many people from other squadrons. Between missions, we would just hang out in our tent area.

We did become friendly with some local kids, who would come to our tents, take our laundry, and bring it back clean. They sold eggs too, and we paid them with lire, cigarettes which they could trade, or candy and chewing gum.

Phil Jensen, a crewmate of Arieff's, told me: "It was fun to give those Italian kids some candy. They were so dirty we'd say why don't you go get a bath. They'd jump in a fountain."

Sometimes we'd go into Taranto. It was founded, according to tradition, by the Spartans, in the eighth century. It had been hit hard by Allied bombs. The social life wasn't much better than in Grottaglie; but, then, there was that good Navy food offshore.

Early in the war, Taranto was the scene of an Allied air raid that soon took on great significance. On November 11, 1940, twenty-one British Swordfish biplanes, based on the aircraft carrier H.M.S. *Illustrious,* used air-launched torpedoes to sink three Italian battleships. A cruiser was also damaged, as were the dock facilities. The Italian Navy abandoned use of the port.

U.S. Navy Secretary Frank Knox was impressed with the way the attack was carried out and recommended to Henry Stimson, Secretary of War, that precautions be taken against a similar carrier-based raid against the U.S. Navy at Pearl Harbor. It later emerged, of course, that Japan's Admiral Yamamoto was another one who was greatly encouraged by the raid and its results.

Taranto was also famous as the original home of Rudolph Valentino.

Although going into town wasn't a great attraction to me, we could go pretty much whenever we wanted if we weren't flying. Lt. Rogers was our pilot; but, on the ground we weren't closely supervised.

There was an official weekly 47th Wing newspaper, *The Bomb Blast,* but my crewmates and I can't recall a specific 449th paper. Rudy Acosta remembers following news like the progress of Overlord on a G-2 map on the base. In general, we didn't talk much about grand strategy. We were more concerned about what the next target was and what the next mission would be like.

Phil Jensen, in the O'Malley crew, reminded me: "When we got back from our missions we'd have a glass of whisky, a hot shower, a hot meal, and we could go to our bed and sleep and nobody would ever bother us."

We did get some U.S.O. shows. "Buck" Rogers remembers in particular one with Irene Ryan, who later played Granny on *The Beverly Hillbillies.* "During her comic act with her husband Tim, she looked at me and said, 'What are you laughing at, Lieutenant?'"

Rudy and I remember an "exotic" Tunisian belly dancer, "Rouhia." He recalled recently, "She was wearing this bra, and one of the strings busted. Those G.I.s were screaming! She fixed it and danced off stage."

Rudy also recalls a man who hypnotized himself and lay on two sawhorses with heavy blocks on his middle. We also heard that Joe E. Brown, who lost a son in the war, came to our base in March 1944, just before we arrived. Over the course of the 449th's stay at Grottaglie, between 1943 and 1945, other famous visitors included John Garfield, Helen O'Connell, Jack Haley, Artur Rubenstein, Irving Berlin, Phil Silvers, and Frank Sinatra.

Despite their role in the war, I had trouble seeing Italians strictly as "the enemy." I grew up in Brooklyn, and my father built houses in an Italian neighborhood there. When I was a kid, there was a daily running of the gauntlet on the way to school when we Jewish kids had to get past some Italian kids. I think it was under the El, the old elevated train line. But those confrontations were mostly purely verbal. They'd call us names, we'd call them names. Overall, my inclination was to like Italians. I didn't know this at the time, but it turns out that a lot of Italians from that region - Apulia - had settled in the U.S. in the early part of the century, especially in Brooklyn!

Part of our base was shared with RAF crews flying Wellingtons and Halifaxes on a variety of missions. Now, of course, I would be curious, and would make an effort to meet them and find out about their lives and where they were from. Back then, it was simply a matter of getting through the day and getting through the missions. We did meet some British troops and the ANZACs, troops from Australia and New Zealand, with those great hats, when we hitchhiked to Taranto.

I know our unit navigator, Hal Strack, got to know some of the British better; but, like Bart Peluso, he was at the base a longer time. He has written me, about some of his memories of some men's attitudes to life between missions, reminding me that some reacted to the situation we were in by taking it as easy as possible, while some wanted to raise hell: "One has to understand that in what appeared to the participants to be perilous times there had to be an air of fatality . . . At that time it seemed that we had about a fifty-fifty chance of making it successfully through a full tour of duty. We were losing about half our crews [but] did not know then that about half of them would ultimately make it back. Faced with somewhat dim prospects of survival, there was a tendency to be more 'devil-may-care' than would otherwise be the case."

And More Missions

One feature I remember of the non-target area stretches of our missions was the scenery. I got a good look at the landscape from the ball turret, as well as from inside the fuselage of the plane during the outward bound and homeward parts of the flight.

Crossing the snow-covered Alps to and from Germany was a wonderful sight. So were Yugoslavia's Dinaric Alps. Since most of our missions involved crossing Yugoslavia on the way to the target, we carried small survival kits with little cribsheets in the Serbo-Croatian language, plus a briefing on which factions were the good guys, mostly the more numerous Partisans of Tito in the south and west, but also Mihailovich's Chetniks in the east. The Croatian Ustachi in the north were as bad or worse than the Germans, and were to be avoided at all costs. The Partisans were communists and they fought with royalist Chetniks, except for both resisting the Germans and Ustachi in common cause as well as cooperating to get our downed airmen across Yugoslavia. Some 449'ers recount being rescued and well treated by the Chetniks as well as the Partisans, who finally won out in the struggle for power after the war when Tito took over all of Yugoslavia.

The briefing for one of our Ploesti missions warned us that if we ended up on the ground in Romania, we would be in enemy territory and shouldn't count on help from the local people. We were advised to head west, toward Yugoslavia, avoiding large towns and the main roads, or any roads that might be watched by the Germans. We were also told, "Be sure to attach your GI shoes to your harness and stuff a pair of woolen socks in them. This is important."

I found kind of intriguing the idea of parachuting into Yugoslavia and meeting up with the Partisans and making my way back to our lines, but I wouldn't have liked the bailing-out part.

I was on a non-effective flight on June 13, 1944. The target that day was the motor works at Allach, near Munich. We were an early return. When our group reached the target, it was covered by smoke and clouds; so the bomb run was made against the city's marshaling yards.

Although no planes from our group were lost that day, and no fighters caused problems, "IHA" flak hurt four men and damaged 26 of 38 planes. Other groups had losses. The Special Narrative Report notes: "B-24 ditched . . . 2 dinghys;" "B-24 going down in spin over target at 1035 hrs, 8 chutes seen;" "B-24 hit in hills just out of target area at 1040 hrs, 5 chutes seen."

Oil was the target again on June 14, when we bombed a refinery at Osijek, Yugoslavia. That day was also the day Roy L. Groeger, who was to die on *The Buzzer,* arrived at the base, a good six weeks before my last mission. So there was quite an overlap.

The "Oil Campaign" continued with a June 16 raid on the Apollo oil storage facilities at Bratislava, now in Slovakia. It was a two-credit mission. Huge fires were reported by witnesses, with smoke 18,000 feet high visible from 130 miles away, according to the Group Special Narrative Report.

This was a day of heavy fighter attacks. On the way to target, twenty-two fighters attacked the formation, from "all around the clock, high and low, mostly singly but in twos and threes in some cases."

FW-190's attacked from the five o'clock level, after dropping their belly tanks. Sometimes, fighters would attack from the side, then turn and attack from behind. There was flak, too.

Of the forty-two planes in our group that took off, two returned early; the rest returned safely, although four men were wounded. Our Group Special Narrative Report lists, under "Observations." "B-24 exploded, six chutes seen;" "B-24 down in flames–4 chutes seen;" and "B-24 smoking, going down and exploded when hit ground–8 chutes seen." Victories claimed: five Messerschmitts destroyed, and one "probable" and one damaged, and two Junkers destroyed.

Over the course of our tour, although flak was always a problem at heavily defended sites, at least the German fighters gradually became less effective. Bob Simons has reminded me that it was in June that year that P-51 Mustangs were really beginning to have an impact on the German fighters. In addition, as Lt. Rogers recalls, the German fighters let up from July on, "because all the German gas was going to the Russian front. They still had lots of pilots and fighters, but no gas. Our raids on the oil depots [were] taking effect."

Rudy Acosta recalls the fighter problem easing to a degree when our escorts started to escort us all they way. That was the beauty of the long-range P-51; they didn't have to turn around and go home miles before we got to the target area. In addition, we simply had more fighters as time went on. The time that we realized that the war was essentially won was when we saw P-51's circling over Ploesti as we approached the target area.

There were some problems when the P-51 first made its appearance. When the gunners first spotted a speck in the distance, we would watch it closely. Our usual P-38 escorts would roll sideways and show their double-tail construction as a tipoff they were friendlies. But there were a few instances where overeager gunners mistook the Mustangs for the opposition. Usually, though, a plane within effective firing range was also within identification range.

Rudy Acosta notes that, before that time, our losses were more from enemy fighters than from flak. Of our fighter escorts, Rudy told me: "They really saved our butts" on the June 16th Bratislava mission. The Fifteenth lost 56 bombers that day." He adds:

> We lost an engine at the target, from flak. It was smoking, white, from oil. We feathered it, and fell behind. We were losing the group. Over southern Austria, we ran into 109s. They made one pass, and some of our escorts showed up.
>
> Boy, they jumped into those 109s . . . before our fighters left three of them came over by our wing and tipped wings to us. We saluted each other.

Of course, this improvement doesn't mean the men who died on *The Buzzer* on December 9, 1944 had it much easier on their later tours. That's because the flak was getting worse as the fighter menace receded. They were still lucky to have come though combat alive.

On June 22nd, we took off for Latisana, Italy, hoping to smash a railway bridge; but my sortie was a "non-eff." Another two-credit mission to Ploesti followed on the 24th. The submarine pens at Toulon were targeted by other 449th units on June 25. The next day, I had another two-credit mission, this one to the Schwechat aircraft factory, in Vienna. No planes went down, but one man was killed and another badly injured by a flak burst exploding just outside the waist window of his plane.

The next day, June 27, we bombed Brod, Yugoslavia. It was an alternate target, and our plane's log lists hits between two marshaling yards, and flames and black smoke indicating oil installation bomb strikes.

Bad weather foiled an attempt on an aerodrome at Zagreb on June 30, and we, like the other crews, brought our bombs back to base. Our unit history notes that cloud cover was a frequent problem during June, but the month had a great statistic, at least for the 719th squadron: no planes lost.

Budapest's Vecses Airport was hit by other 449th units on July 2. My crew went to Giurgiu, Romania, on July 3, to strike oil storage facilities: two more credits. It was the start of a marathon streak of missions that boosted us toward finishing our quotas, even if it left us hardly any recovery time between flights. We flew six missions in seven days. Three of them counted double.

We spent Independence Day 1944 flying to and from Romania again, this time to a rail bridge at Ploesti. On the fifth, we bombed the submarine pens at Toulon again. Among the targets hit was a French battleship. We were part of a force of 319 Liberators and 228 Flying Fortresses that bombed that target and some French rail yards. We were off on July 6, while other 449th units tried again for the railroad bridge at Latisana. The next day, we went to Zagreb, now in Croatia, to hit marshaling yards.

On the eighth of July, for two credits, we attacked Markersdorf Aerodrome at Vienna. After Berlin, Vienna was the second most heavily defended bomber target in Europe. Ploesti was third; so naturally that's where we went on July 9. The target this time was the Concordia-Vega refinery, second biggest in Romania. The 449th got its second Presidential Unit Citation that day.

Pathfinder technology, using airborne radar, which we called "Mickey", was used effectively to counter the usual defensive smokescreen, but we suffered heavy losses. The flak was very bad. Our group put up twenty-eight planes that morning - with four early returns, one plane lost, one missing, two landing at friendly fields, and one crash-landing at a friendly field.

As was often the case at Ploesti, the best we had to go on at first, as far as results were concerned, was a huge column of smoke, this one 20,000 feet high, which could be seen for 150 miles. Interpretation Report No. D.B. 145, issued on July 16th, indicates the damage to the target:

> Very considerable fresh damage has been inflicted on all parts of the refinery. Primary Objectives affected include the main Distillation Unit slightly further damaged, Cracking Plant considerably damaged. Other installations damaged

include the Separation Plant, Stabilization Plant, and several small unidentified buildings and sheds. Very heavy fresh damage has been inflicted on storage tanks. Four large, six medium and four small storage tanks have been burned out and destroyed while at least two other medium tanks have been damaged. At time of photography considerable ground activity is apparent especially at N.E. corner where several lines of hose are playing on a still smoldering tank . . .

One bomber was seen with equipment being thrown out. Its crew was seen to begin to bail out. Another plane had nine men bail out before it crashed. Another crash-landed and burned, killing five men and injuring five.

The citation notes that other groups were unable to bomb that day because of the effectiveness of the smoke-screen; but that, despite enemy fighters and heavy flak losses, the 449th pressed ahead and got the target.

The Presidential Unit Citation read, in part: "The damage inflicted upon this section of the Ploesti fields was a material factor in causing the capitulation of Rumania, in addition to destroying the second largest refinery in Rumania. The outstanding performance of the leaders on this difficult and hazardous mission, the gallant and heroic efforts of all the men in inflicting tremendous damage to the enemy, together with the indefatigable and enthusiastic work of all the ground personnel of the 449th Bombardment Group (H) was an amazing display of esprit de corps and gallantry in the face of overwhelming odds."

After a few days off, during which other 449th units again attacked the Var River Bridge outside Nice, we bombed Budapest, on July 14. Our two-credit target was the Ferencvaros marshaling yards. Our mission was part of a general Fifteenth Air Force attack on Budapest that also targeted refineries and oil storage. The next day, we were back at Ploesti, going after the Romano-Americana refinery, the only one still relatively undamaged at that time.

I remember this day whenever I think about the practice of "blessing the mission." Each briefing ended with a blessing, and the good wishes of the 449th's Catholic chaplain: "Dominus Vobiscum and good hunting."

This was my fifth mission to Ploesti, with all its anti-aircraft guns and enemy fighters. Even the wall map in the briefing room, with its long black line stretching from Grottaglie, across the Adriatic and Yugoslavia to Ploesti, had an ominous look to it. At the briefing, we were told that this would be a big raid, with about 500 B-24s and B-17s taking part. Maybe we'd stop production and this would be the Fifteenth Air Force's last mission to that dreaded city.

We needed all the support we could get from "above." The "good hunting" sounded a little out of place coming from a chaplain; but it was nonetheless welcome. I couldn't help wondering whether the Luftwaffe and Romanian Air Force chaplains blessed their flyers with similar words, in German or Romanian, of course.

From the briefing room we went to the parachute supply shack and picked up our chest packs. The often-repeated joke as the chute was handed over was, "If it doesn't work, return it." Sometimes they didn't work.

By now, it was about five in the morning, just beginning to get light. The sky was clear. None of us enlisted men felt like eating breakfast - except, maybe, Rudy Acosta. Not that he has much good to say now about our food back then.

As we waited by our plane, nobody smoked. We were too close to the plane and all that 100-octane gasoline. I would think about our progress through our missions, in the absence of much real knowledge of what was going on - successes, losses, killed, wounded, prisoners of war. There was some war news in the Mediterranean edition of *The Stars and Stripes,* and we could see what went on around us, including empty tents. I knew I was pretty close to my fifty-mission quota.

A green flare went up. Shit! We were off.

Lt. Rogers opened the bomb bay doors and we got in the plane - tail, waist, and ball turret gunner, to the rear; pilot, copilot, navigator, bombardier, flight engineer, and radio operator to the front.

The engines started with bursts of exhaust. We started to taxi down the runway in a prearranged order. It was a thrilling sight to see those lumbering planes on their way to take-off. I was in the waist, resting, hoping to hell we would not blow up or crash on take-off. It did happen.

Lt. Rogers was ready now. He gunned the engines, and we raced down the runway, slowly lifting off the ground. The landing gear folded into the wheel wells. Slowly, Grottaglie, with its white buildings and airfield with its buildings and tents, began to disappear behind us.

We were on our way, headed for the Adriatic and God-knows-what. Did I pray? No, I couldn't. I didn't know how I didn't believe. Despite the famous line from Father William Thomas Cummings, in his 1942 Field Sermon on Bataan, "There are no atheists in foxholes," there sure was one atheist in a ball turret over Europe.

Our effectiveness over target that day was limited by a truly vast smokescreen.

We had a few more days off. On July 19, other 449th bombers attacked the Neaubing aircraft parts factory at Munich. Our last two-credit mission as a crew was July 20, against Lowenthal Aerodrome and an aircraft factory at Friedrichshafen, Germany. Bob Simons agrees with most of us, that Cinco de Mayo was our toughest mission; but he remembers this one especially well. His nose turret was hit and damaged. Other 449th men were in action July 21, against an aerodrome at Horsching, Germany.

My last mission was July 22nd - to Ploesti.

I ended up with thirty-six sorties, fifty missions—because fourteen of my missions counted double. I knew I was very lucky. I have a picture of Rudy Acosta kissing the ground after his fiftieth. Who wouldn't?

I know our planes shot down many of the German and Romanian fighters that came up after us. Sometimes dozens a day were counted. But, although I know I fired my guns a lot, I couldn't say for sure that I could claim any Messerschmitts or Focke-Wulfs or Romanian fighters myself.

Home! . . . For Me

I left Grottaglie in early August and went to the "reppledepple"—a replacement depot in Naples. Rudy Acosta went, too. He and I were among the earliest in my crew to complete our missions.

The usual way my crewmates left Grottaglie for Naples as their tours ended was by getting a ride on a B-24; Simons flew that way, and so did Rogers. We all successfully made the trip *The Buzzer* was to attempt unsuccessfully in December. Rudy remembers flying in a plane so crowded that he had to ride in the bomb bay. His plane took off, turned around and landed while some mechanical problem was fixed, then took off again headed to Naples.

A newspaper article from my hometown quotes an Army press release quoting me saying, "Of all my flights to date, my trips to Ploesti, Romania, where Hitler has vast oil refineries, were the roughest. Six times our crew faced the ack-ack guns at Ploesti and on every occasion we found that ducking it was almost impossible. We sustained more than a few hits but made it back every time. Even my golden mission was to Ploesti."

I couldn't swear that those were my exact words . . . I've been asked if it was very hard just to turn up every morning for such hazardous duty, but I just didn't see that I had any choice in the matter. Then there was the issue of my buddies—my crewmates.

Rudy told me recently: "I never did feel any pressure, except for take-offs and landings. We took off with planes

heavily loaded with fuel and bombs, and had to clear telephone wires at the end of the runway. Then once we took
off, we'd circle, and form up, and we'd be busy. Once we were
over the water, the Adriatic, we'd test-fire our guns. Once
we were over 10,000 feet, we'd go on oxygen. We'd approach
the target at 20,000 feet. You couldn't see people. We'd be
watching for fighters. I didn't worry about getting killed. I
felt like I was watching a movie. There'd be explosions all
around you, and I'd be praying that we get through it. Let
me tell you, if you didn't know how to pray, you learned how."

At the reppledepple I met a fellow Brooklynite, Dave
Krasner, a paratrooper from Brighton Beach. He was a little guy, full of stories about knifing Germans. He took Rudy
and me into Naples once to show us the sights, which turned
out to be a whorehouse. I remember trading my leather A2
jacket for a German helmet. I'm sure that was a bad deal.
Those jackets are probably worth a lot of money now.

I spent a while in the reppledepple, which was typical;
but my stay might have been made longer because many
ships were involved in the buildup to the August 15 invasion of southern France, code-named Operation Anvil and,
later, Dragoon.

At last, on September 30, we set out for home in a convoy of sixteen ships on a converted Grace Liner, the *Santa
Paula*. It had a few guns placed on the deck. I drew the
highly important role of third shellman on the aft 20 mm
gun. Luckily, we had no problems from the air or from subs.

When they converted a liner to a troopship, they didn't
mess around. The bunks were five high. I don't remember
which bunk I was on, but I do remember being impressed
that the troop bunks were the first racially integrated quarters I'd seen in the Army. This was, of course, several years
before President Truman's order to integrate the armed
forces. This struck me because everything up to then had
been segregated. I trained in the South and was amazed at
the "Whites Only" notices and other signs of Jim Crow. I didn't
go on protest marches about it, then; there weren't any I
knew of. But I didn't like it.

I didn't know it at the time, but on at least one of my missions, our fighter cover was provided by the 332nd Fighter Group—an all-Black fighter unit, the Tuskegee Airmen.

✈ ✈ ✈ ✈ ✈

When the ship pulled into New York Harbor, it was listing to port, because everyone had rushed to look at the Statue of Liberty and the skyline looming.

Rudy Acosta remembers someone being disoriented by, or just new to, big-city ways. Looking at the city streets from the troopship, this guy said to him: "That one car keeps coming around." "What car?" Rudy said. "That bright yellow one." The guy was talking about Yellow cabs.

We docked in Jersey City and went by troop train to Camp Kilmer, near New Brunswick, New Jersey. The train went close to my home. I sent a telegram home saying I was "somewhere on the East Coast." I didn't realize the telegram would be postmarked Camp Kilmer. So my family knew I was very close by. Soon I got a furlough and got to see them.

When crew chief, Bart Peluso, got back to the States, he was about to get on the subway to go home to Brooklyn when a car backfired or something went off, and he hit the deck. A cop came to see if he was OK and asked him if he was just back from the war. Bart said he was, and the cop took him to the subway himself.

Bart had called his wife, and she and his son and father and the rest of his family were right at the subway station in Brooklyn to meet him. He hadn't seen his loved ones for more than a year.

I wish I had known the story of Bart's homecoming when it happened. For decades, we all thought he had died in *The Buzzer* crash. His name had been on the list to fly that day, but he hadn't made the flight. Then some years later, in walks Bart to the 449th reunion in Houston.

Jack Cox got a train as far as Johnson City, Tennessee, then decided to save his money and hitchhike the rest of the way home. When he didn't get a ride, he went the rest of the way by bus.

Buck Rogers got to his hometown in Illinois, left his bag in a tavern near his home, then walked down his street, realizing he was actually living out a longtime fantasy of walking down that street in his uniform, with his wings and medals on. "It did feel good to walk down the street after getting home," he said. "I had my medals on, I was a returning war hero. It was a kick."

The Skinas Brothers

My overseas combat tour was ending as the men who were to die on *The Buzzer* were getting more and more involved in combat, and as men from my crew were still logging their last few missions.

I have the Operational Performance Record, or mission log, for Tom Skinas, a tailgunner who almost flew on *The Buzzer* the day it crashed. He was part of the crew led by Lt. Willam Bache, who also did not fly that day. Skinas' record probably closely resembles that of the other men in the crew who were on their way home, though it was rare for an entire crew to fly exactly all of the same missions.

Surely, Skinas has the strangest story of those who might have been on the doomed plane but were saved by chance. He had been all set to ship out with his crewmates, when he learned that his twin brother had been arrested and charged with manslaughter after killing an Italian marine in a bar fight. He decided to stay and see if he could help his brother - and thus missed the doomed plane.

Tom Skinas wrote me in September 1995, describing how he had always lived in the shadow of his slightly older, much larger twin. "We were of Greek origin, and among Greek families the firstborn, if male, holds a special place. All our relatives would refer to him as 'palikari', which means brave warrior. I have no memory of ever being called a 'palikari' when in my childhood . . . I resented the fact that I was not considered a firstborn male by my parents and uncles and especially by my twin, John, who did not

95

consider me to be his equal. And yet in our own way, we loved each other."

When both men entered the Air Corps in 1942, Tom was five feet, two inches tall, and weighed 105 pounds; John, the firstborn, was a 200-pound six-footer. Tom describes him as "an extroverted, domineering and garrulous individual blessed with rare artistic ability." Separation in the forces proved a good thing for Tom, who said being expected to perform like any other recruit despite his size was "simply exhilarating."

The war did not take them very far apart. By 1944, both were in Italy, flying in B-24s, Tom as a tail gunner and his brother as a radioman/gunner. "I joined the 449th in July 1944 and flew my first mission [July 30, 1944]. My last mission was [December 2, 1944]. I had flown 35 sorties and [was] credited with 40 missions. My crew flew the first five missions on *The Buzzer*. We then received the *Sleepytime Gal* which was the second B-24 to bear that name." It was lost on July 2, 1945.

Tom continued:

Upon my arrival overseas, my brother kept writing to me to request his transfer to the 449th. There was an Army policy that allowed twins to be assigned to the same unit . . . I however, did not request his reassignment, although I never told him that. In my mind I justified my inaction [because] flying combat missions in B-24s was more dangerous than flying C-47s. In late October '44, after returning from a mission, I found him sitting in my tent. Somehow, he arranged the transfer solely on his own. I had very mixed emotions upon seeing him. We had been separated for over two years. We flew three or four missions together but never in the same B-24. Those missions were the most traumatic, for to see your brother's B-24 flying through a flak barrage heightened the fears experienced in those moments.

In November, my brother went to Taranto. There he met a Greek soldier serving in the Greek Army assigned to the British [Eighth] Army. They went to a bar and picked up some Italian girls. Most of the patrons in that bar were Italian marines. The Italian marines resented the girls' drinking with the Allied soldiers. A melee started. My brother was stabbed in the back of his neck and shot in the leg. He in turn shot and killed one of the Italian marines. While the fight was going on, the British military police arrived and beat up everybody trying to restore order.

I flew my last mission on December 2, 1944. On or about December 7, a General Court Martial found my brother guilty of manslaughter and sentenced him to eight years at hard labor. When I got back to the base from Bari, I saw the Squadron Commander and pleaded with him that I be allowed to remain in Italy and not be rotated with my crew. I even volunteered to fly extra missions. He agreed to my staying back. I believe the next day my crew took off on *The Buzzer.*

A few months later, Tom's brother's sentence was reduced to time served, and he was released to fly more missions.

I hadn't known that Skinas and his crew had actually flown their first five missions on *The Buzzer.* So these men not only died in the plane that had carried me on so many missions, they also had faced their first combat in it.

And Still More Missions

Skinas' first mission was July 30, only eight days after my last one. In those eight days, bombers from the 449th flew three missions against oil refineries at Berat/Kucove, Albania, Thalerof Aerodrome, at Graz, Austria, and the Manfred-Weiss Armament Works in Budapest.

The first Skinas mission was to the Budafpuszta oil refinery, at Lispe, Hungary. Next was Aviso, Italy, on August 3. The target was a railroad bridge in the Brenner Pass.

On August 6, the men from my old crew who had not finished yet—including Rogers, Bennett, Girton, Rizan, and Bob Simons—were on yet another mission against the sub pens at Toulon. I know from the Deficiencies and Suggestions Report that their plane's ball turret short-circuited that day. In addition, one of Phil Rizan's top turret guns didn't work, as well as one of the tail guns.

Two of the men who were to die on *The Buzzer* were on that mission: Roy Groeger, in 2nd Lt. Robert E. Underwood's crew, and Joseph Brehun, in Lt. Aldrich's crew.

Flak was heavy, according to my crew's report. The mission's briefing had warned of ninety-six heavy AA guns in the Toulon area. The briefing advised a look at maps showing the safe areas of France; it also recommended Italy and Spain, and warned against coastal regions and the Rhone Valley. Among that day's "Deficiencies and Suggestions" were:

A bit of apparently unnecessary screwing around was noted as we turned on I.P., was that 360 degree turn necessary?

First Aid kit not worth a damn.

Very, very, very, very poor breakfast this morning-rotten eggs.

Skinas' crew was in action over the Alibunar Aerodrome, Belgrade, Yugoslavia on August 7 and over the Vecses Aerodome, Budapest, Hungary on August 9. The Belgrade mission was a diversionary effort, hoping to draw fighters from a major bomber offensive against the synthetic oil works at Blechhammer, Germany. I have the interrogation form showing that Ballou, Erickson, Gettys, and Eckerling were also aboard that day. There was no flak at the target, although some was encountered over Novi Sad, Yugoslavia, and the pilot reports: "bombs were on target . . . the group as a whole dropped bombs on target, on center of field and on the town of Alibunar."

Coastal batteries at Toulon were next, on August 13. These were targeted as part of the buildup to Operation Dragoon. Skinas' first Ploesti mission followed on August 18. The target was the Dacia-Romano refinery.

The infamous Ploesti smokescreen was the target of a new bombing tactic tried on August 17, by other 449th units, and on the 18th. A P-38 fighter went over the target ahead of the bomber force and reported back on any effect the wind was having on the smokescreen, including which parts of the target were remaining clear. These last few days saw successful visual bombing, according to tactical reports.

Before then, other 449th units had been striking gun emplacements at Hyeres, France and Genoa, Italy. On August 15, D-Day for the invasion of southern France, invasion beach 263A was struck. The 449th sat out the last Fifteenth Air Force raid on Ploesti, on August 19. There were no Fifteenth Air Force bomber losses. Other 449th units also bombed marshaling yards at Szolnok, Hungary on August 20, and the Lobau underground oil storage site at Vienna on the 22nd.

Skinas was on a two-credit mission on August 23, also to Vienna, to bomb a refinery in the suburb of Vosendorf. Texas Senator Lloyd Bentsen, who served in the 449th as Squadron Commander of the 716th, was on this mission. His plane came away from Vienna in bad shape and made an emergency crash landing at Vis. Bentsen won a Distinguished Flying Cross for bringing the crew in safely that day. Many years later, the Senator was helpful to me in tracking down my Texas-based former crew members.

✈ ✈ ✈ ✈ ✈

On the 24, Skinas and his crew went on an attack at a rail bridge at Szeged, Hungary. Meanwhile, under Soviet pressure, Romania had officially switched sides, joining the Allies. The next mission, August 26, was to bomb a train ferry terminal at Giurgiu, Romania, to close off one avenue of German retreat. However, the 449th returned to base with its bombs, however, since it could not pinpoint the target.

A railway bridge at Ferrara, Italy was the target for Skinas and crew twice in a row, August 27 and 29. As with the ferry attack, the strategic aim was to interfere with the German retreat. In between, on the 28th, other 449th units went after marshaling yards at Miskolc, Hungary.

The night of the 29th brought the news that Ploesti had been captured by the advancing Soviet land forces. From all accounts, there was some serious celebration at Grottaglie, and I'm sure at bases all over southern Italy. The awful, deadly Ploesti campaign was over.

Here is the official word on the Ploesti campaign:
MEDITERRANEAN ALLIED STRATEGIC AIR FORCE U.S. FIFTEENTH AIR FORCE 205 GROUP R.A.F. PLOESTI DECLASSIFIED SUMMARY OF OPERATIONS RESULTS AND TACTICAL PROBLEMS INVOLVED IN 24 ATTACKS BETWEEN 5 APRIL AND 19 AUGUST '44.

THE AIR BATTLE OF PLOESTI—A GENERAL SUMMARY OF OPERATIONS AND RESULTS

The Air Battle of PLOESTI—one of World War II's greatest sagas—ended 19 August 1944 with the last of 24 attacks on PLOESTI's vital oil installations by bombers of the Mediterranean Allied Strategic Air Force which all told destroyed 90 percent of PLOESTI's productive capacity and virtually eliminated it as a rich source of high grade fuel for the LUFTWAFFE and WEHRMACHT. A fitting climax to this outstanding achievement was the evacuation of 1,135 airmen (1,061 of whom were Fifteenth Air Force personnel) from BUCHAREST on 31 August, 1 and 3 September 1944 by Flying Fortresses and crews which only 12 days previously had taken part in the last PLOESTI mission.

Air operations against PLOESTI by MASAF started on 5 April 1944, eight months after the two attacks of the U.S. Eighth and Ninth Air forces then operating from Middle East bases, and lasted until 19 August 1944. During this almost 5-month period, Fifteenth Air Force heavy bombers flew 6,186 sorties, dropped 13,469 tons of bombs, were escorted by 3,400 fighters.

Twenty daylight missions were flown over what was the third most heavily defended target on the continent (protected by 240-plus heavy guns). The 205 Group (R.A.F.), which, with the Fifteenth U.S. Air Force, comprises the Mediterranean Allied Strategic Air Force, conducted four night attacks against PLOESTI and contributed substantially to the overall success of the PLOESTI campaign.

At the time of the 5 April attack the PLOESTI refineries were potentially capable of a crude oil throughput capacity of 709,000 tons per month.

Actual estimated production at this time was 458,000 tons of crude throughput per month of which 177,000 tons represented maximum gasoline production—approximately one-third of the total AXIS gasoline output.

Attacks between 5 April and 6 May not only cut deep into excess refinery capacity, but also affected actual PLOESTI output. In 6 attacks during this period the throughput capacity was reduced from 709,000 tons per month to 317,000 tons, a reduction of 44 per cent. The success of these operations was particularly outstanding in view of the fact that on several of these missions the effort was divided between the refineries and the adjacent marshaling yards. The result of these attacks, proof that oil refineries could be hit and knocked out with a reasonably [sic] economy of force, was a large factor in the revision at this time of strategic priorities, placing oil at the top of the list and initiating the intensive air campaign by Allied Air Forces against GERMAN oil installations—synthetic and crude.

That the hard fought Air Battle of PLOESTI against fierce resistance from flak and fighters and the most effective smoke screen yet experienced succeeded may be measured in terms of productive capacity denied the enemy. Since the start of operations in April, the capacity of the PLOESTI refineries was reduced by 89 per cent, from 709,000 tons crude throughput per month to 77,000 tons. During this time period the production of gasoline was cut to 15,400 tons per month, a reduction of 91 per cent as compared with pgasoline capacity of 177,000 tons per month as of 5 April 1944.

The loss of PLOESTI oil at a time when all other major enemy oil production centers were being systematically liquidated day by day represents a major triumph in the history of strategic air warfare.

As the summary notes, there were twenty raids on Ploesti by units of the Fifteenth Air Force. Nineteen were daylight heavy bomber raids, and there was one attempt, on June 10, to attack the refinery with dive-bombing P-38s.

According to a Statistical Summary of the Air Force's daylight attacks, prepared by the Twenty-Eighth Statistical Control Unit, there were more enemy aircraft encounters per 100 sorties over the Ploesti area than over any other target zone. This official report agrees with the impressions of my own crew and others, however, that fighter opposition dropped off in July and August. Again, this is not to say that the men of *The Buzzer* crew, and the passengers who served later than we did, had it easy. As the report puts it, "The decrease in losses due to enemy fighter opposition at PLOESTI was offset by a marked increase in losses due to flak during the last two months."

Our own fighters played a big role in reducing enemy fighter opposition, shooting down a great many planes. Long-range escorts flew into danger themselves, with thirty-six lost - one to flak, fifteen to enemy aircraft, and twenty for other or unknown reasons.

The Statistical Summary struggles to put a brave face on our bomber losses in the Ploesti campaign, but it's a hard task. The report says: "In view of the importance of this target to both sides, relatively high losses were to be expected."

How high? We lost 223 bombers against Ploesti from April to August.

The Summary also says: "While our loss of 223 bombers in these operations was somewhat higher than the average loss rate on all operations during this period, it was not proportionately greater than losses incurred in attacks on key targets in other areas.

Moreover, the compensating results in the crippling effect upon the enemy and the recent return of a large proportion of the crew personnel lost, should be given consideration in appraising the cost of these operations."

The work of the 449th and the Fifteenth Air Force was officially recognized:

HEADQUARTERS, FIFTEENTH AIR FORCE
Office of the Commanding Officer

APO 520

201.22   18 September 1944

SUBJECT: Commendation

TO: All Units, Fifteenth Air Force, APO 520, U.S. Army

1. The Commanding General, United States Strategic Air Forces in Europe, has requested that all personnel of the Fifteenth Air Force be commended for their part in the operations of this Command against the Ploesti oil fields. He has stated that our attacks, in connection with similar operations by the Eighth Air Force, have been the most effective blow so far struck against German industry.

2. It gives me much pleasure to pass on this tribute. I realize that our successes at Ploesti would not have been possible except for the skill and industry with which all of you, in both air and ground echelons, performed your assigned tasks. By your work you have made a major contribution to an early defeat of the German war machine.

> N.F. Twining
> Major General, USA
> Commanding

Of course, although Ploesti was over, there was much more still to be done. A name from the Kosovo headlines of 2000 is next on Skinas' log, Mitrovica, Yugoslavia. A railroad bridge there was targeted by Skinas' plane on September 1. Again the intent was to hamper the German retreat. Marshaling yards at Trento, Italy were hit on September 4, and yards at Ferrara were hit the next day. German troop concentrations at Leskovac, Yugoslavia were attacked September 6, and marshaling yards at Nis, Yugoslavia, on the 8th. There was also a 449th mission to Kraljevo, Yugoslavia, on September 2, not involving Skinas. The target was marshaling yards.

September 10 saw a two-credit mission to Trieste, then part of Italy. It was an alternate target. Planes from many groups had set off to bomb targets around Vienna, with the aim of disrupting the supply of arms and equipment to Axis forces on the Italian front. The 449th found cloud cover around Vienna and had Pathfinder ship problems, so instead they attacked ships and harbor installations at the harbor at Trieste. Other 449th planes were in action September 12, against the Allach Motor Works in Munich.

Skinas was next aloft on the 13th, when the railroad bridge at Mezzocorona, Italy was attacked.

On the 15th, the marshaling yards at Larissa, Greece were the target. The Ferencvaros marshaling yards in Budapest were hit on the 17th. The next day, a railway bridge at Szob, Hungary was targeted but missed. Other units from the 449th went after the rail bridge at Kraljevo, Yugoslavia on September 19, and an air field at Malacky, Slovakia, on the 20th.

Skinas was in action again on the 21st, when another Hungarian rail bridge was attacked, this one at Baja. This time a section of the bridge was successfully sunk. There was a return trip to Larissa the next day, and another mission on the 23rd, this time to Italy's Mezzocorona railway bridge. It had been successfully bombed ten days before, but quickly returned to use by the enemy. Unfortunately, bad weather prevented a good follow-up bombing.

That turned out to be a preview of the bad weather to come. Like the rest of the 449th, Skinas and his crew were grounded by poor flying conditions until October 4th, when the unit went after railway lines in the Brenner Pass, at Bressanone, Italy. Hungary's Kamarom marshaling yards were the next target, on October 7. Skinas' next mission was not until October 23, when rail lines in the Brenner Pass, at Bressanone, were hit again.

During that layoff, other units from the 449th attacked Vienna's Florisdorf oil refinery (twice), troop barracks at Bologna, marshaling yard workshops at Vienna, the St. Valentin tank works at Steyr, Austria, and the Sauer-werken (armored vehicles) at Vienna. These missions were part of an effort to strike at Hitler's capacity to produce tanks and other equipment.

It was Friday, October 13, that four planes were lost over Vienna, one of them flown by Lt. Michael Mealey (now called O'Malley). Ellis Arieff, who died on *The Buzzer,* was part of his crew, but was not flying that day. Everyone got out of the plane, Mealey not without some struggle, thanks to the plane's increasing spin. Also aboard was Captain Leslie Caplan, the 719th squadron flight surgeon, the future POW psychology expert and a witness at the Nurem-burg Trials.

I have the Operational Performance Record for S/Sgt. Sam Taylor, nose gunner, a crewmate of Roy Groeger's. Again, while crews' missions do not always match up exactly, there is a good chance that Groeger, who was to die on *The Buzzer,* was on most of Taylor's sorties. If this is so, Groeger's last mission was the October 17 double-credit attack on Vienna-Sauerwerke. His first had been to Ploesti on June 24—a mission I was on. Knowing this really brings home to me how much I had in common with the experience of the men in *The Buzzer* crash, even if I never met them, and even if they didn't all have missions that overlapped mine.

Taylor - and, presumably, Groeger - were also in action against the Scwechat aircraft factory on June 26, another mission I was on. We also shared their third mission, on June 27th, to Brod, Yugoslavia. In July, Taylor was on the missions to Toulon, Zagreb, Markersdorf, the Var Bridge, Budapest, Friedrichsafen-Lowenthal aircraft factory, Horsching aerodrome, Ploesti, Berat/Kucove oil refinery, Austria's Graz-Phalarof refinery, and Budafpuszta.

We had the attacks on Toulon (July 5), Zagreb (July 7), Markersdorf (July 8), Friedrichshafen-Lowenthal (July 20), and Ploesti (July 22). Of course, that Ploesti raid was my last mission. In August, Taylor, and probably Groeger, were on the missions to Aviso, Toulon (three times), Ploesti, Szolnok, Hungary, Vienna, the Giurgiu ferry terminal, Ferrarra, Miskolc, and Cuprija.

In September, they went to Kraljevo, Trento, Ferrarra, Trieste, Budapest, Malacky, and Baja. In October, they finished up with runs to the Brenner Pass, Komarom, Florisdorf refinery, Bologna Barracks, Vienna, and Vienna again.

Skinas also was off when other 449th units attacked a marshaling yard at Munich on October 29. On October 31, there was a non-effective attempt on troop concentrations at Podgorica, Yugoslavia. This was the first mission for Manuel Suarez, according to his mission log. It was thus possibly also the first mission for his usual crewmates, Caldwell, Boswell, Marple, and Ganim. Solid cloud cover caused a turnback.

Suarez' crew went out next on November 3, to bomb oil refineries at Moosbierbaum. Skinas' crew were in action on November 4, when marshaling yards at Munich were again attacked. Julian Caldwell, the eventual *Buzzer* pilot, referred to this mission in a letter to his mother. Enemy troops at Podgorica were hit the next day, when units of the 449th, including Suarez' crew, also returned to Vienna's Florisdorf Oil Refinery—a two-credit mission. According to the same letter from Caldwell, his plane suffered some flak damage over the refinery. Skinas' crew were then off until the 11th.

November 6 was another two-target day for the 449th, neither involving Skinas or Suarez. The targets were the oil refinery at Moosbierbaum, Austria, and the marshaling yards at Sarajevo. Suarez' crew were out again on the 7th, bombing a railway line in the Brenner Pass, at Pinzano, in the Italian Alps. Then other crews struck at troops at Sjenica, Yugoslavia, on November 8.

The target for Skinas' crew on November 11 was Casarsa, Italy, where the Germans had built a bypass around a previously bombed bridge. Both the bridge and the bypass were hit. This attack was part of the aerial assault on the "Brenner Line." Another rail bridge, at Isarco/Albes, Italy, was struck by other 449th units on the 12th, and other units went after marshaling yards at Innsbruck, Austria, on the 15th.

On the 16th, Suarez and his crew hit the Munich West marshaling yards, for two credits. On the same day, other 449th units were attacking troop concentrations at Sjenica, Yugoslavia. Both crews were involved on November 17, when there was a two-credit return to Vienna's Florisdorf oil refinery. Heavy cloud cover made bombing by Pathfinder technology necessary.

Suarez and his crew were out again the next day, bombing Italy's Aviano airfield- which found itself in the news again, fifty-five years later, during the NATO campaign in Kosovo. The Schwechat refinery at Vienna was hit by other 449th units on November 19. The next two missions for Skinas' crew were on November 20 and 21, both against the Sarajevo marshaling yards. Suarez and his crew were also part of the November 20 mission. These attacks were aimed at hampering Hitler's retreat from Yugoslavia. For Suarez and crew, a railroad bridge at Ferrara, Italy was the target on the 22nd; the following day, a bridge on the Sava River at Brod, Yugoslavia was the goal.

The 449th didn't get into the air again until December 2nd. Both Skinas and Suarez were in action that day; it was to be the last mission for both of them. For Skinas, it was the end of his tour. For Suarez, it was only a week until he died aboard *The Buzzer.* Other 449th units hit an industrial sector of Linz, Austria, on December 3rd, and a marshaling yard at Sopron, Hungary, on December 6. Of course bad weather scrubbed a planned 449th mission on December 9, the day *The Buzzer* crashed.

The first 449th mission after *The Buzzer* crash was on December 11, to the oil refinery at Moosbierbaum. It was the 177th mission of the 449th. The bomb group fought on until its 254th mission in late April 1945, just over a week before V-E day.

A Vet In Speech Class

Back in the States, I spent a while thinking I'd be shipped to the Pacific, like many returnees. I spent time at a number of bases around the country before starting work at Eglin Field, Florida, for a while, in the photo lab. There I saw photographs of Peenemunde, Werner von Braun's rocket site.

The services had a point system for deciding who was up for discharge first. You got points for being overseas, points for flying, and so on. Not long after the war ended, my points added up to the magic number I needed, and I was discharged.

I had developed a real distaste for flying. I had no trust in airplanes. Some of the guys in my crew always loved flying; some were washed-out air cadets. For a while at Eglin Field, I was determined never to fly again.

I'd seen too many planes going down in combat and in crashes, even going back to training days. This was a pretty common feeling. Several of the men who died on *The Buzzer* had written in letters to their families that when their tours were done they didn't want to fly again, at least not for a while. Just the same, when I got the chance to hop a flight back to New York City to be discharged, I took it.

My honorable discharge came October 21, 1945, at Newark, New Jersey. In case any of us thought it was "goodbye to all that," our "Information For Veterans" pamphlet advised us that failure to report to our local draft board within ten days of discharge was a Federal offense!

More than anything, what I wanted to do when I got out of the service was get married. I'd been introduced to Rita Cahn, who was to become my first wife and the mother of my three children, while I was still in uniform. I was very much under the influence of the romantic dreams and music of the era, not so much the Big Band swing as such romantic ballads, as Dinah Shore sings, "You'd Be So Nice to Come Home To".

I was shy when I was young. I remember going to the famous Stage Door Canteen in Los Angeles and being one of the many guys standing on the perimeter, making comments.

Now, Rudy was an "operator." He was a real Zoot Suiter, watch chain and all. I certainly envied him; he was always gung-ho. Even in Italy, he always seemed actually disappointed if a mission was scratched.

I went back to school on the G.I. Bill and took the Civil Service test for Junior Professional Assistant Geologist, but there were no jobs. I married Rita and graduated from Brooklyn College in 1946 on $2,000 per year, thanks to the G.I. Bill. But before I could graduate, I had a stern test to face.

Back when I had enlisted, in September 1942, I was a senior with only one semester to go. Brooklyn College had a requirement of two semesters of Speech. I passed the first semester, which dealt with the mechanics of speech, as a sophomore. The second semester, though, required speaking in front of the class. Now, as I said, I was painfully shy. But, the war fixed that. By enlisting, I was able to put off Speech II indefinitely.

When I returned from the war and enrolled again, I hoped that, somehow, the actual speaking requirement of the Speech course might be waived in return for my having flown fifty combat missions. No such luck.

As it turned out, when I gave my speech, a light look at some aspects of cooking, I got very positive attention, not only from the teacher but from the women in class. I couldn't do anything about the latter except enjoy it, since I had married just before the semester started. But, for me, that change has always been a sign that the thirty-seven months I spent with my surrogate family in the Army had transformed me from being a kid to a man.

With some uncertainty, I joined my father's new business, building single-family homes in New Jersey. My children—Jane, Nancy, and Charles—were born in 1948, 1952, and 1953. Now I have six grandchildren.

I think it was June of 1955 before I heard that *The Buzzer* had crashed.

In early 1967, Rita and I were divorced. In late 1967, I married Nancy Slane.

In October 1985, I went to the second reunion of the 449th Bomb Group, in Dayton, Ohio. It was my first reunion. There, I met Texas Senator Lloyd Bentsen, who later helped me with my research for this book.

Buck Rogers had stayed in the service, and served in Korea. Shorty Carlson also stayed in. Jack Cox had become an architect, like so many, benefiting from the G.I. Bill. Bob Simons, a butcher before the war, had later managed a steel plant in Luxembourg.

I revisited Italy a couple of years after Nancy died. She died in 1989. I had never been back to Europe since the war. I went to Grottaglie to see if I could find the base but everything was so changed I couldn't locate it. I eventually got someone to show me the site of the base but it was unrecognizable to me.

The fifth reunion of the 449th was in April 1991. In the winter of 1992, I found out about the discrepancy between stories of a crash in the Bay of Naples and the burial sites and records I'd discovered. In April 1993, I contracted with DCP Productions to produce an oral history video about my crewmates and their experiences. I invited Rogers, Carlson, Hinds, Acosta, Cox, Simons, Girton, and Peluso to Princeton for the taping of what became *B-24 Bomber Crew*. Girton was ill and Hinds's son was near death, but the rest of my surviving crew members came.

I don't recall the actual day, but the idea formed that I would have to do more. I would have to find out what I could about what happened to *The Buzzer* and who the men who were killed were and what their lives had been like.

Citizens of Oliveto Citra discussing crash of *The Buzzer*

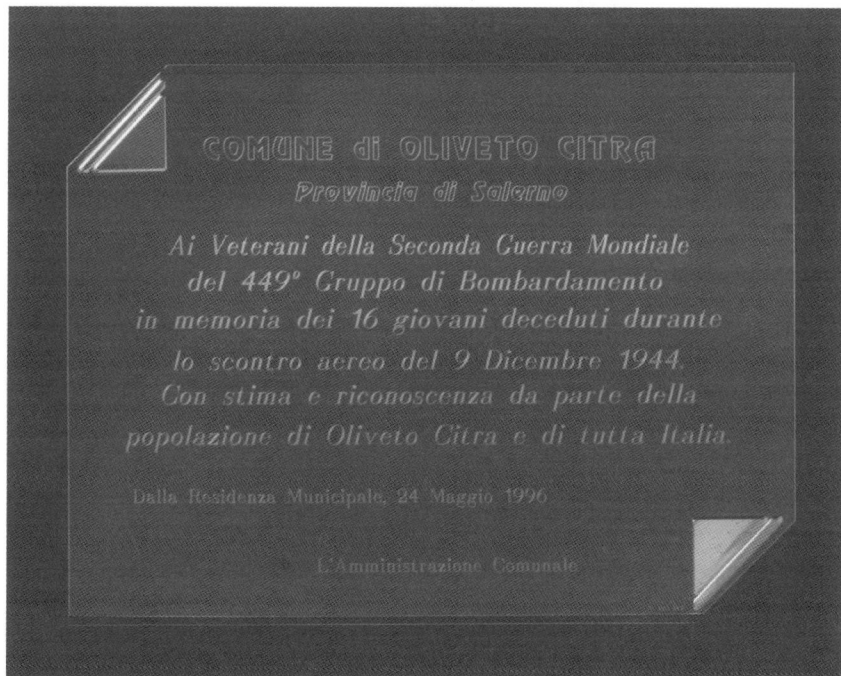

COMUNE di OLIVETO CITRA
Provincia di Salerno

Ai Veterani della Seconda Guerra Mondiale
del 449° Gruppo di Bombardamento
in memoria dei 16 giovani deceduti durante
lo scontro aereo del 9 Dicembre 1944.
Con stima e riconoscenza da parte della
popolazione di Oliveto Citra e di tutta Italia.

Dalla Residenza Municipale, 24 Maggio 1996

L'Amministrazione Comunale

Memorial plaque presented to 449th Bomb Group veterans

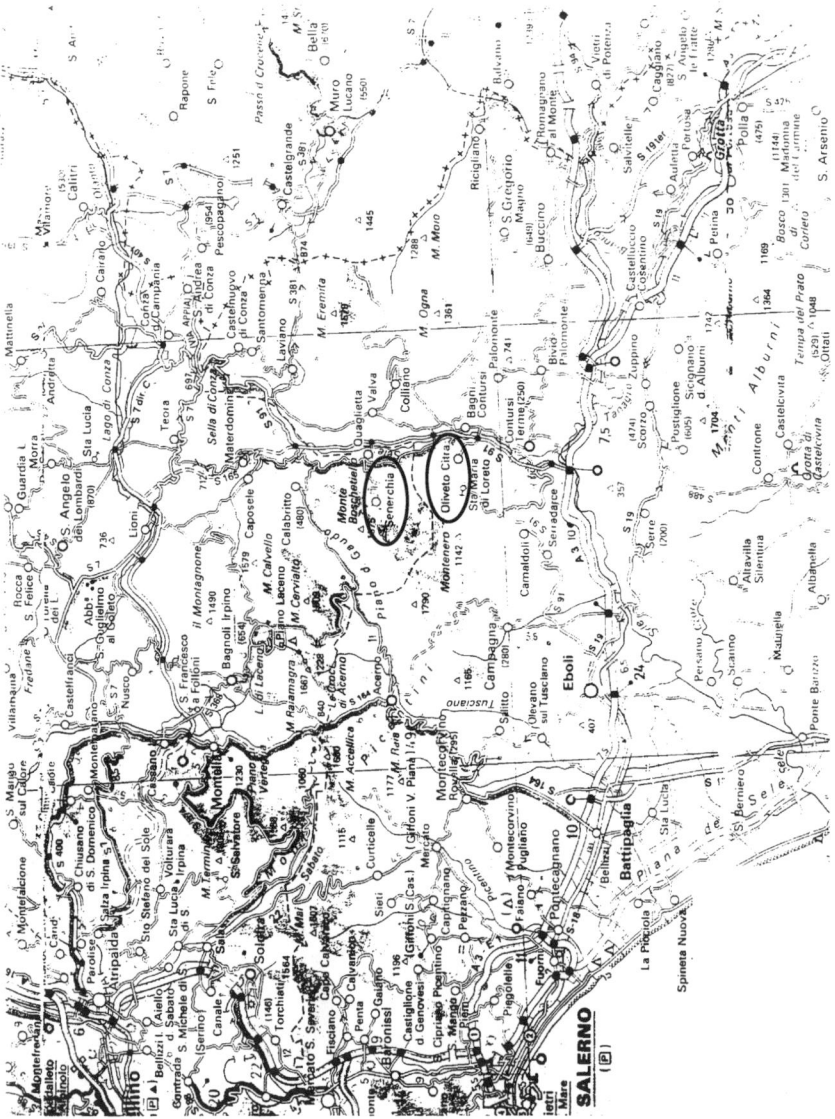

Map of *The Buzzer* crash area

Farm bucket made from oxygen tank retrieved from *The Buzzer*.

Oxygen tank retrieved from *The Buzzer* used as a farm bucket

Removing vines from shed roof made from bomb bay door of *The Buzzer*

Part of *The Buzzer* fuselage used as coop enclosure

Wedding dress made from a parachute from *The Buzzer*

Armor plate retrieved from *The Buzzer* wreckage

Paper money retrieved from *The Buzzer* wreckage

Part of *The Buzzer* retrieved in Italy

Sicily Rome American Military Cemetery Nettuno. Four of *The Buzzer* crash victims are buried here.

Sixteen Men And A Plane

Ballou, Doyle, Eckerling, Erickson, and Gettys were all from Bache's crew. Their pilot, William Bache, was not on the flight; nor was their ball turret gunner, Tom Hazen nor their tail gunner, Tom Skinas. Groeger was from Underwood's crew, and Brehun from Aldrich's. The five crew members the night of the crash were all from a ship called *Touch Me Not*.

A strange thing emerged when I started trying to find out what happened to *The Buzzer*. Although it became clear that graves registration officials had reached the wreckage and recovered the bodies, the first the bereaved families heard that the plane had been found, on land, was from a letter from Amelia Clemente, an American-born resident of Oliveto Citra.

Amelia was the wife of a local area doctor, Vito Clemente, and she corresponded with several of the bereaved families, mixing details of the crash site, her colorful interpretations of postwar Italian politics, and requests for money and various goods.

The area of the crash was not on the scheduled route, but on the direct route. Did the pilot ignore the plan? I'm not sure. Squadron navigator Hal Strack told me that the crash location might be a coincidence. Under the flying conditions that day, the plane might have been trying to follow the safer route and drifted off course far inland.

Like the exact cause of the crash—icing, navigational error, drastic mechanical failure this remains a mystery.

There were a great many non-combat plane crashes during the war, and this one was in a very difficult place to reach.

Having set out to find out about *The Buzzer's* end, I quickly became absorbed in a task that probably took me more miles than my three trips to Italy and several trips to Romania combined: finding out what I could about the men who died aboard the Liberator that had carried me safely home on so many dangerous missions.

This has brought me some frustration in some cases, rewarding luck in others. Naturally, it has brought me in contact with a great deal of sadness, and with people whose love for their lost ones seemed no less by all the decades since the accident. An interesting side affect has been in some families the children or grandchildren of the deceased have taken a new interest in what family members did in a real war.

Everyone has been welcoming and eager to do what they could to help me.

This is what I found.

Julian L. Caldwell

"I'm going to fly one of these days . . ."

Second Lieutenant Julian Caldwell was *The Buzzer* pilot on the day of the crash. He was the sixth of ten children. He had four brothers and five sisters. Both his parents had both been teachers when they married in 1913. But they quit teaching to farm in Lodge, South Carolina. The farm remained in the family until 1993.

He was born March 9, 1921, six miles out in the country from Lodge, which is about twenty miles west of Walterboro, in the southern part of South Carolina, well inland from the coastal city of Charleston.

His sister, May, two years his senior, remembers Julian and their family:

"Dad had a two-mule farm with about 75 acres clear land and 210 acres in pastures and woodlands. He raised cotton, corn, grains, beans, peas, watermelons, rice, sugar cane, peaches, pecans, apples, pears, figs, plums, persimmons, potatoes, etc. Cows and hogs and chickens. We children did a lot of the work on the farm while attending school."

The work included picking cotton. The school, which had 250 pupils in eleven grades, is now a vacant lot; but the cotton fields are still around in the community. The school was all-white, with a "colored school" nearby. In the days when there were separate schools, I don't recall any trouble between the races. We hiked down to their church that had picnic tables outside for picnics (whites only) - no problem!

117

"Julian attended school at Lodge eleven years, graduating in May 1939, along with a sister, Susan. When Julian began school in grade one he complained of "tummy aches" a lot to get to stay home with Susan, who was a year younger. Then, as soon as the bus would leave, he got O.K. He also said some of the big boys teased him and he'd cry when mother said he had to go to school. She finally gave in, and let him stay home until Susan was old enough to go too - all was O.K. then".

"He was a rascal as a kid - Mom would "whip him" - she whipped all of us. We weren't too bad - we were too busy to be bad."

According to May, Caldwell's mother wouldn't let him play football because she was afraid he would break a bone.

"Julian joined Carter's Ford Baptist Church in August 1933. Susan did too. Our parents carried all of us to church regularly, sometimes by mules and wagon and we picked up neighbors on the four miles way and enjoyed it.

"After graduating from High School, Julian began thinking of what he could do to make some money. He joined the C.C.C. [Civilian Conservation Corps] and later the National Guard in Walterboro. I don't remember him wanting to go to college. Very few young men around went to college back in 1939. Julian had two sisters in college, and it would have been very hard to have three in college at once. We wanted to be teachers, and he wanted to fly.

"I'm a little older than Julian and I remember when we were out in the fields working and a plane would fly over - Julian would say 'I'm going to fly one of those one day and eat breakfast in one city, dinner in another and supper in another.' I really got tired of him saying that! As it seemed so far out! However, he did fly and fly in ten-twelve years and made us all real proud of him."

Caldwell joined the Air Corps at the beginning of 1942, and, as was the pattern, was stationed eleven different places before even leaving the U.S. in 1944. Fort Jackson, South Carolina was followed by the Aviation Cadet Center at San Antonio, Texas, Kelly Field in Stamford, near San

Antonio, Texas, Goodfellow Field, in San Angelo, Texas, Lubbock Flying School, in Lubbock, Texas; and Randolph Field, also near San Antonio Texas.

Then he was sent to Turner Field, in Albany, Georgia. By this time he had become a flight instructor. He had a food allowance of 70 cents a day and spent $1.25. Then it was back to Texas, to Bryan Field, and back to instructing at Turner Field. Then came Maxwell Field, Alabama, and combat crew training in Pueblo, Colorado.

May says: "While he was an instructor at Turner Field . . . he had to do some extra flying so he would fly to Anderson Field in Walterboro in a B-24, about 100–120 miles. When he'd come to Walterboro in the big planes he'd come over our house at Lodge and circle and head for Walterboro. We knew to go meet him to bring him home for a short visit. The neighbors enjoyed seeing him circle over too, and some speak of it even today in remembrance.

"Sometimes he had real difficult times - long hours, not enough rest and sleep. He said while instructing at Turner, 'Combat duty could easily be considered a holiday compared to this.' He was responsible for as many as seven flyers in his class, and it was dangerous with greenhorns in planes.

"When Julian was flying the B-24s, the Lockheed Constellation crossed the U.S. April 17, 1944 in six hours and 58 minutes at 355 miles per hour. It was thirteen feet longer than the B-24 Liberator. He sent us a newspaper article on this important feat.

"Julian began dating one of my teacher friends who was teaching at Lodge with me. To show how mischievous he was, he brought her by our home one night and stopped and got a watermelon from *our patch* without telling her it was his home. She thought he was stealing it, and was upset about it, but laughed about it later.

"As time went on he was training for overseas duty and decided he wanted to get married to the teacher soon, so he volunteered to go overseas so he could get through his thirty missions and get back home - he only got to do 27 before the fatal one. . . ."

"June 10, 1944 in Pueblo, Colorado, Julian got a general power of attorney, so he knew he would soon be shipped overseas.

"When in Pueblo, he said [the] weather was so hot during the day, but when they flew at night at 2,000 feet he nearly froze.

Julian was back at Turner Field on August 31, 1944. He turned in his baggage the next day and mailed suitcases home. He knew he'd be overseas any day. The next the family heard he was "somewhere in Italy," as of October 15, 1944.

"He asked for more blankets, as it's the cold and rainy season and he lived in a tent with no floor . . . Hopes for a permanent tent."

This is the weather I was lucky to miss.

Caldwell wrote to his mother October 23, 1944: "We are having quite a bit of rain now, so there is nothing but mud and cold weather. Our tent is not much good either, so we plan to build a little stone hut when we can get a truck to haul the blocks. We don't have any lights except candles and we still don't have a heater so the only thing to do at night is get between some blankets. No mattress or pillow. Soon, Caldwell and a friend, with some Italian help, built a hut out of the local limestone. It took about a week.

"The weather is getting pretty cold over here and especially in this tent with no heat. I will soon have heat though as our little house is about finished and when we get in it we will make a gas heater with two steel cans and some hydraulic lines. We had quite a time getting all that stuff together, but we have it now, so what we need now is time to work with it. Where it gets cold is at high altitude flying. We have electric heated suits so we keep warm but we have had a few oxygen masks freeze up in flight."

"They have a theater in town for us so we usually go to a show each night even if we have seen the picture a couple of times months ago. I saw three in the Naples area that I hadn't seen before but over here there has been nothing new so far.

"The most disgusting thing I have seen over here yet is boys that graduated from cadets one year after I did and are all 1st [lieutenants] now and a few that finished four months after me are captains. That goes to prove what I always said that all an instructor gets for a year's slavery is plenty of hell and no consideration.

"I flew yesterday for a while and will fly a little more today if the weather is okay. I will probably get more longer trips pretty soon. I went to services in the post chapel last night. We had several services on deck while we were at sea. I sure would like to get some mail soon. Maybe I will if they will wake up at headquarters and send it on to our group."

It's worth remembering that in the letters home written by Caldwell and others that strict wartime censorship rules prevailed. Some of the men's letters even refer to it. There was no return address other than "Somewhere in Italy," which wouldn't have given much away if the letter fell into the wrong hands.

I still have my Pamphlet No. 21-1, "When You Are Overseas." It urges soldiers to use their common sense if the stated rules don't cover a subject that might be sensitive. It also says that censorship takes at most forty-eight hours, and is not responsible for holding up mail. Slow mail was a frequent gripe among servicemen.

Ten prohibited subjects were spelled out in the pamphlet:

- military information like the location, strength, materiel, or equipment of Army units
- details about military installations
- anything about transportation
- anything about convoys
- movements of troops, aircraft, or Navy or merchant shipping
- plans, forecasts, or orders, "whether known or just your guess"
- effects of enemy action

- writing about a casualty until released by the Adjutant General, and then using only the casualty's first name
- attempts to write in any code could be severely punished
- your own location or any clues that could give it away

Enlisted men posted their letters unsealed; officers could seal theirs, but the letter could still be subject to censorship examination at base, rather than unit, level. Enlisted men who wanted the same treatment (say, for a letter with especially personal contents - could request a special blue envelope.

The pamphlet also warns against loose talk when home on leave; and advises taking only essential papers into areas where capture is possible.

Many of the letters home from Caldwell and others were V-mail-V—for Victory mail. This was a special system for the Armed Forces. Letters were reduced onto microfilm to save space on ships or planes, then enlarged and printed for delivery Stateside.

Like most troops overseas, he loved getting mail from home; but it was slow. One of his letters reports a letter mailed in South Carolina on September 18th not reaching him until early November.

Caldwell's family still has several letters from their mother written in the late fall of 1944; the envelopes were stamped "Return to sender"; handwritten above Caldwell's military address is the word "MISSING."

In one of his last letters, he reports that it was very cold, and that he went to the movies in Grottaglie. In a letter to his mother, dated November 5, 1944, Caldwell wrote "I was over Munich yesterday and Vienna today." He was referring to sorties to bomb marshaling yards in Munich and the Florisdorf oil refinery at Vienna. It seems a strange echo of his youthful forecast of three meals in three cities.

The same letter reports: "I didn't have any trouble over Albania or Munich but my right wing and engine picked up a few pieces of flak today. I am rather tired tonight - as you see I had two long days yesterday and today. I slept pretty well last night though as I was so tired I went to bed at 7:30. I feel a little better tonight but I won't be up much longer. Sure hope I don't have to fly tomorrow.

He wrote home after missions over Germany, Austria, and Italy: "The more flights I get now the better I like it, for we have a required number to fly and the sooner we get them done, the sooner we go home."

In addition to letters, May still has a booklet, "Directions for B-17 and B-24 Combat Crews," which lists her brother as Airplane Commander Crew #14, and a pilot's flight log. His last letter was dated December 4th.

Two of Caldwell's brothers were serving overseas when *The Buzzer* disappeared. Mendel was on the U.S.S. *Mink,* a forward crew Navy tanker with aviation gasoline and diesel oil, anchored in a harbor at Biak in the southwest Pacific. Alvin was a staff sergeant in Weisbaden, Germany. An older brother was married and was not in the war. Teenager Buddy had not yet entered the war, but had been advised by the three serving brothers to join whichever service they were in.

As with the other men who died on *The Buzzer,* news was slow to reach home. Seven months after the accident, on July 17th, 1945, the latest word from the Government was still that Caldwell was missing. A telegram announcing his death arrived July 31st.

On August 24th, Rose and May went to see "the teacher," the woman Caldwell had planned to marry. They returned her letters to him, and she gave them a picture of him.

Many of the bereaved family members, especially parents, corresponded with one another for some time after the accident. Sometimes they shared practical details of getting information from the Government; sometimes they simply tried to console one another.

Just as military service brought my crew and the men of *The Buzzer* into contact with people from different parts of America, and American society, the crash brought the families into contact with people they might never have encountered.

On June 6, 1946, Nancy Caldwell wrote to Pauline Suarez, mother of Manuel Suarez, Caldwell's flight engineer, "I am going to ask that Julian be sent home and buried in our family plot. The War Dept. did not let me know about where they are buried in the United States Military cemetery, Naples Italy . . . Julian's grave is Plot L Row 7 Grave 74. They told me funeral services were conducted by a Lutheran minister Chaplain C.O. Anderson of Laurel, Montana.

"I wrote to Chaplain Anderson and he told me Julian was buried in a grave by himself . . . That he conducted a full religious service at the grave of each one who [was] killed in that plane crash, that is, for each of the Protestants: Psalms 90:2–6, 12; Romans 5:12; Hebrews 9:27; Luke, 12:35–37, 40; St. John 11:25, 26; and Corinthians 15:53–55 and 57 were read at his grave. The interment service was held after the closing prayer. He wrote me words of sympathy. I appreciate his letter.

"I miss Julian more as the days go by. We can not understand why all this had to happen. I am sure that God had a Divine plan in mind. I try to go on and you must too. Let us hope to be with them someday."

Caldwell's sister Susan was closest to him. She was away at college, May was canning at North Greenville College with a sister, Edith when the news arrived of his death. Caldwell died at 23.

Caldwell's name is among those on a monument built in 1990 at River's Bridge State Park, Walterboro, S.C. honoring the known World War II dead of four South Carolina counties (Callison, Allendale, Bamberg, Hampton), as well as those of Korean and Vietnam conflicts.

On March 12, 1949, Caldwell's body came home by train to South Carolina. There was a steady, ongoing program to disinter servicemen buried abroad and, if requested, bring their remains home.

The undertakers met the train at Yemassee and drove the body back to Walterboro, accompanied by a soldier and family members. He was buried near Lodge, at Carter's Ford Baptist Church, on March 20, 1949. "Peace at last!" says May.

I asked May how many people were there. "One to two hundred," she said.

Once, long after the war, May was in church and thought she saw a man who looked like Julian Caldwell might have looked by then - a few decades older. She said she couldn't wait for the service to finish so she could find out. Of course, it wasn't him. Other people I spoke to among *Buzzer* relatives have had similar experiences, years and years after the war.

When I was trying to reach relatives of *The Buzzer* men, using the Missing Air Crew Reports (MACRs) as my starting point, I often proceeded by placing ads in the local newspapers of the airmen's hometowns. May said that just five minutes after she read the ad I had placed in the Walterboro paper, she got a call from me. I had called other Caldwells in Walterboro, then Lodge; finally reached her. "And we've been buddies ever since" she says.

I have been lucky enough to visit Lodge several times, to meet with May and other members of Caldwell's family, to have breakfast at Bee-Box's, and learn more about their brother Julian.

When traveling to meet relatives of the men who died on *The Buzzer*, I have usually shown people material I've gathered about other airmen. May says, "We enjoyed seeing the boys that were with him. They seemed like a nice bunch of boys."

Although the family no longer has their old property, and the old house has been leveled, a garage remains, built for Julian's 1939 Ford. Perched on it is a birdhouse he made.

John T. Boswell

"Even as I write all this it seems impossible."

Second Lieutenant John T. Boswell was Caldwell's copilot the day of the crash. His listed next of kin was his mother, Mrs. Grace L. Boswell, of Cleveland, Ohio. She wrote to Mrs. Caldwell, mother of her son's pilot, on May 21, 1946. Her letter mentions Amelia Clemente and her promises of information in exchange for money, clothes for her children, and various beauty products for herself.

Mrs. Boswell wrote: "If you will excuse this typewritten letter I will do better next time. I received the letter you sent me from Mrs. Clemente in Italy. I want to thank you very much for sending it to me. This is the first real thing that we have found out about the accident. While it was terrible to read, I suppose to know these things is better than to sit and try to think them out for yourself.

"I do wonder how you got the address of this lady in Italy? Was it from the Cranmer fellow that is mentioned in the letter? If he went there and talked to her and there is any more information that you can give me or anything at all about John, would you write and let me know."

The "Cranmer fellow" Mrs. Boswell refers to was William Watson, son of Mrs. Hazel Cranmer and brother of Paul Watson, another *Buzzer* casualty. Mrs. Cranmer corresponded with a number of the other bereaved families, and her son William, who was also in the services, tried to get some information in Italy.

Mrs. Boswell continues: "She mentioned that she had been to Julian's grave at Naples. I have written three times to try to find out the grave location & have never received an answer. Do you know whether John is buried there with Julian?"

"Even as I write all this it seems impossible. I still can't realize it has happened. Our precious boys to have been taken that way. I feel very close to you people as John was so very fond of Julian. He talked of him the whole time he was home on his last leave. He said that the whole crew thought they had the best pilot that could be had and that they would bet their last penny on him. John spoke so well of Julian and of course I always felt that I knew him. I do wish I could see you and talk with you. I feel that it would help both of us very much. Do you think you could ever get this far up in the country and come to see me? I surely would love to have you or some of the family visit me.

"I am a long time sending you a picture of John but did not have one until now. I had to write to a place in Texas and have this one made. I have the one you sent of Julian, the one of Albert Marple, one of Joe Shiel[d]s [the bombardier] and of John, framed and on my dresser.

"I suppose you will be swamped with letters from all the people you sent the copy of [the] letter to but if you have time let me know what to do about sending Mrs. Clemente something. Shall I send money or some of the things she mentioned?

"Thank you again so very much for the letter. I hope to hear from you as soon as you find time to answer this letter."

Boswell is one of the men buried together in Jefferson Barracks National Cemetery in St. Louis.

Albert E. Marple

"And then he volunteered . . ."

Second Lieutenant Albert E. Marple was from Burien, Washington. He was *The Buzzer*'s navigator. His sister, Bernice Quamme, told me about him:

"Well he was fifteen months younger than I. When we were growing up many people thought we were twins. We were very close. He was very bright, exceptionally bright. Back when he was in the Air [Corps] he was given a trophy labeling him best Air [Corps] student. He was always at the head of his class wherever he went.

"He graduated high school here in Hettinger (North Dakota) and then he went on to Jamestown College and got his Bachelor's Degree. Later he went to the University of South Dakota where our parents had gone to school. He did teach a while. He was a summer band director for one school, and he taught there. And then his hometown called him back to teach here, and he told them he was in the draft and maybe he wouldn't be here long, but he came anyway.

"And then he volunteered for the service. He didn't have to, because he had just got an appointment from Washington to do some chemical research. He would have done that, but he had just volunteered, so he went into the regular Army and he was in the band. He wasn't seeing any action, so he mustered out. I don't know how he managed that, but he was free for one day and then he joined the Air [Corps]. And then he got his wings in Texas. That would have been in 1944, I think, and then he went overseas shortly after that.

"He had a terrific sense of humor. He could put me on the spot a thousand times if he wanted. It was partly because he was a brilliant student and all - successful wherever he went. He was a Red Cross Life Saver instructor when he was still in college. He went to different camps and that was part of his summer vacation, and doing life saving.

"Another thing that he did that was interesting was he was a night baker in the bakery. He and another fellow from the high school were hired there, and so for that summer and several summers he came back and was a night baker. So, if something I baked didn't come out, he could tell me what was wrong with it."

In the band, Marple played French horn and trumpet. "He could play just about any instrument in the band. We had an orchestra here first and he played the violin. And when we turned into a band and he went away from here he probably played a brass instrument. He and I played French horn together in college . . . everyone in our family played the violin."

"He was engaged to be married when he went overseas. And, he loved my kids. I had two children by the time he left home. He wasn't afraid. When the oldest one was only a few months old, he took her to town, took care of her, he even took her into one of the bars. He was made for taking care of kids. And they were just crazy about him.

"We come from a long line of teachers. My parents were both teachers.

He majored in chemistry in college and he started off being a pharmacist. He worked for his uncle who was a pharmacist. But one summer, he figured that if making banana splits and stuff like that was pharmacy, he didn't want it.

"Anyway, he didn't pursue that for long. So, he went into teaching. We lived in town because mother taught here. But he got interested in the farm because I was raising chickens. He did buy a cow before he left and then he left them to me.

"We were very close. We were more fellow collegians than a brother sister relationship. We even had pictures of him and me - we were both on the paper staff - so when they were taking pictures of the reporters and stuff for the annual, they put us both in the same picture. He was not a big kid. In fact, I was bigger than he was. When we were in high school and walked through study hall together, I couldn't really look down on him, but I was taller than he was. But out of school, he was taller than I. He played football and basketball.

"He went to Jamestown College. It's a Presbyterian school. It's a private college and we both had scholarships enough to pay our tuition all four years. And I have a son graduated from there and I have a grandson who just graduated from there. In fact, I just went back for my Sixtieth Reunion, or the sixtieth anniversary of my graduation.

"I'm having a hard time, even yet, getting over it. I lost my mother in '36 and my father in '49, my husband in '62. And my brother's death haunts me about as much as anything. We were almost like twins . . ."

Marple is buried in the Sicily-Rome American Military Cemetery, Nettuno, Italy.

Manuel Suarez

"In case I'm counted as missing I'm sure to get back."

Staff Sergeant Manuel Suarez, of New York City, was the flight engineer on *The Buzzer.* He was the first *Buzzer* victim whose family and background I tried to investigate. The Missing Air Crew Report (MACR) listed S/Sgt. Suarez's mother, Pauline Suarez, as the next of kin, and gave her address as 56 East 103rd Street, in Manhattan, in a neighborhood known as El Barrio, East Harlem.

One day I had to go to Montefiore Hospital in the Bronx for a checkup. On my way back by subway to Penn Station, I realized I could change trains at 125th Street. in Harlem, and get the Number Six to 103rd Street and Lexington Avenue, only a few blocks away from 56 East 103rd Street, the address I had for Mrs. Suarez.

I was full of hope and anticipation as I started out from the subway exit. Partly, it was exciting seeing part of the city I really didn't know. Even more, it was the prospect of meeting Pauline Suarez. My own mother was ninety-six years old and in good mental and physical shape that year. I thought: this could be my first meeting with a family member of one of *The Buzzer* crew.

However, when I got to East 103rd St., there was no #56. I double-checked the Suarez address. The building had been razed, and must have stood where I could now see the George Washington Carver public housing project. I asked two men sitting on the stoop of #28 if they knew the

Suarezes, but they didn't. It was a big disappointment. The prospect of using the phone book was daunting, because there were quite a few Suarezes.

Walking back to the subway, I had the idea of placing a personal ad in the Spanish language newspaper, *El Diario,* which produced no results. I eventually hired a professional researcher and people-finder, Karen Alderson, who helped me find the people I was looking for, some as far afield as San Diego. That's where she found Frank Suarez, Manuel's brother. He wrote this statement:

"I was Manuel's younger brother by four years and clearly remember him as strongly dedicated to his family and ultimately his country. Although wracked by severe asthma and bronchial problems during most of his life, he always bounced back from what seemed like his ultimate asthma attack [thanks to] my mother's tireless devotion and curative powers. Like our family, other Mexican-American families that I knew seemed particularly vulnerable to this affliction.

"Manuel was very protective of his brothers and sister and at an early age could outsmart antagonistic groups of youths bent on mayhem. I personally witnessed an incredible incident in which I thought we would surely be robbed of our money during an errand to the grocery store. We were quickly surrounded by six to eight older youths. Manuel had quickly hid the money in his jacket when they approached and he cleverly diverted attention while being searched by expressing empathy with their objectives and saying there were easier pickings just around the corner. The money wasn't found and definitely not surrendered to this gang. That evening my mother was able to serve us a dinner of pork chops, rice and beans.

"If I wasn't with him during the attempted robbery, he could have easily run off, but he stayed with me since he thought I wouldn't be able to run fast enough - an unmistakable sign of his courage and daring which was to manifest itself during his brief and tragic life. Like all the brave airmen of the 719th Squadron of the 449th Bomb Group, who flew, fought and subsequently died on *The Buzzer* during the deadly air campaign against Hitler's supplies and other flights, Manuel had that same special resourcefulness and vision.

"It was this kind of personal initiative and fast thinking that enabled him to achieve the goals he eagerly wanted—to fulfill the dreams of his mother, Paula, to reach our potential and a better life that had eluded our father. There were no jobs available during the Great Depression, especially for young kids in the "Barrio." But this didn't stop Manuel from bringing home badly needed money to help his family. Manuel eagerly sought possible earnings after school and on weekends by selling wholesale purchased shopping bags at retail prices at "La Marketa," a large semi-open air market in the "Barrio," shining shoes downtown, and at age seventeen working at a garage doing automotive work.

"It was this later work and automotive studies at high school that prepared Manuel to achieve a high score when tested by the Army for mechanical aptitude after he enlisted at the age of under nineteen. Manuel was later sent to an Army Air Force school where he was trained as a flight engineer and "understood how everything worked on a B-24 bomber," passed his exams and flight training.

Manuel Suarez' father was born in Cuba in 1896 and came to New York in 1916. There he met the airman's mother, Paula, who had come from Mexico as a nanny to a prosperous Mexican family. She had once jumped a fence to escape from a charging bull on her uncle's ranch in Tlacotalpan.

According to Manuel Suarez' nephew, Frank Jr., Manuel's mother found leaving Mexico "heart-wrenching . . . she was torn between staying in her familiar homeland or going to a strange country for a better life."

Frank Jr. also provided some details of his grandmother's emigration: "Before arriving in the land of opportunity, Pauline Suarez had to endure a long and perilous sea voyage filled with storms and high seas. The passage to the new world was made all the more dramatic because the voyage was made during the hostilities of World War One.

Upon approaching the American coastline, the ship's crew spotted a German U-boat, but the seamanship of the crew and good fortune enabled the ship to complete the passage."

Frank Sr.'s statement continues:

"Even though he had come from an established Cuban family, Beny Sr. was neglected during his early years and left Cuba to work as a merchant seaman. During a voyage to Veracruz, Mexico, he was impressed by this Caribbean looking city, its Cuban-like atmosphere and music, and its friendly people. Obviously, when he met our mother Paula in New York [whose home Tlacotalpan was a resort a day's journey from Veracruz] . . . he was favorably impressed. They were subsequently married and though life was difficult for them at times they endured and had bright, nice-looking children. Beny Sr.'s early and untimely death during the first years of the Depression profoundly affected our lives and ultimately helped reinforce our family's spirit of self-dependence, self-determination and perseverance in spite of subsequent tragedy that seemingly has doggedly pursued our small family.

"Our older brother Beny Jr. was the first to feel culture shock when he went to first grade in public school with Spanish as his primary language and was told by my mother to curtsey to the teacher. He was immediately targeted by other kids in his class who would harass him or try to beat him after school. Fortunately for him a sympathetic teacher showed him how to speak English and gave him a good academic foundation, subject by subject. He also learned not to be ashamed to adequately defend himself. Thanks to him we all learned to converse in English from the start and the beauty of Spanish almost disappeared from our home except when we spoke to Mom. Beny Jr. was a whiz and had an answer for all our questions. By the age of seven or eight I was reading Beny Jr.'s science fiction magazines and listening to his well rounded and intelligent comments—so did Manuel and Virginia."

According to Frank Jr., his grandmother told him of the impact of Pearl Harbor. "the Japanese attack electrified the Barrio. . . . My grandmother's strong love of country, courage and self-determination undoubtedly influenced my uncle Manuel Suarez' character. It was that set of shared strongly held beliefs and values that motivated my uncle to enlist." In Frank Jr.'s words, "He traded his family life for eagerly anticipated letters from home."

Manuel Suarez registered for the draft, and in the spring of 1943, got one of the notices so many other young men were getting. His family still has a copy, dated March 19, 1943.

"ORDER TO REPORT FOR INDUCTION

The President of the United States

To Manuel Suarez

Order No. 13235

GREETING:

Having submitted yourself to a local board composed of your neighbors for the purpose of determining your availability for training and service in the armed forces of the United States, you are hereby notified that you have now been selected for training and service . . . "

"You will, therefore, report to the local board named above at 103 W 110th St., New York City at 5.20 a.m. on the 10th day of April 1943."

"This local board will furnish transportation to an induction station of the service for which you have been selected. You will there be examined, and, if accepted for training and service, you will then be inducted into the stated branch of the service."

"Persons reporting to the induction station in some instances may be rejected for physical or other reasons. It is well to keep this in mind in arranging your affairs, to prevent any undue hardship if you are rejected at the induction station. If you are employed, you should advise your employer of this notice and of the possibility that you may not be accepted at the induction station. Your employer can then be prepared to replace you if you are accepted, or to continue your employment if you are rejected."

"Willful failure to report promptly to this local board at the hour and on the day named in this notice is a violation of the Selective Training and Service Act of 1940, as amended, and subjects the violator to fine and imprisonment . . ."

Frank Sr.'s statement recalls:

"On furlough before going overseas, Manuel was, as always, confident and unusually happy. He brought home several records such as Harry James's album which included "I Cried for You" and a record with the song "Louise"—the lovely sentimental tune sung by Maurice Chevalier. These platters my sister, Virginia, and I re-played constantly— almost as if to capture his spirit after he left to rejoin his group.

"Beny Jr. at this time was also in the service, working as a radioman for the Army Air Force Flying Tigers behind the Japanese lines in China. The harsh reality that my brothers were at the opposite ends of the world was slowly beginning to sink in as well as the idea that their coming home was going to take a very long time. I used to walk by the apartment building where Beny used to live after he was married, hoping to bring back the spirit of happy times when all our family was together. Naively I didn't know that we would never really be united again. Like our area of the "Barrio" that was later bulldozed to make way for faceless housing projects, we would have to rebuild our lives from the devastating rubble our dreams were to become."

Manuel Suarez was born February 17, 1925. He had enlisted before he was eighteen, and would die before he was nineteen.

A friend and former classmate of Suarez, Bill Dassinger, wrote him from Camp Stewart, Georgia, on February 14, 1944.

"Hi Square:

"Well here is that former school pal of yours writing from the same old dump at Camp Stewart.

"How are things going with you in the Air Corps. Every thing is going the same with me. There have been a few changes in the outfit I am in. A 40 mm. Outfit sure carries a mean punch. We have the 40mms, 50 cal machine gun, M.5, (four 50 cals mounted to one turret), M-1 rifle and now we got a Bazooka. So you see we can take care of ourselves in a tough spot. It's been raining down here all week and soon we are going on a 15 day maneuvers. We'll be digging in water up to our knees. If it rains while I'm out, then I'll be in for a tough time. That's all for that. Square I got my high school diploma without going to the last term. Every once in a while I get a letter from Jesse Hartmayer. He expects to go in soon and so does the rest of the gang. If they think the Army is a soft life they better think again . . ."

✈ ✈ ✈ ✈ ✈

Suarez seems to have been truly stuck with the "Square" nickname. The letter from Dassinger is addressed to Manuel Squarez, and one from Leo Leal, working in Connecticut, and sent to Suarez at Keesler Field, Mississippi, opens: "How is square from nowhere."

The same goes for a letter from another friend, Jesse Hartmayer. The letters show a close circle of friends trying to keep in touch as they are scattered by war.

Suarez' family still had an engine-starting checklist from his time in the service. I've included it in the Appendix. It reminds me that even though there have been many technical advances since the Forties, the Second World War, particularly for bomber crews, was a pretty high-tech business.

Like most servicemen abroad, Suarez wrote home frequently.

Italy September 9, 1944

"Dearest Mother,

"Have arrived safely and am fine. Things here are well, but we sleep in tents. I guess I'll be eating spaghetti and having some of that Italian wine.

"Hope you are getting my War Bonds and the $40 allotment. I hope everyone is well and in good health. I guess this war will be over soon from what I've seen. Tell Benny to write and don't worry too much as I'm fine. Give my regards to everyone, and will write to them soon.

"Well Mother take care of yourself, as I close this letter with all my love.

Your loving son,
Manuel"

"Somewhere in Italy" October 17, 1944.

"Dear Mom,

"I'm now at my permanent camp and I'll be home sooner than you know. I'm living like a king now. We have three Italian kids, who clean up for us and also our laundry. I'm drinking plenty Italian wine, as it's pretty good here.

"Don't worry about me too much because I'm fine. We have to make 50 missions. They may be pretty rough. In case I'm counted as missing I'm sure to get back. We live in a tent, but it's fixed like a palace. I now have a different address. So don't forget when you write."

I have wondered if that sentence, "In case I'm counted as missing I'm sure to get back". came back to Suarez' family after he disappeared, and later. Like the other airmen, he was officially missing for a long time, half a year, before his death was announced.

Nov. 2, 1944

"Dear Mother,

"I'm just as happy as can be, since I am fine, and living the life of 'Riley'. Well at least I'm a sergeant now.

"You see I can afford to write a regular letter now. (ha ha) I do hope you have received my V mail letters, since I expect to hear from you soon. I already have in a couple of missions. After the fifth mission we receive the Air Medal. Well if you buy the Daily News regular you're liable to see my name in the papers with a big write up.

"The food is pretty good and most of everything is okay here. I expect two more promotions during my stay here. Well Mother tell Vincent I'll pull my rank on him if he doesn't write to me soon.

"I'll be sending you some money soon. So don't be working too hard. Well mother I close this letter with a bomb load full of kisses and hugs."

Nov. 6, 1944 Somewhere in Italy

"Dear Mother,

"I'm fine and hope to find everyone in the best of health. I've completed five missions and they are quite rough. I now will receive the air medal.

"It sure is cold up there. But somehow, you don't feel it once you're over the target. But the happier moments are when the plane hits the runway, and once more everything is okay. I do hope to be home real soon, maybe six months. If I can possibly get all my missions in.

"Well mother I now ask you to do me a little favor. Will you send a donation for me to the church on 14th St. At the end of this month I'll send you most of my money. The reason, no place to spend it. By the way I'll be a Staff Sgt. also. Well Christmas will be around soon. And I want you to buy yourself the nicest looking dress as when I come home I want to be looking at the best mother in the world. Well I close with all my love, Do write soon.

November 12, 1944 Somewhere in Italy

"Dearest Mom,

"Wishing to find everyone in the best of health. As I am fine and in good spirit. It's been pretty cold lately. But I do manage to keep more than warm. We built a gasoline stove lately. And it sure keeps us warm.

"I hope you have received my letters lately as I've been waiting for some time for a reply. As I would like to hear from you a little more often. I was figuring on receiving some hair oil [vaseline hair oil] and try and see if you can get some film for me as I would like to send a few snap shots . . .

"So do try and send it soon. Well mother don't forget to buy yourself that new dress. As I may be home before you know it.

"So I close Mother with a big kiss and all the love in the world."

Nov. 14, 1944 Somewhere in Italy

"Dear Mother,

"Received your letter postmarked Oct. 23 and [it] was swell to hear from you again. I was happy to hear you are getting my $40 allotment. But I must say you are only getting a $18.70 war bond, not a fifty. Don't worry if you have not received it because you will get it.

"I'm sending you a $50 dollar money order. Well do anything you please with it. Write and tell me as soon as you receive it. I'll be sending home more money at the end of this month. Tell Carmen I wrote to her.

"I just received a letter from Vincent saying he is fine. You should have [written] to him, as the card I sent him was blurred.

"I took some pictures lately so in the coming letters you'll all be seeing my pictures. I close with love to all."

Nov. 17, 1944 Somewhere in Italy

"Dear Mother,

"I'm fine, and do hope everyone is well at home. I've been quite busy as now I have 8 missions completed. I have 42 more to go. But we'll get there as we've got the best pilot this side of Europe. I sent $50 in my last letter. So I do hope you get it before Xmas as it is a present from me.

"In your last letter Virginia wrote to my friend Pvt. Balogh. I would be very glad if she wrote again and gave him my present address. I still haven't received your package. But I know they must be on their way. Tell Carmen I'm sorry I haven't written, but it's because I'm too damn tired after a mission.

"I should be sleeping, but I must write you since I know you want to hear from me often.

"I'm making about $140 a month now but since I expect another promotion I will then be making about $175. By the time I make Tech. Sgt . . . I'll be making over $200 dollars a month which ain't hay. Well mother tell me if you have received any of my 25 bonds. I close my letter and do hope you are well. Regards to Carmen and all."

"Your son,
Manuel"
"PS Write soon!"

Nov. 18, 1944 Somewhere in Italy

"Dear Mom,

"I'm fine and hope you are fine, I now have completed my tenth mission and only have 40 more to go. You can see, I'll be home soon now. I'll be busy again tomorrow as it will be a busy day again.

"I just finished drinking a bottle of Rupert's beer, and it never tasted so good. Well now, I have to wait till next week for more. I didn't have a chance to pick up my pictures I took, but if I get to go to town tomorrow, I'll send you a couple.

"Well mother, I do hope every one is in fine health. As for Frankie, I hope he's still as smart and doing well in school.

"I have to get up real early again, but I do get a lot of sleep after all. It's just that you don't want to get up on a cold morning.

"I hear Vincent is going overseas. But he will have a good deal at that since he will put in some communications on the ground. So I guess he's better off than me. I close with all my love and kisses."

"Your son
Manuel Suarez"
"PS Write soon"

Nov. 19, 1944 Somewhere in Italy

"Dear Mom,

"I'm happy and fine, and hope to hear everyone is well. Well now I have 11 missions. I won't be flying tomorrow as well so I guess they're giving us a little rest.

"I'm sending you the picture I've been telling you about. I rather came out cute, as everybody tells me. I'm wearing my flying jacket. You can see us boys in the Air Force have rather expensive jackets. I hope you are hearing from me regular since I've been writing regular. I just received a Xmas package from Mrs. McGloin, and it certainly was pretty nice of her . . ."

Nov. 23, 1944 Somewhere in Italy

"Dear mother,

"I'm fine, and had a wonderful turkey dinner as we celebrated Thanksgiving we bombed the enemy with 2,000 pounders and they do make quite a lot of noise, when they go off.

"I now have 14 missions and am quite happy to get in so many in such a short time. I'll be sending you some more money at the end of the month.

"Do tell me if you are getting that $18.75 bond every month now.

"By the way Mother are you still working or have you quit. If things aren't too well you can always change my bonds.

"I enjoyed my turkey dinner, as it's been about the best I've had in the Army, so far. We have a little dog who is our mascot. It sure is a cute thing. We expect to bring him for a ride one of these days . . ."

Manuel's mother wrote to him on November 30, 1944: of course, with the slowness of mail, many of these letters will have "crossed."

"Dear Son,

"I received your most cheerful letters and was mighty glad to hear you are well, and everything under control. I have so much to say I really don't know where to start. First I want to congratulate [you] We are all proud of your splendid achievements in your daily routines . . . We all certainly hope you all can keep up the good work and in due time you'll be back with us. The pictures certainly were a real surprise for me. I never saw you looking any better. I can see you still are strongly attached to us in your young boyish way. I am so grateful you take time out to write to me. I really and truly appreciate it. I'm dreadfully sorry if my mail isn't very regular as you know I'm quite a busy person. Vincent wrote home and according to what he tells me he won't be shipped overseas as he did not pass his physical examination. He is stationed 60 miles from San Pedro. We haven't received your War Bonds yet. I was shopping around for your films No. 1828 so far I haven't been able to get it as it is a bit difficult. But don't worry about it because I'll find it if it is the right number. When I do get it I shall send it together with your pill and hair tonic. I was not able to get your favorite brand of Vitalis. Please write to Carmen as soon as possible and congratulate Victor as his birthday was November 26, 1944 but was celebrated Dec. 3 on account of a few obstacles. Please my dear son take good care of yourself."

December 2, 1944 Somewhere in Italy

"Dearest Mother,

" . . . I have completed 16 missions and am happy to know I'm getting closer to my goal. I made Staff Sgt. that is three up and one down. But that isn't all, for next month I'll be Tech. Sgt. with the help of God.

"I received your letter and was thrilled as that is the first letter I got from you in English.

"I'm very happy tonight well I just am. I only hope you don't miss me on Xmas but mother I'll surely be thinking of you.

"I may not finish my missions in Italy. But since I do not know I only hope for the best. I hope you have received the picture I sent you.

"Let me know how things are. Well mother give my regards to Helen and Carmen. I'll close with the biggest kiss & hug this side of the ocean."

Manuel wrote home again on Dec. 6th.

"My dear Carmen,

"I hope to hear you are in the best of health when you receive this letter. As for me I'm fine.

"I now have 16 missions and an Air Medal for outstanding achievement during aerial participation against the enemy. I'm out on a pass and enjoying myself at a Red Cross Club.

"I sure wish I were home for Xmas, but as I know I won't I'll be thinking of you all. And I do hope you enjoy yourself. I myself will celebrate. So if you happen to be with Mother . . . Well I'll be home soon again. So don't any of you cry.

"I'm now a Staff Sgt. Well I guess I can order Vincent around now.

"Well Carmen, best wishes and best of everything to all. So I close with all my love, and do hope to hear from you."

On December 7, 1944, Manuel's sister Virginia wrote him a letter he was never to read:

"Dearest Brother,

"Here's hoping when you receive this letter it will find you in the very best of health and especially in good spirit. I just can't seem to believe it, that time has passed away so terribly fast. Every day that passes, we all anxiously and eagerly await your letters. Isn't that something to look forward to? Every moment of the day we always have you in mind, plus a fear in our hearts, for the very dangerous task that you are undertaking. Gosh Manuel I just can't seem to put it to words how terribly much we all miss you. I know it's your duty to be there like the rest, but oh! How I do wish we all would be together like good old times. But you needn't worry just have faith in God that's the main thing, for it is

He the only one who judges all of us, good or bad, bright or dumb. I'm sure . . . the entire crew must have done their utmost to accomplish each and every mission. We all know they are quite rough, and it's kind of cold in the heavens.

"We all realize these hardships which you all are undertaking too bravely and take for granted it's just another days' work. We folks back at the home front sure are mighty proud of each and every one of you. I do hope you will soon receive your Christmas parcels as they contain the very articles which you need. We haven't received any of your War Bonds yet. Manuel just buy the $17.50 Bonds as I am also buying Bonds. If you can possibly send the cash it's much better. On the other hand if you can't buy the Bonds. As soon as I get film No. 1828 I shall send it immediately to you.

"Well since Christmas is just around the corner, we all sincerely wish from the bottom of the heart, a Merry Christmas and a Happy New Year. Try to write to our brother Vincent. Today we received a letter from Pat Balogh, he became ill and was sent to the hospital and missed the shipment overseas. God only knows where they are now, France probably.

"He certainly was surprised to hear you were a Corporal but he doesn't know you are a Sgt. now. He hopes you'll make general before you're out, quite a chap isn't he! Well my dear I believe I've taken up quite a bit of time from you with my silly chatter. Now I close this letter leaving you in God's Care and Trust. Love from Mother and Francis. Remembrance from Carmen and . . . my gentlemen friend. The one from St. Moritz Hotel."

"Love,
Sis"
"Virginia M. Suarez"

Virginia wrote again on December 13th—four days after the crash. Of course she knew nothing of it yet.

"Dearest Brother,

"I was delighted to hear you are well, even though slightly bored of existing conditions away from home. I still acknowledge the fact you are a long way off, from fifty missions, but time will tell and you shall soon be home again, away from the bizarre horror and terror of the tumultuous European skies. By the way you stress the fact that you have been over Yugoslavia, Germany, Austria and the great white Alps, it makes itself clear that you are not there for sport but for the dangerous business of dropping calling cards saturated with explosives!

"Now to get down to earthly matters. I want to divine your excellent judgement on the topic last discussed. We received all your Greeting cards—also the War bonds—the ones you purchased in the month of October. They were indeed very lovely and thoughtful of you. We donated the ten dollars to the church as you told us to, eight went for flowers, two went for Mass. The chosen day for the Mass was Tuesday the 12th. About the films I tried securing them for you but they haven't been on the market for quite some time. As soon as I find them I will send them to you. Pvt. Henry B. wrote to us. He told us his outfit was ready to make a change of station so they told him to get rid of all addresses of any sort. He tried to memorize it but soon forgot it. It so happened he got sick and was sent to the hospital, missing the shipment. He doesn't know you are a Sgt. now. He said you certainly are getting up in the world. Vincent wrote and is well. Have you received our Christmas parcel yet? Now I close this letter hoping it will leave you in the best of humor, and spirit and may God Bless you and take care of you."

"Regards from all,
Love,
Sis"
"PS Answer soon."

Like the other families, the Suarezes were notified that Manuel Suarez was missing just before the New Year. Like the others, they endured months of waiting before eventual notice of their relative's death. Many official documents were involved, but the families still lacked information.

The Suarez family still has a two-page, single-spaced typed government briefing, "Information For Next Of Kin Of World War II Deceased" concerned with details like the order in which soldier's remains were returned to the U.S. and shipped around the country to their final resting places.

It includes the information, "The remains are escorted home individually by a service man who is of equal or higher rank, of the same branch of the service, of the same race and sex as the deceased."

Manuel's mother received many letters from the other next of kin. Fowler Doyle's widow wrote her. Hazel Cranmer, Paul Watson's mother, wrote several times, reporting on the basic crash information her son Billy (William) had found in his visit to the site, sending photographs of her sons, and offering condolences:

"It is so hard to think of our boys not coming home now that the war is over—but God knows best—may he comfort your heart in your sorrow as he does mine. Remember we shall meet them one of these glad days and shall never part again."

Sylvia Arieff, Ellis Arieff's widow, also wrote, "I have faith that they are all right somewhere. I know it is hard, but we can help each other a little by exchanging any news we might get about our men."

A plea for any more information than sparse official communications offered also came from the Ballou family. The Groegers and others tried to compare notes on the letters they were receiving from Amelia Clemente. They wrote to Mrs. Suarez that they wished all the next of kin could meet once in a while; the Groeger's from Chicago, had recently visited the Ganims in Cinncinnati. They passed on Hazel Cranmer's account of Mrs. Clemente's account of the fate of the plane. They said they had passed on the information they had to the *Chicago Tribune*. They hoped the Tribune's man in Italy would be able to find out more.

In November 1945, the Groegers wrote Mrs. Suarez, "Many thanks for your kind letter and the dear picture of your beloved son Manuel. He is so young and sweet looking;

it just seems unbelievable that these 16 godloving young boys are gone; however, let us feel, that they are not gone forever, but just away for a while, and that, some day, we will all see our boys again, in that great place of the unknown world called heaven."

"We are very glad to know your oldest son has recently returned from China; if he should happen to come to Chicago some day, be sure and tell him to stop at our home for a few days and get acquainted."

The Groegers told her that the *Chicago Tribune's* Rome correspondent had been sent an account of what the parents knew so far, including the name of Mrs. Clemente.

Mary Ganim, Albert's mother, wrote on December 9, 1945, the first anniversary of the crash, "Dear Mrs. Suarez,

"I have thought of you many times in the past year and have often thought of writing to you but just did not. We have heard from many of the families or wives of the boys lost on the plane a year ago today. I have thought about you especially because my son Albert was such a good friend to your son, he always wrote home about him, and mentioned any number of times that he was going to have him come to Cincinnati after the war was over, and they came home. He called him Pancho . . . I have a picture with the three boys together and wondered if you also had one, it is a snap shot taken in Italy October 18, 1944. In almost every letter Albert mentioned Pancho, we did not know his name until we received the list of the men on the plane from the War Department."

"Mr. Groeger was in Cincinnati . . . he is a very much upset man over the loss of his only son . . ."

"My daughter was in New York during the summer . . . she was there when the plane crashed [into] the Empire State Building, it upset her considerably and when the confirmation of Albert's death was received she came home."

This refers to the famous incident in late July 1945 when a B-25 medium bomber, lost in thick fog, crashed into the 79th floor of the Empire State Building. Fourteen people were killed. Quite coincidentally, the B-25 was from the regrouped remainder of the 47th Wing and 449th Bomb Group, by then in Nebraska, Charles "Jeb" Stuart, the last 719th Operations Officer in Italy, planned on going on that flight to Stewart Field at the U.S. Military Academy and then on to Long Island, with the intent of spending the weekend in New York. When they were preparing to take-off, a jeep came out to the airplane, and he was told to get off as he had been reassigned to a B-29 outfit and had to now go there. Otherwise, he would have been on that airplane when it struck the Empire State Building.

✈ ✈ ✈ ✈ ✈

"She and Albert were very close and it was hard on her especially being away from home, she always thought and hoped the boys would be found, that they might have fallen into friendly hands and be safe, so the Government confirmation of the death of the boys on December the ninth has been very hard for her although she as we all know that Albert is happy in Heaven and God knows best, and must have wanted them to permit their death it is still hard to take."

Mrs. Ganim's letter complains, as do many, of the lack of detail forthcoming from official sources.

"We are of the Roman Catholic Faith so we find consolation in prayer as all people do naturally. We had a Mass for Albert this morning and another one tomorrow morning and one for Christmas just before the day."

Mary Ganim wrote Mrs. Suarez again in February 1946: " . . . It is nice to know we have something in common, both being Catholic we can understand, and our Faith is such a comfort in times of trials and sorrows." She too wanted a picture of Manuel, and enclosed one of her son Albert.

In 1946, Pauline Suarez got a note from Albert Marple Sr., thanking her for her letter and pictures. Mr. Marple continues, "I am glad to hear you have one son at least left. I have none, nobody to perpetuate my name. I have two girls. One is married has two children and lives on a stock ranch in N. Dak. The other is a sophomore in Macalester College in St. Paul, Minnesota. I am alone since their mother passed away June 1936 when our home and contents burned to the ground and she died from the burns 12 hours later."

✈ ✈ ✈ ✈ ✈

Nancy Caldwell wrote in June 1946: She had sent all fifteen sets of next of kin copies of a letter from Mrs. Clemente asking for shoes for her child. "Yes, I sent all fifteen a copy and I thought it explained itself but I had not thought of the little boy getting too many pairs of shoes. Well, if he is that lucky, I think she will pass them on to others who need them. I sent everything she asked for and doubled the amount of coffee and thread. She asked for black and white cotton and I thought she meant thread. I sent her 14 spools of mixed numbers of thread. Also two pairs of socks for her son and a little sweater for the expected baby. I sent a good coat my daughters had outgrown, three or four packs of needles, some candy, three powder puffs."

"Mr. Groeger sent me a similar letter from her back about February. Some one of the boys' uncles had sent it to him and I had asked him what he had found out. In that letter she asked for used clothes to give the poor civilians who went down to find out about our sons. I sent her a box then of old clothes: two coats, a sweater, a shirt and some pants. I do not know if she has gotten them. Mr. Groeger wrote last week that they had sent her four packages and that she had received two of them.

"I received the picture of your son. Thank-you so much for it. I think he is a lovely boy, if I may say it that way. I have seven, eight with my own son. They are all fine looking."

"Our sons' flying away together makes all of them dear to me."

In January 1949, the Groegers wrote to Manuel's sister, who had married and was now Mrs. Virginia Dimas. She was in San Antonio, Texas.

They were able to inform her that Manuel had been one of the victims who was identified, and that he was buried in the U.S. Military Cemetery at Naples. They also alerted her to a possible claim against the Government.

"I received a copy of a Congressional Bill No. H.R. 3722 which is to come before this 81st Congress, in the House of Representatives. It relates to authorize payment of certain personal claims of military personnel and civilian employees of the Army or of the Navy Dept. . . . in case of their deaths, to their survivors."

The Groegers thought Virginia or her mother might want to file a claim to recover lost personal property of Manuel's.

The Groegers wrote Mrs. Suarez in March that year, after his body had been returned to the U.S., " . . . Your son is now laid at rest in the soil of our good old U.S.A.; the country for whom he had fought and died—and his soul now in heaven with god almighty watching over him; and may we all meet up in spirit with our dear ones some day, which may not be far away, as this would be a reward for our sorrows which we have endured on *this* earth." The Groegers suggested writing to the Quartermaster General in Washington to secure the return of Manuel's ID tags.

Mr. Ballou, Ralph's father, wrote Mrs. Suarez from Cedar Rapids, " . . . We were in Calif. [for] the Gold Star Mothers Convention last June, and called on Mrs. Cranmer, had a nice visit and also a fine time at the Convention. It was wonderful. They are having the Convention in Atlantic City, next June, but we have not made up our minds yet as to going."

"Three years have passed since that fatal crash, Dec. 9, and it will sure be hard to get over, and never forget. We never had any personal effects returned. Did you?

"We would like to hear a lot about your town and state and of course would like to see it, and may try to if we go east next spring. I was in New York once [when] I was in World War I and we left and returned to New York."

Manuel Suarez is buried in Long Island National Cemetery in Farmingdale, New York.

Albert Ganim

"It will be seven months tomorrow since my Son is missing over Italy."

Staff Sergeant Albert Ganim was twenty-one when he died aboard *The Buzzer*. He was the radio operator. He was the son of George Ganim and the former Mary Ann Farrell. He was born in Cincinnati, Ohio. The family lived in the city's Walnut Hills section, and Ganim attended Roger Bacon High School and the University of Cincinnati before joining the Army Air Force in 1943.

When he died, he had two sisters, Betty, aged twenty-two, and Helene, aged eighteen. His brother George was fifteen. Much later, George spoke about his brother:

"We got along fine as young boys. I was fifteen or sixteen when he went into the service. He was very intelligent. And, I'm not just saying that. He won scholarships in high school and all that. He joined the Army Air Force and he was going to the University of Cincinnati, and he probably would have been very successful. He was interested in medical school or something in that order. He comes from a family of doctors. My two uncles are doctors . . . And he went into the service and he wrote me letters."

Ganim won his silver gunner wings on graduating from the gunnery school at Harlingen Army Air Field, Texas. Like so many airmen he completed training in a Liberator bomber at Pueblo Army Air Base, Pueblo, Colorado.

He wrote George from Italy five days before he died:

Dec. 4, 1944

"Dear Brother

"I'm writing this amid the din of music from a brass band, clinking glasses, laughing and singing. The club is just two tents away from our house and tonight they are celebrating the squadron's first anniversary with a big party.

"I was up there a few minutes but it's too much of a rat race for me. They have about 200 GIs and about 20 girls to dance with them. The girls look like they are half scared to death, and I don't blame them. What a mob.

"How are you doing fellow? I hear that your high school is the best as far as football teams are concerned. I'm glad to hear of it. You could have made the team even if you were a little too light. But Purcell always did go in for big heavy teams.

"As fast as you are growing, you should be right in there next fall. I hope you are getting along OK with your studies and not finding them too tough. Get all the help you can from Betty and Helen.

"I'm a staff sergeant now. I was promoted the first of the month. I still have one more stripe to go, then all I'll have to do is stay on the ball and keep them.

"The crew has 16 missions now. Thirty-four to go and then home again. It seems like a lot, but [BLANK] ago we had fifty to go. I've been saving all the details in my memory, so I can tell you all about them when I come home. Censorship is too strict to tell you anything really interesting.

"I don't know if I told you before, but I received your last letter about two weeks ago. It was very interesting and well written. Your English is becoming very good while mine degenerates with every day that passes.

"I'll bet you're a knockout in the new suit you have had made. When I get out of the Army I'm going to spend the first week at home shopping for new clothes; with your assistance of course.

"I received a letter from Helen tonight. She tells me you have acquired a keen interest for poetry. Will miracles never cease?

"A notice was on our bulletin board tonight stating that I am to receive the Air Medal. Don't get any wrong ideas now, I'm not a hero. They are given out quite freely to flying personnel.

"How's business at the Drug Store? I think it's a good idea to work there so you can earn a little spending money. Do you still have all the Hill-Billy trade from the neighborhood? I used to get a bang out of some of them when I worked there.

"Keep up the good work kid and write when you get a little time. I'll be thinking of you."

Love,
Al

George continues:
"See, when the plane crashed, it crashed December 9th, and we got a telegram 'Your son is missing' period. We didn't get any confirmation. I know the war was on and there was all kind of crashes, but I'm going by my poor mom and dad because I have five children, I have four sons, and if it had happened to me, I don't know what I would have done. There's a telegram, but we never heard anything. And my dad would write to different people, and the congressmen, but they never found the plane. The plane hit and they never found it until maybe in July. And, naturally, the remains were all over the ground. So, that's how we found out. But the waiting period was just unbelievable. As a teenager, I didn't feel as a parent would, but now I think of how bad it really was, it really shook them up."

Albert's mother Mary wrote the War Department on July 8, 1945:

Dear Sir:

" . . . It will be seven months tomorrow since my Son is missing over Italy. To date we have received no word from the Government, and are naturally discouraged since the end of the War in Europe, and the prison camps all liberated, it looks and seems a hopeless story now. I have a letter written on December 5 by my son telling me he had been awarded the air medal and would send it to me as soon as he received it. I have not received the medal the only thing received was a Diary which arrived the other day. Albert had more things to send home I am sure of. He took pictures of the family and friends and some books we would be interested in having because they are his. We did have mail and Xmas packages returned . . . "

She soon received word of an award won by her son:

The War Department, The Adjutant General's Office
31 August 1945

"Dear Mrs. Ganim:

"I have the honor to inform you, that by the direction of the President, the Air Medal has been posthumously awarded to your son, the late Staff Sergeant Albert Ganim, Air Corps. The citation pertaining to this award is as follows:

Air Medal

"For meritorious achievement in aerial flight while participating in sustained operational activities against the enemy from 31 October to 16 November 1944."

"The decoration will be forwarded to the Commanding general, Fifth Service command, Fort Hayes, Columbus, Ohio, who will select an officer to make the presentation. The officer selected will communicate with you regarding your wishes in the matter.

"At the time your son received the Air Medal, his grade was that of Sergeant and the decoration will be engraved with that grade.

"May I extend my deepest sympathy to you in your bereavement.

Sincerely yours,
Edward F. Witsell
Major General
Acting The Adjutant General"

The Roger Bacon High School Alumni News for November, 1945 featured Ganim on its front page:

"S/Sgt. Albert Ganim '42 is 32nd Gold Star

"As Bacon alumni everywhere were saddened to learn that Albert Ganim '42 became the 32nd graduate to lose his life in service they expressed the hope that it would be the last for World War II.

"'Abie', as he was affectionately known by his classmates, was a student at U.C. when he enlisted in the Air Corps in 1942. A staff sergeant gunner and radio operator on a B-24 Liberator with the 15th Air force in Italy, he was flying his 18th mission on Dec. 9, 1944, when his plane failed to return. Not until late this summer was Sgt. Ganim's death officially confirmed. The plane, the War Dept. announced, had encountered bad weather and crashed into a mountain on a flight from Taranto to Naples, Italy."

Here is more evidence that the true story of the crash into an Italian mountainside, not into the Bay of Naples, was widely known in the year following the event; but somehow the story got around among the unit's veterans that the plane hadn't been found.

The school newspaper story continued:

"A requiem Mass at which the Rev. Principal, Fr. Vincent Kroger, OFM, officiated was offered by the Alumni Association shortly after the official announcement was made."

An August 27, 1946, letter to Mrs. Ganim from The Adjutant General apologized for her having had no reply to a 1945 request for details about her son's death. It provided the address of the 449th's chaplain, and, apparently on the subject of Mrs. Clemente, said, "I am unable to advise you concerning the information received by the father of a crew member serving with Sergeant Ganim, direct from Italy in return for clothes for the needy."

In the autumn of 1949, George Ganim received a telegram notifying him that the remains of his son were on their way back to the U.S. The telegram confirmed that since individual identification was impossible, Ganim's remains with those of seven other airmen would be buried as a group at Jefferson Barracks.

The telegram also made clear that next of kin who wished to attend the burial would do so at their own expense, and that "PAYMENT OF SEVENTY-FIVE DOLLARS INTERMENT EXPENSE ALLOWANCE IS NOT REPEAT NOT AUTHORIZED SINCE BURIAL IS IN A NATIONAL CEMETERY."

George Ganim wrote back on November 1, 1949, to ask if the records of his family dentist and the expertise of his physician brothers could be used in one more attempt to identify Albert's remains, so that he could be buried in the family plot.

He also criticized the telegram for emphasizing what the Government would not pay in the way of expenses.

In asking for a chance to have the remains reexamined, he added: "I wish you to know that I realize that my rights and interests are in the same category of the rights and interests of the next-of-kin of my son's comrades, and that in sharing their bereavement and in being respectful of their wishes, I may ultimately yield to the Government's plan of interment."

A reply came, dated November 9:

"Dear Mr. Ganim:

"Colonel G. H. Bare has forwarded to this Office for reply, your letter of 1 November 1949, in which you raise several questions incident to the identification and final burial of your son, the late Staff Sergeant Albert George Ganim, whose remains are a part of a group to be buried in the Jefferson Barracks National Cemetery. Before answering your specific questions, may I say how sorry I am that the initial notification you received from the Port informing you of the imminent arrival of the group appeared to stress unnecessarily the practical aspects of non-payment by the Government of travel and interment expenses. We in Washington, who are responsible for the inclusion of these items in the telegrams have recognized the impact of the message as a whole on sensitive families, but have decided that it is the lesser of two evils to spare those relatives who might incur burdensome travel expenses under the erroneous impression that they would receive some reimbursement from the Government. It is not an easy task to convey all of the necessary information within the limits of a telegram to the large number of families with whom we must deal and whom we are not privileged to know personally.

"In order to explain to you the reason why only a group identification of your son and seven others was possible, I should like to recount certain facts available from our records. As you probably have been told before, your son was one of five crewmembers of the B-24 aircraft, "The Buzzer," which departed from Grottaglie, Italy, on 9 December 1944 on a ferrying mission bound for Naples, carrying eleven military passengers. The plane crashed into the peak of a mountain near the town of Oliveto Citra, Italy, killing all aboard. At the time the remains were recovered and buried in the United States Military Cemetery Naples, Italy, it was possible to identify and bury individually three of the crew and five of the passengers; however, so fragmentary were the recovered remains of the other eight, that they were interred in two graves in the Naples Cemetery as the only recoverable remains of your son and seven others.

"Prior to the final acceptance of the group identification, the remains in the group were carefully reprocessed late in 1948 in an Identification Laboratory in the Mediterranean Graves Registration Zone. Our records contain a complete and detailed report listing the fragmentary commingled skeletal parts present; the findings are signed not only by the Officer in Charge, but also by Dr. Alexander

Lenard, M.D., of the University of Vienna, who was the Supervising Anthropologist at the Laboratory. Both certified that individual segregation could not be accomplished because of the badly fragmented, incomplete, and intermingled condition of the remains. It was not possible for the technicians to accomplish any dental charts. Under these circumstances the group identification as originally established has been confirmed, and the remains have been returned to this country in two caskets.

"I sincerely regret that it will not be possible to arrange a conference in Cincinnati to discuss the findings or to permit examination of the remains prior to their burial. However, our records here in Washington are always available to scrutiny by anyone having a close interest who desires to go into the details of the case; furthermore, we shall be glad to confer at anytime with you, your brothers, Congressman Elston, or any member of his Washington staff.

"In closing may I say that we appreciate the generous attitude you voice in the last paragraph of your letter, in which you express consideration for the feelings and interests of the seven other American families with whom you are irrevocably bound in the tragic loss of a beloved son.

"Sincerely Yours,
E.V. Freeman
Colonel, QMC
Chief, Memorial Division"

Not only did families have to wait until almost five years after the accident to have their loved ones' remains returned to the U.S., but some families were confronted with thinking about the detailed effects of a crash, fire, and long winter and spring of exposure on their loved ones' bodies, to the extent that so many men's remains could not be separately identified.

I am not blaming the Government for this, just the poignancy of the facts. As far as the long delay before repatriation goes, one has only to think of how many dead had to be removed from Europe, the Pacific, North Africa and elsewhere.

As I have mentioned, Caldwell, Boswell, Marple, Suarez, and Ganim, the flying crew of *The Buzzer* when it crashed, were part of a regular combat crew, about a third of the way into their missions.

Naturally, I have been concerned with the effect of the loss of the men in that crash on their families and loved ones, but I shouldn't underestimate the impact on the rest of that crew of losing five men like that.

According to Francis A. "Hank" Riefer, of Fairmont, West Virginia, their nose gunner, the rest of the regular crew, who flew on the *Touch Me Not,* were Joe Shields, bombardier, from St. Louis, Missouri; ball turret gunner "Shorty" Treahorne, of Ohio, tail gunner John Sailor, of Pennsylvania, and a top turret gunner called Spratlin.

Ganim's brother George said, "My brother is buried in a group grave of the remains of some of the boys in Jefferson barracks in St. Louis. He was the last boy killed in the Second World War from Roger Bacon High School. They do have a plaque, it doesn't have all the names on it. What luck to be the last one, well anyone, but the last one hurt even more."

William G. Stevens

Ten Missions In

Lt. William G. Stevens was the son of William Stevens, of 2931 North Mason Street, Chicago, Illinois. He was a pilot with a crew and plane of his own. Before the war he worked as an electrician. At twenty-seven he was older than most of us out there. Stevens had married Anne Miller Murdoch on January 24, 1942.

He had started working for a company called Liquid, which manufactured components for B-24s and B-17s, in February, 1941. He joined up the following October, as a private in the 1st Armored Division at Fort Knox, Kentucky. He was transferred to the Air Corps eight months later, gaining his wings at Mission, Texas in February 1943.

He was an instructor at the gunnery school at Laredo, Texas, until going to Italy in October 1944. He completed ten missions before the crash. Stevens is one of the eight men buried together at Jefferson Barracks National Cemetery.

Francis G. Baldwin, Jr.

"He was going on a joyful mission . . ."

Baldwin was twenty-five when he died, widowing Mrs. Anne Murdoch Baldwin, of 5 Madison Lane, Hyde Park, Ohio. He also left a nine-day-old son he'd never seen, Francis G. Baldwin III. He was on the plane because he was going shopping for gifts for his wife and newborn son. He had just been made First Lieutenant on December 4th.

Baldwin was a Liberator copilot. He had completed about thirty missions over Germany, Austria, and other Fifteenth Air Force targets. He was awarded the Air Medal with Oak Leaf Cluster and the Distinguished Unit badge with Oak Leaf Cluster.

The grandson of a brigadier general and son of a major, Baldwin joined the Air Corps in January 1943. The family had even earlier links with the military. A Baldwin was captured by Indians, one fought in the Civil War and in Italy for Garibaldi, and one was gassed in the First World War.

He got his wings in April 1944, graduating as a Wing Commander, in the top ten percent of his class. He went overseas that summer.

Baldwin's mother, Mrs. Anna Louise Baldwin, lived in Maryland, and his father lived in Sarasota, Florida. He had a brother, William I. Baldwin, in Cincinnati, and a sister, Mrs. Mary Louise Van Doren in Detroit, Michigan.

Francis Baldwin was born July 16, 1920, in Milford, Ohio. He went to Milford Public School and Cincinnati

Country day School. His family moved to Terrace Park when he was ten, and he attended Terrace Park School. Then came Walnut Hills High School.

If war had not intervened, Baldwin might not have followed the family military tradition. After finishing high school he attended the Central Academy of Commercial Art, and became a commercial artist, winning enough success to operate his own studio.

According to his friend Louise Walker, he was freelancing, doing assignments for local companies and advertising people, and producing things like gifts and playing cards. She also said his father, the Major, was "quite artistic." Louise Walker and her husband, William, were at Baldwin's wedding, and vice versa.

When I met his son, Francis Baldwin III, now in his 50s, he told me "People kept looking for the artistic side in me . . . but there's appreciation only."

Baldwin's crew arrived at Grottaglie from Tunis on September 14, 1944. He was the copilot in the crew of Alvin E. Charnes. The navigator, Lawrence "Larry" Hamblen, Jr., was a help to me in gathering information about Baldwin. Hamblen, a first lieutenant, flew fifty-one missions from October 4, 1944 to March 8, 1945. He once saved the life of nose gunner Myron Potter by crushing the ice in the gunner's face mask, putting him on a portable oxygen bottle, and carrying him across the catwalk above the open bomb bay doors to the flight deck for help.

Hamblen sent me this:

"REMEMBERING FRANCIS G. BALDWIN

"First met Francis G. Baldwin, Jr. (Baldy) at Westover Field, Mass. Where Alvin E. Charnes (Al) the pilot selected his crew. Baldy was chosen as Co-Pilot, both had many hours as instructors. I was chosen as Nav. After all the crew had been selected, we went to Chatham Field, Savannah, Ga., Aug. 44. During the time we were training, one weekend Baldy's wife Ann came for a visit. She was six months pregnant and didn't even show—they seemed very happy.

"After training we went to Mitchell Field, New York to pick the B24J plane to go overseas. While at the air base for a few days Baldy introduced me to the New York Subway, scallops, and Tea at the Waldorf Astoria.

"After we arrived in Italy we made several trips to cities close by. Baldy being a commercial artist knew which paintings were good and he was going to help me buy some to ship home and also buy some for himself.

"Baldy got a cablegram telling him he had a son born Dec. 1. So he was going to Naples to buy gifts for his wife and baby boy. I was to go with him but had to fly a mission (it was later scrubbed because of bad weather). Before Baldy left on that fatal *Buzzer* flight he went back to the tent and Al Charnes asked if he could go with him but Baldy told him he had gotten the last seat place.

"When the Buzzer and none of the men came back, they had several search parties trying to locate them. On one trip Virgil Hillstrom (R/O WG) [that is, radio operator/waist gunner] on Charnes' crew thought he saw the plane in a deep ravine but next day could not see because of the snow.

"I always felt close to Baldy and was so saddened when I had to pack his things up to send home and to write a condolence letter to his wife Ann.

"It was a very sad time."

Larry Hamblen learned later that he did not send all of Baldwin's personal effects home. Their pilot, Al Charnes, personally delivered some to Baldwin's parents at Siesta Key, Florida, near Sarasota.

Louise Walker, Baldwin's friend, told me, "I can't tell you the dates, I just remember that we came home that Christmas of '44 because Mr. Walker had a brother who was in the submarine service and his submarine had been lost in the Pacific and his mother was told that he was in a missing status at that time . . . there were three [submarines] that were supposed to rendezvous together and only one got back, they were taking soundings in Tokyo Bay. So we came home that Christmas to be with mother in

Oklahoma City, so that is how we happened to come home that Christmas and went over to see [Baldwin's] wife, Fifi; her real name was Ann but we all call her Fifi and she was at home at her parents with her new baby and we went over to see her and to give her our condolences and to talk about both of these boys, brother and F.G being lost more or less at the same time and both of them having been in that wedding. That was in December of '44 at Christmastime."

William Walker, Louise's husband, was in the 20th Bomber Command in Guam, also flying B-24s. He also had one run in a B-29. He told me: "We were doing weather because we were losing too many fighters. They put us out there in weather reconnaissance, nothing too exciting . . . We were glad to get back though, I'll tell you."

The *Times-Star* of Cincinnati carried a joint article announcing the deaths of Albert Ganim and Lt. Francis Baldwin Jr.

Bill Baldwin, with some friends, started an American Legion Post named in honor of his brother. Carlisle Murdoch, Baldwin's father-in-law, wrote to the Post Commander in October 1946:

"Dear Sir:

"Mrs. Murdoch and I wish to present to your Post an American Flag and standard in honor of our Son in Law the late First Lieutenant Francis George Baldwin Jr.

"No finer boy ever lived and what little we can do to keep his memory green in the hearts of his friends can never be enough.

"Please secure for the Post the *best* Flag—silk if possible— that you can get with a suitable standard and cover. I am sure you will be able through the Legion to procure a much better Flag than we can get elsewhere . . ."

Baldwin's son, Francis George Baldwin III, who goes by F. George Baldwin III, lives with his wife Susan in Alabama. He was legally adopted by his stepfather John

Hunter after his mother remarried, but kept his own name. Baldwin's wife remarried three years after his death.

We met at a 449th Reunion in Biloxi in October 1998.

He grew up not hearing much about his father. "He was never discussed," he told me, adding "I have the strong sense it was as if it was yesterday to my mother, all her life."

He never knew his father, but as he learned the story of what happened, including the long wait between the "Missing" notice and the death notice, he knew the impact it must have had on his family. "I could only think about what my mother was thinking, and my grandfather."

Later he was taken aback to read a letter from his grandfather about the night the news arrived that Francis was indeed dead. Apparently, Baldwin's father was so opposed to the Roosevelt Administration that he was on the verge of moving the family to Brazil rather than living here under the New Deal. Baldwin's father describes in the letter getting the news, going outside, looking up at the stars and being thankful that his dead son wouldn't have to live in a country run by F.D.R.

"Dad was gregarious," Baldwin's son told me, adding that he knew his father had a strong sense of humor. "When I would misbehave as a kid, my mother would look at me knowingly, as if to say, 'If you're not careful you'll grow up like him.'"

Baldwin's son was ineligible for the Vietnam draft when he finished Yale in 1966, as a sole surviving son. "I was pro the war, but I was engaged, and had no desire to enlist." He said he considered that a gift from his father.

Overall, he thinks the Government did as good a job of informing the bereaved families as could be expected, with a vast war going on, and the crash being in a relatively inaccessible area. "Each person thinks of their own situation as being specific and unique but . . ."

By writing to the American Battle Monuments Commission, I was able to find out that Baldwin, like Marple and Erickson, is buried at the Sicily-Rome American Cemetery, Nettuno, Italy.

Ellis Arieff

"I don't take anything for granted anymore."

Ellis Arieff's former pilot, Michael Mealey, now O'Malley, said this about him:

"The world should learn about Ellis Arieff, the human being. In addition to being a highly intelligent, selfless person, he was conscientious to a fault. He never denied any of my many requests that he assist our young and unsophisticated crew members. To say that he was the most popular and respected member of our crew may be an understatement in his case.

"Sylvia, his wife, was from the same human mold. At the airfield from which we departed, she tearfully implored me to bring *her Ellis* back safely; her manner and message were most compelling and are etched in my memory. My first phone call, after returning to New Jersey from our German prison camp, was to Philadelphia. Upon learning from Sylvia about her husband's fate, I experienced my greatest personal grief of those horrible war years."

Ellis Arieff was born in Philadelphia on September 8, 1918, to Jacob and Matilda Arieff. He had five older sisters—Lillian, Eve, twins Hattie and Rose, and Mildred.

His widow, Sylvia Fisher, says, "Ellis was the baby of a family of six children, and the only boy. They were a wonderful, warm, caring family. They took me in as one of their own."

He attended Gratz High School, Philadelphia Normal School for teachers, and Temple University. After college he worked as a salesman for his brother-in-law, Eve's husband, at Weiman Jewelers. He was drafted into the Army Air Corps.

Mrs. Fisher was born Sylvia Binder. She attended Tyler School of Art and Temple University. She describes a wartime romance:

"I was a girl of the times as most of us were and he was stationed in San Antonio and he wanted me to come out and visit him and after a lot of begging and crying and carrying on, my parents finally let me go after they found another young lady who was going out there, and she came from a good family. The two of us went out there to our boyfriends. And of course it was very nice, it was during Christmas week vacation, I was going to college then. And he was a man and he wanted to sleep with me. And I was so indoctrinated that I couldn't do it unless we got married. So we got married in Texas and there it is.

"I, of course, never told my mother or father. He came home a couple months later and we got married again. It's a true story. My father would have been extremely upset because he thought things like that were not nice, to elope, or to not get married with the family. He never found out. I never told my father, absolutely not. My sister found out. She's six years younger and she was looking through my bag for some change and found my wedding ring in my purse, so she was sworn to silence. I told my mother later. His family never knew. He was the youngest child of six children and the only boy in the family. I haven't been in touch with them for a long time. They were very kind to me, they were very good people."

That was 1942. Ellis Arieff received his diploma from the Air Corps Officer Candidate School in Miami Beach, Florida, on August 5, 1942.

His widow recalls: "I joined Ellis in Texas after I finished college, and we spent about one to one and a half years living in different places, as he was assigned, many in Texas, one in Utah [Salt Lake], one in Wyoming [Casper.] Our years of travel, of being on our own, seeing the country, were a great adventure."

Crewmate S/Sgt. Thomas W. Sommers, of Arkansas, describes a scene before Arieff went overseas: "We skipped most of our advanced training; we were in Casper, Wyoming in advanced training, we had been there a week or two and . . . all the officers came by and came into the barracks. We were all champing at the bit to go overseas and we were young. And my pilot said if he could get a full crew here then we would leave. And so he got most of his crew, radio operator, mechanic, whatever right there in that barracks. Well Arieff was with him and he was a super guy. That guy was one of the best guys I ever . . ."

Sommers also recalls pilots arriving in Wyoming being told "'Don't fly down Main Street, don't buzz the eighteen wheelers, and for God's sake don't shoot up the rancher's cows.' You think this did not happen?"

Mrs. Fisher: "When he was sent overseas, I drove home to Philadelphia, to stay with my parents until he returned. But, as you know, he never did.

"That was awful. Somebody rang the bell one night. It was somebody in the Army, I guess, he was in uniform. And he came in and he told us he was missing in action.

"This is funny, we lived on a boulevard next to people who were, I guess, famous in their way. His name was Doc Irving and her name was Princess Yvonne, a fortune teller and they were big performers at the Million Dollar Pier in Atlantic City. She was a 'mind reader' with a crystal ball and he was a magician. And they were pretty well known. And we would get carloads of people from all over the country who would come to her for readings.

"And so one day I said Yvonne, tell me is he alive or where is he, and she said come on you know it's beyond my abilities, I do not know!"

Arieff was a bombardier. Crewmate Sommers says that Arieff was separated from his original crew and was soon flying lead ship. Thus, he was not with some of his crew when, on October 13, 1944, they were forced to abandon ship over Yugoslavia after bombing the Wiener-Neustadt marshaling yards near Vienna.

As O'Malley remembers it, "He was my original bom-
bardier, he was with me right until I got knocked down over
Vienna on October 13. He was not with me that day because
he was in a rest camp with my co-pilot and my navigator.
Those three guys were smart enough to go to the Isle of
Capri whereas I said I don't want any rest, I'm going to fin-
ish my tour before Christmas. So I got my ass knocked down
October 13 and they were sunning their butts at Capri."

O'Malley's crew was, relatively speaking, lucky. Although O'Malley recalls a huge struggle to push himself out
of the plane against the force of its spin, all of the crew of
the *Nancy Jane II* that day survived bailout. Two who had
broken legs were spirited out of the country by partisans,
and the rest became POWs.

Soon after he hit the ground, he recalls, "A German soldier came over with a big rifle pointed at me saying 'For you
the war is over.' We were POWs until the following May
when we were liberated. We had almost no food. It was a
bummer, period."

"I was just a twenty-one year old kid who didn't know
that every time we left the ground we could be killed, until
I became a prisoner and that was an event that shaped the
rest of my life."

Among O'Malley's crew that day was Capt. Leslie Caplan, a Jewish doctor who later survived the grim 1945
death march of POWs across Europe and wrote major texts
about the psychology of the POW experience. Caplan was
the 719th's flight surgeon, at thirty-six vastly older than
most of the airmen around him.

Caplan refused to be held with other officer POWs, in-
sisting that he remain with the enlisted men who needed
his medical care. Eventually he persuaded the Germans to
let him work. After the war he testified at the Nuremburg
War Crimes Trials.

Phil Jensen was Ellis Arieff's roommate in Italy. He
was part of the crew that came overseas with O'Malley and
Arieff. In the days following the crash of *The Buzzer,* Jensen
was one of the men who flew search missions.

Arieff, he says, had two Purple Hearts to his name. Although Arieff was not on the October 13th flight that was shot down, he was forced one time to bail out and make his way back the to Allies with Partisan help. He got his first Purple Heart for an injury suffered during the course of his bailout and return. Then, after returning to active duty, he fell victim to a common affliction for bomber crews: frostbite.

I asked Jensen about the time Arieff bailed out over Yugoslavia. "I wasn't on that mission. Ellis and some of the other people were married and they wanted to get their missions done so they could get back home. But I was on R&R. When I got back I heard some of the crews were lost and Ellis was one of them."

Jensen told me, "Arieff and another man, as I recall, they parachuted into Yugoslavia and a bunch of guys came running up and said, come with us quick. So they took off running and there were two or three of them that were kind of crippled and Ellis wasn't able to, I've forgotten just what happened, but they weren't able to run away. So the ones who ran away, they turned them into the Germans and Ellis and this other guy were turned over to the partisans and they were back in Italy in a day or so."

Then, according to Jensen, after Arieff returned to flying missions, "He was on a bomb run and his heated suit ran out and he wasn't able to change it in time and it was terribly cold up there, 60–80 degrees below zero. We always had spares so if you felt your hand getting cold you'd just get a spare, but he wasn't able to do that as we were on a bomb run, and his boots ran out so he got frostbite on his feet. The suit connected with buttons, you just plug the whole thing in the socket in the plane."

"He couldn't fly anymore because his feet were frostbitten, exposure to the cold just made it worse and he was recovering but they said you can go home."

Jensen thinks Arieff had done well over half his missions by then.

And the fatal crash?

"He was on his way home. He had two Purple Hearts and his missions were terminated and he was headed to Naples."

As for as the Army's failure to produce an official report on *The Buzzer* crash, O'Malley says " . . . that's just a typical reaction from the services that were over-deluged with responsibilities that they should have accomplished but didn't. It's too bad about the lack of recognition, but such is a drop in a very large bucket. There are too many people who were killed who didn't even get the appropriate medals."

In 1999, Sylvia Fisher requested Arieff's Purple Heart medals from the Government; she is entitled to them as his widow. So far she has only received one, so either his friends were mistaken about his receiving two, or the Government records are in error. His medals are American Defense Service Medal, American Campaign Medal, European-African-Middle Eastern Campaign Medal, WWII Victory Medal, Honorable Service Lapel Button WWII and Air Medal.

Sylvia Fisher describes the lack of news that she and other loved ones endured, "Just 'missing in action', that he came out of Bari [actually Grottaglie] on his way to Naples and the plane just disappeared, they didn't know where it was. At the time, I think they told me who the other people were and we would write to each other. Nobody knew, there was no information coming from the government. They didn't know. How could they be responsible when they didn't know what happened to the plane. As you found out later, it just disappeared. I think they said something, the wings had iced up."

I asked her, was this after they found the plane?

"No. They said ice had formed on the wings. I remember I was very upset. I was working at the Naval Depot at the time doing illustrations . . . I'm an illustrator, I'm an artist. I was working on the manuals and I was very upset because in the manual I was drawing things that showed they had de-icers on the plane and I wondered why there had not been one on his plane. Now that you tell me all this, I can't understand why they let that plane go out after the other planes came back and aborted their missions because the weather was so bad. It makes no sense."

So just as my mother, Sybil Yedlin, worked on diagrams for machine guns I fired, Sylvia had worked on illustrations of de-icers. But the chances are *The Buzzer* did not have de-icers, which were introduced on B-24Js very soon after the plane was built.

Mrs. Fisher still keeps a letter from the Fifteenth Air Force dated 18 August 1945:

Fifteenth Air Force
Office of the Commanding General
A.P.O. 520
"Dear Mrs. Arieff:

"I regret I must confirm that your husband, First Lieutenant Ellis Arieff, 0–560560, was killed in an aircraft accident on December 9, 1944.

"As stated in our last letter to you, dated December 31, 1944, your husband was a passenger on a non-operational flight which failed to reach its destination. The cause of the crash is as yet undetermined. The wreckage was found near Oliveto Citra in Southern Italy in uninhabited mountain country. The force of the impact rendered identification of many of the passengers impossible. However, definite identification was made of your husband's body. Grave location will be made known to you as soon as conditions permit.

"The manner in which Ellis carried out his assignments reflects honor not only on himself but on the Air Force which he served so well. May I take this opportunity to extend my heartfelt sympathy in your loss."

Very sincerely yours,
(Signed) William L. Lee
Brigadier General, USA
Commanding

This letter is similar to one received by next of kin of victims of the crash. Many also received letters from H.H. "Hap" Arnold, the Commanding General of the Army Air Forces.

When Sylvia remarried, it was to another bombardier-navigator, Leon Fisher.

"It's funny, I'm not good with numbers but I have never been able to wipe out his [Ellis's] serial number from my mind. I don't know Lee's and I've been married to him for forty-five years. He was a bombardier navigator in England and he flew his missions and got home before I knew him. I met him here. He came back and started going to Temple and my younger sister met him at Temple and thought he was too good to let go so she arranged a date.

"When I was remarried, it was a little embarrassing. We kept in touch with [Arieff's] family, and it was a little odd. And then the Army got in touch with us and said that we could have the body brought to this country if we wanted to. His family decided they wanted it brought here. And so they did. And Ellis is buried in Roosevelt Cemetery out on the boulevard with his family. There was a service and of course I went and it was one of the hardest things I ever did. I was eight months pregnant. But of course I went, I could not go. They were very very sweet people. He was a very sweet man. It was a shocking thing to me that something like this could happen. It affected me the rest of my life. I don't take anything for granted anymore."

Sylvia thinks Arieff might have been a pilot but for anti-Semitism.

"Somebody said to me, the Army discriminated against Jews. They washed out more Jews as fliers and put them into navigation bombardier positions. [Ellis] wanted to be a pilot. Leon was turned down for pilot training, which is weird because he happens to be one of those people who is very adept at things and he's always been a sportsman, drove cars, I mean he had the facility for this kind of thing, he was washed out too.

"The war changed this country completely. When I went to live in Texas, they didn't know of anything Jewish out there. You wouldn't have known it as much as I do because I was a woman and I went to the store and I bought things and I brought them home. They thought I was crazy when I went to try to buy sour cream. Sour cream! That's what they throw out, you know. And there were no such things as bagels or rye bread or anything that now is everywhere. It was different, completely different.

There seem to be different opinions as to why Arieff was aboard *The Buzzer* when it crashed. Phil Jensen thought he was on his way to Naples and home; and Mrs. Fisher wrote to Mrs. Suarez, after the crash: "My husband was a passenger and the flight was supposed to find out whether he could fly high altitude missions again. You see he was released from the hospital on the 8th of Dec. where he had just recovered from frost bite."

I also remember hearing from someone that despite being grounded by his frostbite, Arieff could continue to draw flight pay, which was Lieutenant's pay plus fifty percent, and was taking a ride from Grottaglie to Naples for that reason.

Jensen: "I was very fond of Ellis and Sylvia, nice people, we visited them in Casper. I didn't get really well acquainted with her but I knew Ellis and he was a grand guy. It was so sad that he'd gone through all the shooting and lost out in another way."

Paul F. Watson

"Well he never showed up."

Private First Class Paul Watson was from Los Angeles. He went through bombardier school in Nevada. His mother once visited him there. According to his brother William, who spoke to me in 1998, Watson went on to serve as a gunner.

William Watson lives in central California, in a town called Coarsegold, between Fresno and Yosemite. "I left home originally when I was thirteen years old . . . Don't misunderstand me, I loved my family and all, but on account of the Depression and everything I was out trying to find where I could do better than I was."

He told me that Paul worked some before joining the Service, and was also, like Julian Caldwell, in a Civilian Conservation Corps camp for a while.

In the service, Paul Watson's postings included St. Petersburg, Florida, Buckley Field, Colorado, Lowry Field, Colorado, Las Vegas, Nevada, Salt lake City, Utah, and Alamogordo, New Mexico, all between January and August 1943.

William was trained to fight in the Pacific. "We were sent to seven different camps here in the States and given special training for jungle warfare, survival, weaponry, you name it. We were supposed to go to MacArthur and at the last minute they broke us up into combat units and sent us to Europe. I belonged actually to the 66th Black Panther Division. But it was broken up and the division itself was sent to England and . . . the battle of Normandy. When I came back to the states, I was discharged as the 66th Black Panther Division."

Paul's brother ended up attached to the 458th Engineers. "I had a fifteen man crew that [was] used strictly for demolition, anti-mine stuff and enemy weapons."

William was attached to the engineers by a roundabout route, he said. " . . . when it was time they were sending me home, they were looking for somebody for the supply depot and . . . they found that I had a parts supply store in a gas station. And they took me off of the boat, took me down by . . . Naples and stuck me in a seven square mile depot and put me in charge of it because the officer was leaving for the north." I was a T/Sgt.

Paul was an bombardier gunner, not a regular air crew member, according to William.

"I was waiting for him to come to Rome, because he was going to have R&R before they sent him home . . . my word from him was that they were bringing him to Rome and I went to Rome and was waiting for him."

I asked what happened.

"Well he never showed up . . . I went back and I never found out what the heck happened. I got a letter from my mother that he was reported Missing In Action . . .

I asked if the two brothers had been in close touch during the war. "He is about like me, he wrote his wife and wrote my mother but didn't write me very much. And well, you're both in a war . . . and you got your mind on other things."

Their mother, Mrs. Hazel Cranmer, "was definitely very devastated by his death at the time. But it was such a prolonged thing because they never declared him dead for so long . . . when she heard from the lady [Mrs. Clemente] . . . I think she accepted more clearly that he was dead. And by the time that she got notified by the War Department it wasn't a shock anymore."

"That woman from Oliveto Citra contacted my mother . . . and told her what happened, and she wrote me and I went up to see the woman. In fact I went up there a couple of times.

"I don't remember the exact date but I got a vehicle and found my way up there and talked to her for quite some time. I never met her husband, he wasn't there at the time. But I talked to her extensively and she told me what happened and so forth and then she wrote me a couple of letters. She wrote my mother mostly."

I asked him about the trip up there; he said it wasn't so bad in a four-wheel drive, and that he didn't see bridges in that area wrecked by bombing. I was there and back in one day from Naples. "Down in [Salerno] they bombed pretty extensively, but I saw no evidence up there, you know, where they were and their home was intact." I put some pressure on Graves Division in Naples to go get them or list them as finally dead. It took a lot of time before they followed up.

Watson told me that according to Mrs. Clemente, the people who went down to the wreck brought back some personal effects. " . . . and one of the things was my brother's watch." She reported that she took the watch down to Naples when she informed the military of the site of the crash and turned it over to them.

He was in Italy for three years. "We hit North Africa but we were transit. We were going through North Africa and just bounced over to Sicily but we were right behind the push. And then . . . just after they passed Anzio and went on up to Naples and we came to Italy there. And then I went with them following them doing my little thing or my group thing clear up past Rome. And then they pulled me out and brought me back to . . . just outside of Naples."

I asked him what he thought of us Air Corps guys.

"Hell, we were all in a war, you know . . . Part of my training was paratroop training and we were down in Fort Benning and Fort Bragg and took paratroop training and then never had to make a combat jump. We went to seven different camps getting specialty training after we had our basic.

"And we had all kinds of training. Most of our work overseas was . . . we had to go, you know, blow something up. But other than that was to de mine areas and debooby trap. When they were going to move into an area, we had to go out ahead of them and find the mines."

I said that must have been risky.

"Well, yes it was. We didn't have mine detectors at that time. You had to get down . . . with bayonet. But at the last end of the war they came out with those mine detectors and made it pretty easy, but you know you've got to be damn cautious. And when they move into buildings and stuff, you have to go and check them, make sure they weren't booby trapped. And a lot of them were."

William Zartman, an armorer in the 719th, knew Paul Watson. He says Paul was on his way to rest camp on the final flight. "Me and Richard Weber and him were to go to rest camp. And he chose to fly and we went by truck."

William Watson knew Paul's wife, Freda, who later remarried and went to live in the Los Angeles area. Another brother, Edwin, served in the Pacific.

Watson's mother Hazel Cranmer was one of the most active correspondents among the next of kin in the years following the accident.

On March 4 1945, she wrote to Mrs. Suarez, hoping to exchange news.

"My boy was on his way to visit his brother who had gone to Italy just a short time before. Mrs. Arieff says her husband was on the plane for an altitude test. I was glad to hear that as I had made up my mind the plane had cracked up in the mountains, but now I think they probably had gained enough altitude to clear the mountains, so now I think they were probably forced down in neutral territory. My other boy over there said he thought they were somewhere in neutral territory as there is a lot of it there and no enemy territory where they were going over.

"What was your boy flying for that day? What was his mission?"

Of course the plane did crash into a mountain. In the long months of "Missing" status the relatives must have entertained all kinds of possible ways their loved ones might still be alive. Even the official word of death could not drive out hope in every case, even though some were resigned to the worst even before it became official.

Mrs. Cranmer got this reply to one of her letters to the authorities, after her son had been declared dead:

12 August 1945

"Dear Mrs. Cranmer:

"This is in reply to your recent letters regarding your son, Private first Class Paul F. Watson, who was killed in Italy on 9 December 1944.

"I wish it were possible for me to share your hope that your son is alive, but my knowledge of the reliability and accuracy of reports of this nature prevent my doing so. Such reports are determined to be authentic before being furnished to this office for transmittal to the emergency addressee. You may be assured that positive identification was made before the report of your son's death was submitted to this office. I deeply regret that there is no alternative but to accept the facts as reported by the commanding general of the area. All amnesia victims have been identified and the persons designated by them as the ones to be notified in an emergency have been notified . . .

"Edward F. Witsell
Major General
Acting The Adjutant General of the Army"

Aug. 21, 1945 Hazel Crammer to Mrs. Caldwell
She wrote to Caldwell's mother on August 21, 1945:

"Dear Nancy,

"Your kind letter came today and I thank you for your sweet expressions of sympathy and prayer to Our Father. Yes, He can and does comfort and I do sincerely pray the Father to comfort your heart, too. I did hear more through my other son in Italy and he says the Intelligence Office there investigated as far as possible by going to visit and interview an Italian lady who lives near the mountaintop where they crashed, and who wrote to Mrs. Erickson saying her son and your son and eight other boys were around there.

"On the C.I.D. investigating they found out she only had some very meager information from some of the belongings she had found of Donald Erickson's. My boy says it took the C.I.D. man 48 days to make the trip to the town where she lives and back, and that the country there is extremely rough and that the bridges, etc, have been blown up by the enemy and have not been repaired. One has to go on foot and even then it is hard to get through.

"I also had a letter from Brig. Gen. Lee, Commanding 15th Air Force, A.P.O. 520 in answer to one I wrote to him in trying to learn more. He says the plane crashed into an inaccessible mountain peak with such terrific force as to kill all instantly and so as to make identification impossible. This, to me, clears up all the mystery about the crash.

"Those mountains are very rough and very high and probably that particular peak wasn't flown over too often, and until they got this Italian woman's letter, they had no idea where to look. I, too, have been very much upset and find this hard to take, but Our Heavenly Father surely knows what is best for all of

"With sincerest sympathy,
Hazel Crammer"

On October 3, 1945, she wrote to Mrs. Suarez:
" . . . How is your other boy? Did he get to come home again? My other two boys are still overseas, one in Italy and the other in the Pacific. I do hope they can come home soon. The one in Italy is afraid he will be kept over there another year as he is in the army of occupation. But the other in the Pacific hopes to be home by February. I hope he can. He has been overseas two years in February, and in the service five

years. The other boy has been over in Italy a year now and in service three [years] next month."

She also wanted to enlist Mrs. Suarez' help in contacting Alex Eckerling's sister. She was in the process of collecting pictures of all of the men who died with Watson.

In another letter to Mrs. Suarez, after Manuel Suarez' body was repatriated, she wrote:

"I was so glad to hear from you and to know your boy Manuel has been brought back home. My Paul hasn't yet and when they do bring him back, it will be with the other eight [seven] who are buried with him. You see, he is one of the eight who have never been positively identified and were buried all together in the same grave. They intend to bring them back all together soon. Mr. Groeger's son is one of the eight buried with them. Thank you for the nice card of remembrance you had made for your son. It is very nice.

"It is so lonesome without my husband. I am thankful I have my baby son with me. He is 15 years old and goes to school but he is my youngest and the only one at home with me. He is such a comfort. He never runs around. He comes home as soon as school is out and either makes model trains or listens to the radio, or both. If he has homework, he does that. But he never cares to run around town like so many boys. And he never goes out at night unless he goes next door to our neighbor's house. They have television and sometimes he goes over there. He sure is good to me. I don't know what I would do without him."

She wrote the War Department on May 27, 1947:

Quartermaster General
Memorial Division

"Dear Sir:

"Yours of May 19, 1947 at hand and I certainly want to thank you for the information in it regarding where our boys are buried. It is the first I have had from the War Dept. about where they were buried.

"You mentioned the fact that it had been impossible to identify the boys. I was wondering if the following bit of information would help any.

"Due to an injury in childhood, Paul had a bony protuberance about 2 inches long on the upper part of the lower bone in his right leg. It is formed of the substance that usually oozes out of broken bones and tends to heal them together. An X-ray revealed the bone had been broken, or rather split lengthwise, about two inches and the substance had oozed out and hardened and later became a part of the bone in his leg. It was rather noticeable in the side of the calf of his leg.

"If that leg was found you could be sure it was Paul. Of course I understand the bodies were in pretty bad shape due to the crash and the fire that followed but there might be a chance of finding this little identifying mark.

"I do not know, of course, if this had been noted on his physical records on file with the War Dept.

"Thanking you again for your information and your sympathetic interest I remain
Mrs. Hazel Cranmer"

This letter came to Frieda Watson, Paul's widow, from the War Department:

5 December 1947

"Dear Mrs. Watson:

"The Department of the Army desires that you be furnished information concerning the resting place of your husband, the late Private First Class Paul F. Watson, A.S.N. 39 274 212.

"With deep regret I must inform you that, although the records of this office disclose that the remains of your husband were reverently interred, it was not possible, because of the manner in which he met his death, to identify his remains individually.

"The remains of your loved one and other fallen comrades are currently resting as a group in United States Military Cemetery Naples, located in Naples, Italy.

"The American Graves Registration Service exhausts every possible clue which might lead to the individual identification of United States deceased personnel, however, if further research fails to establish their individual identity, the remains of this group will be returned to the United States for final interment in a national cemetery designated by The Quartermaster General. All legal next of kin will be advised at a later date of the national cemetery in which final interment will be made and will also be notified of the time of burial.

"May I extend my sincere sympathy in your great loss.

Sincerely yours,
Thomas B. Larkin
Major General
The Quartermaster General"

Mrs. Cranmer wrote this letter October 28, 1949:

A.G.R.S.
Memorial Div.
Washington, D.C.

"Dear Sirs,

"Yesterday I received a telegram from Col. Bare telling me that my son's body is en route to the United States for burial at Jefferson Barracks National Cemetery in Missouri.

"He is part of a group burial and as that is centrally located for all the next of kin, the Army chose there.

"But I am a widow with very limited finances and have no money to go to the burial services. I want to go so very much. I wonder if you could either help me out on this, or tell me if there is any one who could.

"I realize that it would cost at least $200 for the fare on the train, eats on the train, etc., and a hotel room while in Jefferson Barracks, Mo. The fare round trip to Saint Louis from Los Angeles for coach, $87.65 on the Santa Fe and Mo. Pac. For sleeper, $124.65 + $18.11 for berth. This is on their Grand Canyon train to Kansas City, and coach from K.C. to St. Louis. Then eats on the train and while in St. Louis.

"I am unable to work and earn the money now. I hope to be able to work when the Doctor gets through with me. But I cannot now. If I could work, I would not need to ask for help on this.

"I hope I can go to my son's funeral. But if I can't, I will try to be content with the knowledge that he is back on home soil again.

"I appreciate very much that the Army has done and is doing for my beloved son, Paul.

"Thank you very much.
Sincerely,
Hazel Cranmer"

This was the reply:

11–4–1949
"I can readily understand your natural desire to attend the services to be conducted at the time of the final burial of the remains of your loved one in the Jefferson Barracks National Cemetery and I regret I must inform you that there is no authority whereby the Government can provide financial assistance to those next of kin desiring to visit a national cemetery for the purpose of attending the interment services of the remains of their loved ones.

"The Superintendent of the National Cemetery will notify you of the time and date of the services, and I sincerely trust you may be able to make the necessary arrangements to enable you to be present.

"I regret that I cannot furnish you with a more favorable reply.

And finally this official word, seven years after the war in Europe ended:

10 April 1952
Mrs. Frieda M. H. Watson
11407 Wright Road
Lynwood, California

"Dear Mrs. Watson:

"Reference is made to the interment of your husband, the late Private First Class Paul F. Watson, and his comrades, which was made in Grave 148-B, section 82, Jefferson Barracks National Cemetery, St. Louis, Missouri. It is regretted that because of the fact it was impossible to identify individually the remains of your husband, you were deprived of the comfort and consolation which you might have been afforded by interring his remains at home.

"It is felt that you might like to have the enclosed photograph of the stone which has been placed at the grave.

"You are assured that the grave will always be cared for in a manner fully commensurate with the sacrifice your husband has made for his country. Any desired information concerning the grave or the cemetery will be furnished upon request."

"Sincerely yours,
JAS. F. WATT
Lt. Colonel, QMC
Memorial Division"

Fowler C. Doyle

"All of us searched for three days."

First Lieutenant Fowler C. Doyle, from Lexington, Kentucky, was a passenger on *The Buzzer*. He had been William Bache's copilot. Like the others in Bache's crew, he was on his way home after completing fifty missions. Like Baldwin, he had a child at home he would never see. His son, Larry, was about six months old.

Doyle's sister, Betty Doyle Eilert, of Louisville, Kentucky, told me she had thought her brother was a pilot, not a passenger, in the crash. She provided me with a list of surviving relatives, and said it was a relief to know more about what had happened to her brother's plane.

She also wrote me: "I want you to know that Fowler flew his missions from September to December as he wanted to come home to meet his son, Larry David Doyle, for the first time. Larry was born before his father left the States but he was not given leave before he left for Europe."

Doyle himself was one of six children. After graduating from Henry Clay High School, he attended the University of Kentucky. He enlisted in the Army Air Forces on June 19, 1942, and got his commission at Lubbock Airfield, Texas, in February 1944. He went overseas on July 17, just five days before my final mission. In the course of his tour of duty, he was awarded a Unit Citation Badge and the Air Medal with three Oak Leaf Clusters.

His son, Larry, told me: "I was born in June of '44 and he was overseas and killed in December of '44, so I never did see him. And then my mother remarried early, and like I said, I was never told much of anything. The family sort of drifted apart that way. And, the pictures I had, both my grandparents are dead. I never knew much about it other than he was going to school and he went into the service and wanted to be a commercial pilot when he got out. I guess that's what I gather, I don't know if I can add much . . . I really can't add anything. I go to his grave site and that's about it because there isn't anybody to tell me anything."

I asked what he felt about losing his father that way.

"He was never there to be taken away from me. I was never told about it, and I didn't really think about it until I got older. And, my kids, they grew and they watched the tapes. . . . I go out all the time to the grave, but I really don't have any feeling whatsoever."

How did he find out what happened?

"I had pictures and my mother, from time to time, [described] who this one was and who that one was, and I had a couple of his books of people he was in with. Like I said, nobody in the family talked about it.

"I was always just told that it crashed in Naples, Italy, and they brought him back on the train. Really, I was always in the dark on it. I think he was only twenty-one when he was killed."

John Doyle, the youngest of Fowler's five siblings, has few recollections of his big brother: "He got married and then he went into the service. That's about all I remember."

Mrs. Mitchell Stamper, like Mrs. Baldwin, was widowed with a very young child. She wasn't sure what to make of the first communications from Mrs. Clemente.

"This Italian woman called my mother-in-law and told her, she said your son has 'been around here' and she named all the boys on the plane and so that made us feel good because we thought he was alive.

"And so we went on to the beach and then came back and then it wasn't very long, I went to my aunt's and while

I was up there my mother told me . . . this Italian woman had said that she hired mountain climbers to go down in there because they left in bad weather from wherever they were and he left with another crew.

"He didn't go with his original crew and . . . it was bad weather and ice froze on the wings and it forced them down in this ravine.

"I was the only one out of the sixteen that got a letter from the War Department saying that Fowler was the only one who wasn't burned beyond recognition because all the boy's parents, they either wrote to me or came to see me . . .

This would seem to contradict the stories of Erickson surviving the crash by several days. And, of course, Doyle was not the only victim to be individually identified.

"This Italian woman, I guess she got everything that they had, everything that you could pick up and of course, all I got back was some letters that had footprints on them and then she started asking my mother-in-law for sugar, being it was rationed and baby bottles and all that kind of stuff that she couldn't get over there. So Mrs. Doyle sent it to her.

"If she had written to me, I wouldn't, I wouldn't have sent her nothing.

"I don't remember [when I was first notified,] I was so torn up, you know. Larry was little and out at Mom's and you know a thing like that I just . . . well, you just go all to pieces."

Captain Bache wrote to Mrs. Doyle from New Orleans on January 5, 1945, just after the men had been declared missing and long before they were declared dead.

" . . . I know that you want to know the full story of what happened. Here it is: As Fowler told you, we all finished our missions and were ready to come home. I had been recommended for a promotion to Captain, so I could not leave when the rest of the boys were ready to go. Fowler, Erickson, Gettys, Ballou and Eckerling decided they would go ahead and leave and Kaufman and I could catch up with them in Naples a few days later.

"Naples, where we had to go to catch either a plane or a ship for the States, was just a one-hour ride from our field, and Fowler and the other four boys made arrangements to fly there with another crew in our squadron, who were also going to Naples at the time.

"They all took off, and that night someone came and told me that they never landed there, whereas I said, they should have gotten there in an hour. I went right over to Operations and checked up and it was true. I had them send to all the fields in the area, but they had not landed at any of them.

"The next day I took up a ship and flew over their course for seven hours, trying to find some trace of them. We flew back and forth, time after time, but could find no sign of them or of the ship. Many other ships from the Group went up just as I did, searching, and several other airfields in Southern Italy sent up numerous ships to aid in the search.

"Naples sent out land-searching parties on foot, and the British sent out air-sea rescue planes, just in case they might have strayed out over the water and been forced to ditch. All of us searched for three days. We covered every mile of Southern Italy thoroughly, but could find no sign of them nor of the ship. Myself and the other boys in our outfit flew for twenty-eight hours in three days, trying desperately to find out what happened to them, without success.

"From our field to Naples, their course wasn't within hundreds of miles of any place where any action is taking place and there is absolutely no possibility that their disappearance might be due to enemy action. That flight should have been just as safe to make as it would have been to fly around the city of Lexington, so don't fear that they might have run into trouble from that source.

"As to what happened to them, and why we could find no trace of the ship, I have thought and thought, hour after hour, and I can only tell you what I *believe* happened.

"I checked up on the weather on their course, after they failed to reach Naples, and found out that they had to fly through some pretty bad weather. They had to fly over a mountain range, six thousand feet high, and to get over it they had to fly in an overcast. And it was pretty cold that day. I think they must have started picking up ice on the ship and had to sit it down.

"The reason we couldn't find a trace of the ship would be because of the mountains. As diligently as we searched, it would have been awfully easy not to spot a ship in those mountains, ravines, trees, and passes.

"And that's just about all that I can tell you, I'm afraid. All we can do is wait and hope and pray that he and the rest of the boys eventually come through it safely. I know how worried you and Fowler's Mother and family must be Mrs. Doyle, and I can't tell you how bitterly sorry I am that I must write you this kind of a letter. I got to know Doyle well, and I thought an awfully lot of him, both as a pilot and as a personal friend, and to have to write his wife this kind of a letter is one of the hardest and most distasteful jobs I have ever had. He really did a swell job in combat."

Doyle's remains were laid to rest in the U.S. Military Cemetery, Naples, after they were discovered. In 1949 they were removed back to the United States for private burial.

Joseph Brehun

"That was the last I saw him."

One family I visited had suffered an appalling double tragedy. I first got in touch with members of the Brehun family in 1995. Joseph's sister Marie spoke to me about her brother, and I was explaining why I'd started this book, and she said: "Another tragic thing was that just exactly one week before Joe was in the plane crash, his brother John was killed over in Germany."

I said "Oh my God, in an air . . ."

She stopped me. "It wasn't an air crash; a mortar shell hit him in the spine and he got injured on November 30th of 1944 and died on December 2." It was in the Hurtgen Forest. Joseph died December 9 in *The Buzzer* without knowing what had happened to his brother.

Joseph's sisters still talk about the sight of a taxi coming down their street. Telegrams arrived by taxi then, and a taxi usually meant bad news for someone.

A third brother, Francis, serving in the Navy, was moved to relatively safer duties after this. I spoke to Francis in 1995. I asked him when the military had told him what happened to his brother Joseph.

"They didn't let me know until I got home. My ship went through the Brooklyn Navy Yard . . . I was in convoy duty between New York and England and through the Mediterranean and that area and I got back to Pittsburgh and I called my sister because she lived there in Pittsburgh and she told me about the crash."

That was his late sister, Anne.

"When I used to pull into port I would get a three day pass, a 72 hour pass, and I'd take a train to Pittsburgh and then contact my sister and walk around town a little bit, maybe have dinner together then I'd take a bus into Uniontown and visit."

First Lt. Joseph Brehun, navigator of the homeward-bound Bache crew, came from New Salem in Pennsylvania. His father Nicholas was a miner and his mother, Julia, a devoted wife, mother and homemaker. His sister Anne's husband left the mines to fight in the war and was directed back to copper mining by a Government short on manpower below ground.

New Salem, south of Pittsburgh, is the sort of mining community where it would not have been unheard of for more than one family member to die in accidents. However the Brehuns suffered a different kind of loss in late 1944.

Like Doyle, Brehun was one of six children. John and Joseph died in the war and Anne died in 1973. Marie, Rita, Francis are still alive.

Brehun had been a good student, top of his class in all subjects. He graduated from high school in 1939 and went to St. Vincent's College. He loved to listen to opera on the radio on Sunday afternoons and loved both shooting and shooting pool. He also played baseball, and had a good knuckleball.

Brehun was drafted, and after he went into the service his family never saw him again. He trained, went overseas, did his missions, and was coming home when he was killed.

I visited a large, friendly gathering of Brehun's relatives in Uniontown, Pennsylvania, in 1999, and asked them what they thought of bereaved father Louis Groeger's opinion that the loss would have been easier to take if it had been in combat. They didn't agree; as they saw it, both brothers were in harm's way as part of their war duties. They felt that after fifty missions, Joseph had certainly seen plenty of combat.

Joseph's family knew also that Joseph was offered, at or near the end of his missions, a captain's rating which he refused. They believe he turned it down so he could finish his fifty missions with his crew which he did. He was on his way home when *The Buzzer* crashed. One of those "might have beens" is that if he had taken that job, he probably would have survived the war.

The family is devoutly Roman Catholic and their praise of Joseph's character as a young man often included comments on his faith. Joseph's sister Rita, who went to Oliveto Citra and found herself thinking-somewhere in these mountains I lost a brother, was in Italy on a pilgrimage.

The Brehun family showed me around their town: old coke ovens, and the miners' "patches," groups of small houses built by the mine owners and rented to the miners.

Brehun might have appreciated Rudy Acosta's rat-shooting efforts: he once woke up in Grottaglie to find a rat sitting on his chest. On the plus side of his wartime location, he was able to follow his love of opera to live performances in Naples.

As I found with other crew members, I might read records and even letters they wrote and received but it was when I met their relatives that the men became most real to me.

Brehun's sister Rita told me: "I remember my brother taking us the day before he went into the Army (I never saw my brother in uniform) . . . my sister and I . . . to 'Fantasia'. And they sat through it twice. Of course I was so small so I just curled up and went to sleep and he took us to a big spaghetti dinner afterwards and I remember I couldn't eat it and we took the last trolley home at midnight . . . and that was the last I saw him."

I asked Brehun's sister how their parents had dealt with the wartime losses. She said "I suppose you just live through it. Everybody has to."

First Lieutenant Joseph Brehun was buried with his fellow airmen in the group service at Jefferson Barracks National Cemetery in St. Louis, having first been part of the group burial in the United States Military Cemetery Naples.

The family said they were somewhat comforted by the fact that Joseph was buried with his comrades-in-arms, even in a common grave. All of them attended the service except Anne who stayed home with her small children.

Roy L. Groeger

"Roy was a heck of a nice person."

First Lieutenant Roy L. Groeger was a bombardier. He was one of those who had finished their missions and was headed home.

I learned this from Ralph Tamm, a schoolfriend of Groeger's:

"Roy Groeger and I went to grammar and high school together. Both schools were in Northwest Chicago. He was from a one-child family, so Roy's death was devastating to his parents. My sister met his parents after Roy died and they were quite devastated. That was really a shame. I felt really sorry for them. Roy was a heck of a nice person and very intelligent. And, he was always at the head of his class; we expected great things from him.

"Roy tended more toward intellectual pursuits rather than sports. Even if he would have liked to compete in sports, he had the heart but didn't have the necessary athletic capability. Also, our Chicago high school had more than three thousand students—stiff competition. Everyone liked him as a person and respected him for his intellect.

"My sister said she traded stamps with Roy and was envious of his collection because he traveled with his folks every summer to 'exotic' places like Mexico and Canada. She also thought his father traveled on business quite a bit but couldn't remember his father's occupation—we think it was related to finance. She knew his mother to be a kind and gentle person."

Groeger's father, Louis, was thirty-nine when Groeger was born, on February 1, 1924. Groeger went to Lloyd Grammar School, Class of 1937, and Foreman High School, Class of 1941.

Did Tamm know what Roy had planned to do after the war?

"No. I don't have information on what he did after high school. He may have attended a university before he enlisted in the military. . . . I know that his father was involved in the market somehow. He was business oriented, I guess. I knew Roy fairly well, but you know how things are, I don't know details about his family or anything. We used to call him 'Pussy.' He had freckles that looked like whiskers, you know, a friendly type of thing, not derogatory."

Lorraine Mazerick, of Carpentersville, Illinois, was in several of Roy Groeger's high school classes. She sounded a constant theme. "Well, Roy was a very private person."

In high school, Groeger was in the National Honor Society, served as features editor on the school paper, and took part in a stamp collecting society and a current events club. He spoke at his high school graduation; the theme of his address was intellectual freedom.

As a senior, he and classmate Paul Caputo wrote the following for the school paper (*Foreman News,* June 11, 1941).

"Being of Reasonably (?) Sound Minds. . . ."

"We, the members of the senior graduating class of June, 1941, being of REASONABLY sound minds and bodies do hereby make, publish, and declare this to be our last will and testament:

First: To the freshies, because we "love" them, we hereby bestow upon them

    (A) four dozen season passes to the elevator

    (B) all our un-canceled ninth periods, some
        are first editions (very valuable)

    (C) eight sets of final exams

Second: We bequeath to the fastest runner in the sophomore class, the pretty girl in locker 1319.

Third: To the gourmet juniors who revel in gastronomic delights at the Sugar Bowl and Leo's Place, we leave the remainder of our supply of Tums (for the tummy)

Fourth: The new seniors will inherit:

    (A) a newly vacated and decorated (with gum) auditorium division compete with five broken seats

    (B) our card file of excuses and alibis; you'll need'em

    (C) those guys in white suits who parade around the stage during assembly

Fifth: To the miscellaneous departments and inhabitants of Foreman, we leave the following items:

To the gym department we bequeath the fifteen unused bars of soap with which we failed to wash.

To future chemists go our slightly worn gas masks and fire extinguishers

To the math students we leave the following:

1. 2 stubby pencils.
2. 1/2 sheet of notebook paper.
3. 1 copy of Einstein's "Theory of Relativity."

To those who like to roam the halls, we leave the new girl guards.(Wow!)

To the football team we leave a package of Wheaties to make for huskier linemen.

To Mr. Maloff we leave a bottle of Welch's grape juice and a box of Ry Krisp.

We haven't got much left to leave, but you'll find the remainder in the Lost and Found. (First come, first served).

(Last but best of all, we leave behind us our undying gratitude to the faculty, and to our companions who have made our brief career here at Foreman, a memory of our lives which will remain close to our hearts.)"

                    Roy Groeger and Paul Caputo,
                    Executors

In November 1998, I spoke with Sam Taylor, nose gunner in Underwood's crew.

"I flew right over top of Groeger. That's why I worked with him quite a bit. I was up there with him. I started flying in May of 1944. We were a replacement crew out of Casper, Wyoming. I think our first mission was to Ploesti." Taylor said his crew went to Ploesti three or four times. I asked when he first met Roy Groeger.

"In Casper. We flew all assembled to Salt Lake City and of course they issued a number there and the pilot—I met the pilot, he came up through the train hollering for my number."

He and Groeger were part of the original Underwood crew and Groeger was the only one who was killed. I asked why he was the only man from Underwood's crew on the plane.

"Well, the . . . enlisted man, as you probably knew, finished ahead of the officers, simply because we flew extra on new crews, so we got ahead of the officers, all the enlisted men finished and I came home in November. Our ball turret gunner, he stayed over there and he was assistant crew chief on a B-25 for some officer that just flew out—so he stayed a few months longer. And I don't know when the other officers came home, but I guess Groeger just came home the first shot he got.

"Because he didn't like that war at all. That is just one thing that he just didn't care for. None of us did, but we went on and he just wasn't happy over there."

Taylor described a similar experience to mine where officers were concerned - very little contact outside of missions and our one rest camp. His crew didn't even go to rest camp together. I asked if he knew anything about Groeger.

"No, I didn't know much about him. He seemed like a kind of strange guy. He seemed like a pretty good guy, but I don't know, I understood or kind of surmised that he just had a little bit different life than the most of the rest of us. I think he surely came from some wealth . . . most of the guys on our crew were just poor old boys just trying to get along. He—I don't know—he was a pretty good kind of a guy, he used to take me up to the bomb sight they had set up out there and showed me how that thing worked. And messed around. I don't know. I guess just something to do, because I looked through a bomb sight a few times when we was up there but I never bombed anything . . .

"I think he surely was educated. He seemed like a pretty shrewd kid and he read quite a bit. Well so did I. We did a lot of reading. Read everything that you could get your hands on. But he seemed like he knew where he come from all right. That's why I thought, you know, he had a pretty good background and had some education."

I mentioned that Groeger's father had been active in making contacts among the relatives of other men killed in the plane. He said "I never heard him mention his mother or his dad or any part of his family. I never heard him mention a soul."

I said "That is sort of strange, isn't it?"

"It is. Yeah it was. He was—I don't know he just wouldn't tell you anything about his life. Because I come from a big family and you know it is part of my life. But he just didn't tell anything about himself at all. In a way I kind of liked the guy, but you just couldn't get close to him.

"He was a little guy. He just didn't like being over there. He didn't want any part of that war and I think if anybody was scared on the crew, he was probably the one because he [was] bitter when we had to fly missions. He was griping all the time."

Groeger's pilot, 1st Lt. Robert Underwood, said, "It's strange that Groeger's father thought his loss would have been more bearable if Roy had died in combat, while his son was the most—vocally—unhappy about being in the war."

Groeger's crew flew a new plane over to Italy and didn't have a regular plane of their own. Taylor thinks they may even have flown a mission or two in *The Buzzer*.

I know Groeger was part of a crew that hit one of my old targets, the sub pens at Toulon, in southern France. I have the interrogation form from that August 6, 1944 mission. He was bombardier, as usual, in Underwood's crew, and Taylor was nose gunner. The form says the flak was intense, accurate and heavy, and the bombs "fell into smoke, tgt seemed well hit."

The Deficiencies form for Groeger's plane that day notes: "#3 turbo and RPM gauge out. Left front bomb rack wouldn't release at altitude, was OK on ground. Ball turret door wouldn't open properly. Nose turret elevation won't work at high speed."

After Groeger was reported missing, his father wrote to the *Chicago Tribune* in hopes their correspondents in Italy could shed some light on the mystery of the missing plane and crew. He wrote to the other families asking for details about crew position, rank, bomb group, and final destination.

He wrote this to the War Department soon after learning of his son's death:

August 9, 1945:

"Attention: Edward F. Witsell, Acting the Adjutant General

"Dear General,
"Relative to your Western Union Telegram C.S. 213–69 Govt. WUX Washington, D.C. 30 657P 1945 July 30:

"We are thankful for your promptness in notifying us of corrected report which you have just received, stating that our son, Lt. Roy L. Groeger -703484, Bombardier; of the 449th Bomb Group, 719th Squadron, of the 15th Air Force, Italy, who was previously reported missing, was killed on the 9th of December 1944.

"Up to this date, we have heard that five of the missing boys have been killed on that B-24 Liberator on a non-operational flight, between Grottaglie and Pomigliano, Italy. There were *sixteen young men* on that plane, and we would like to know how many more were killed and how many more were saved, *if any!* And, could you give us the names of those killed and those alive?

"We, the nearest of kin, are in communication with each other and do the best we can to console one another; however, the load would not have been so heavy to carry had our boy gone down fighting, and I think I can speak for the rest in this spirit. I just cannot understand why these boys received such a terrible pay-off, after having so heroically done their bit—What was wrong?

"We would appreciate getting all the details pertaining to this catastrophe, such as, the weather conditions at the time of the take-off; and, did the accident indicate the boys had bailed out, or did the plane crash, and near what town or city, and at what altitude?

"Would like to have the name and address of the Commanding officer, so we may get in touch with him regarding personal matters, such as their personal belongings, etc. Roy mentioned at one time that he had received a little reward for his efforts. I believe he had reference to some medals. Did he have them with him?

"Wish I could obtain the names and address of all the boys, with whom Roy went on his *last bombing mission,* and would it be possible to receive a group picture with their bombing plane. We see so many of these pictures in homes, magazines and newspapers.

"Trusting my requests are not too numerous,
"Yours very respectfully,
Louis C. Groeger"

Groeger's father wrote this to Major James L. Prenn, office of The Quartermaster General, Memorial Division, Washington, DC:

September 25, 1946

"Gentlemen:

"With great appreciation I acknowledge your kind letter of September 19, 1946, in reference to the remains of our son First Lieutenant Roy L. Groeger now temporarily buried in a Military Cemetery in Naples, Italy.

"About a year ago, we were told, our son died of broken bones and burns which caused us to believe he was definitely identified. There were sixteen boys on this B-24 Liberator at the time of the crash, and we would like to know the names of those identified and those not identified, and also how long it will be before we will get to know the details pertaining to this non-operational flight disaster? (Most of these boys of a letter to him, which I received from a lady in Salerno, Italy, who claims to have sent Italian mountaineers to the mountain top where the plane had crashed.

"Hoping our son will be definitely identified.
"Yours very respectfully,
Louis Groeger"

Major Prenn responded on November 1st His letter stated that identification had been made of Arieff, Baldwin, Caldwell, Doyle, Ballou, Suarez, Marple, and Erickson, and had still not been made for Brehun, Stevens, Boswell, Gettys, Eckerling, Ganim, Watson, and their son.

Major Prenn's letter added: "A copy of your letter has been forwarded to The Adjutant General, Washington 25, D.C., for direct reply relative to the name and address of the Commander in Charge of the ATC of the 15th Air Force at Grottaglie, Italy, and circumstances surrounding the death of your son, as that office has jurisdiction over matters of this nature."

✈ ✈ ✈ ✈ ✈

In a June 1947 letter to Mrs. Suarez, the Groegers reported sending eight gift packages to Mrs. Clemente in Italy, "as she has been very nice in writing letters to us, and has also put some flowers on *all* our sixteen boy's graves."

The Army sent the Groegers a letter like those received by the other bereaved, describing no progress in separately identifying eight of the bodies, and saying that the choice of Jefferson Barracks was central for the families involved.

Groeger's father wrote often to the Department of the Army Quartermaster General. He tried unsuccessfully to have the upright stone maker at the common grave changed for a flat one. He also asked if the Government would furnish transportation to the gravesite for next-of-kin or if he would have to bear the expense, when the bodies came home in May of 1949.

The inscription on the back of a wartime photograph of Roy Groeger reads:

"1st Lt. Roy L. Groeger (Bombardier)
449th Bomb Group
719th Bomb Squadron
15th Air Force, Italy
Born - February 1, 1924
Took off on December 9, 1944, to that great promised land, we all hope someday to reach, and may they all, who have gone with him, rejoice with each other.

His Father and Mother
Mr. and Mrs. Louis C. Groeger"

Donald A. Erickson

"He did not have a care in the world."

If such distinctions can be drawn, T/Sgt. Donald A. Erickson's reported survival of the crash by several days makes his story the most heartbreaking. Members of his family think news of his prolonged suffering hastened the death of his mother, and many inhabitants of the Oliveto Citra area told me they thought Amelia Clemente had been wrong to even tell the family the news.

Tom Skinas told me:

"Donald Erickson was an individual whose facial expression suggested that he did not have a care in the world. He had no enemies - only friends. But during our missions in any given situation which required his technical knowledge and skills his concentration was something to behold. For a big and heavy set individual he moved fast and if you didn't get out of his way he would bowl you over. We were most fortunate in having him for our engineer."

Erickson was part of the Bache crew, on his way home. His sister, Mrs. Evelyn Dunlop, said he had done more than forty missions and would have to go back after Christmas. This may be true but it is also possible that there was some confusion because he had done his fifty mission-credits in forty sorties. He probably was top turret gunner as well. His sister told me he always said "Boy, if the plane goes down, I'm gonna jump out of the top."

When Erickson was killed, his father, Alvin A. Erickson, was 45. His mother, the former Hildur Hallof, was 43. His sister, Evelyn Ann, was 18.

Erickson was born in South Dakota and brought to northern California as an infant. He went to Turlock High from 1938–1942. He enlisted in the Air Force in 1943.

Evelyn Dunlop still lives in Turlock, California. She and her brother grew up on a 40-acre farm a mile and a half from town. She recalls: "My brother Donald and I were only a year and a half apart in age. There was only the two of us and he was always there for me when we were growing up. Before he left for the service, he asked my mom and dad to be sure I had my own car to drive. He didn't want me riding with any reckless boys. Because of his request I drove the family car the thirteen miles to and from Junior College everyday. He was the greatest brother to me."

Evelyn Dunlop still has many of Donald Erickson's letters home from his time in the service:

Feb. 18, 1942 On USO Stationery

"Dear Annie,

"I was very pleased with the letter you sent me and I am sorry that I told you not to write. I received orders when I got here that I should write no letters from here because I would leave too soon. The reason I haven't left is that the Army has plenty of cadets but they don't have any openings at the present for primary flight training. We have to wait here until a class of cadets graduate from a primary flying school and we will then move to a training base. They are giving us air cadets a course in math and physics while we are waiting for shipping orders. They are giving us a terribly stiff course but not as bad as I expected it to be.

"I can't wait until I go up in a plane which will be in a month or two if I don't get out of here pretty soon. I have qualified and have been accepted since the first of February.

"I did a bit of drill this morning and I received a typhoid shot in my arm this afternoon . . . They have given me four different vaccinations so far and my arm is stiff tonight so my writing isn't very neat.

"I worked in warehouses yesterday and handled hundreds of packing crates which were filled with uniforms. These crates were very heavy to lift because they each contained 500 pairs of wool socks and others contained heavy overcoats for use in Alaska and cold climates. I have gotten two letters from Jimmy Arthur. I may get a pass in 18 more days if I stay here."

"Love from Donald"

Erickson was stationed at Keesler Field, Biloxi, Mississippi for some time.

April 30, 1943 10:30pm Air Corps Technical School Keesler Field, Mississippi

"Dear Evelyn,

" . . . This afternoon I went with Gibson and another P.F.C. and we went down to the place where the soldiers can check out G.I. rowboats for two hours at a time.

"The place was closed because the Sgt. who checked out the boats was waiting to get paid. You know it was payday here today. I don't get paid again for a month. I got paid last on the fifteenth of March and haven't been paid since. The cadet business got my records all mixed up so I don't know what I am going to do to get it straightened out.

"I was leaving the boat pier when an Army truck driver asked if any of us wanted a ride back to our camp. I jumped in back and a bunch of "New Jeeps" who are taking their five week basic drilling got in too. I raised my head up as I was sitting on a bench in the truck and looked at Bill Brown from Turlock sitting across from me . . . He couldn't believe it was me when I started talking to him. He said that I was so sunburned and rugged looking that he didn't know me. He said I had aged something terrible since he seen me last. Bill said I look over twenty in my coveralls with P.F.C. stripes on.

"He has been in the Army about three weeks and is still a rookie—about half done with pack and rifle drilling. Bill is colorblind so he can't be a gunner. He is going to try radio. The sucker. Bill hadn't seen anyone change so much in four months as I have done."

I don't think Erickson was right about his friend here - I know I was a gunner, and I am colorblind.

May 12 1943 11pm
Air Corps Technical School
Keesler Field, Mississippi

"Dear Annie,

"Today was my day off so I have been on the beach at Biloxi and down town on a pass all day. I could get an overnight pass once a week if I had any relatives or friends here that would write a letter to my commanding officer telling him that I was welcome to stay overnight at their house when I am not on duty. This school runs just like a high school course. The "Student Instructor" gives me a mock-up mechanical arrangement to work on and at the end of my seven hour session he gives me a test on my work to see what I have learned about it. Last night I peeked in his grade book and seen that I have a 90% average so far. I heard that some fellows who cut up and get continuous low grades were shipped out of here to go on air corps pick and shovel gangs. The army is anxious to get more airplane mechanics that they really make us toe the mark or else get kicked out.

"The majority of the boys in my outfit are New York Jews and Southerners who are Catholics. The chapels here are sure swell and they are very neat both inside and outside.

"This camp was a large swamp two years ago when they started building it up. The day before yesterday I talked with an Erickson boy who was from Oregon. He was in the Medical Corps and looks after a ward at the field hospital. He heard me coughing and said I should try and get over my habitual "Mississippi Miseries" before it turned into bronchitis or pneumonia. According to him the hospital is full of spinal meningitis and pneumonia cases. This afternoon I took some pictures of myself with my big camera of course I had a buddy snap them.

"I got a permit to use a camera on the post from the Provost Marshal or "MP"s as I call them [when] I first got here or else my camera would have been confiscated during short term inspection.

"When I get my pictures developed I'll send you some. I took the enclosed funny picture this afternoon at a studio in Biloxi."

August 9, 1943 3:00A.M.
Air Corps Technical School
Keesler Field, Mississippi

"Dear Annie.

"I finished the twelve day phase on Test Blocks tonight so now I have only thirty-two more days of school left. The final examination tonight on the Test Block Engine Operation branch consisted of preflighting the engine and checking for range of operations on the governor. It sure felt funny to be in the cockpit of a B-24 D Liberator checking the engines. The engines are Pratt and Whitney fourteen cylinder and do they make a roar when they are running.

"My ears sure ring after being around a engine that is running half open. I always feel a bit scared when I pull the huge twelve foot propeller through. Two boys got killed a few months ago by an engine that kicked back. It is best to be very cautious when turning . . .

"I went to New Orleans on my last pass but I stayed there only a few hours and came right back. I took the Greyhound bus when I went and rode the L & N Streamliner back. The trains and buses are sure crowded now days. All I seen on the train on the way back to Keesler Field was soldiers and sailors.

"I visited the waterfront at New Orleans and got a good look at the Mississippi River where it flows between New

Orleans and Algiers. Algiers is a French community directly across the Mississippi from New Orleans. I seen large piles of bananas on the docks that had just arrived from South America.

"I sure enjoy the *Readers Digest*. The boys in my barrack all read it when I get it. I spend my leisure time laying on my upper reading my lessons or the Digest."

August 11, 1943
Air Corps Technical School
Keesler Field, Mississippi

"Dear Annie,

"Today is my day off so I have time to write a few letters. I got a Special Pass last night at 1:A.M. when I got back from school but I was so sleepy that I didn't care to go anywhere. I had planned to go to Mobile Alabama on this week's pass but as things are I will probably go next week. I am going to try and see all of the country that I can around here before I ship out in about a month. I have only thirty more days of school

left now before graduation so that means that I will not be able to be out on more than three or four more passes before I ship out to either Aerial Gunnery in Texas or factory school in San Diego or Willow Run which is Ford's new bomber factory. There is no hope of me getting a furlough until I get assigned to a Bomber crew.

"Thanks a lot for the swell birthday present. Now I am the owner of a $25.00 bond. You are sure a swell aunt to always remember me on my birthday. That sure is a cute birthday card that you sent . . . Two boys in my squadron from New York spent a summer in Pine Crest in 1939 when they came out to California on a trip visiting relatives in San Francisco. I have got accustomed to the heat in the four months I have been here so I don't sweat anymore. The new men coming in from up North sweat until they look like they fell in a tub of water."

Erickson went not to Willow Run, home of so many B-24s, but to Laredo, Texas, for aerial gunnery school. In an October 6 postcard to Evelyn, he describes liking the home-like climate, and describes plans to cross the nearby Rio Grande for a trip into Mexico.

During Erickson's tour in Italy, he was involved in a dramatic incident about which little is known outside of a photograph from Egypt. Evelyn Dunlop wrote me:

"Forgot to mention [a] picture my brother sent home from Egypt to us. It seems their plane was hit and my brother went out on wings and repaired some things and had removed gloves and frozen his fingers or hands. The crew was sent to Egypt to rest and relax. Then returned for more bombing missions."

I think it goes without saying that either Erickson was fooling his sister or she misunderstood something about the details of an incident; in any case, Erickson would not have been "out on the wings."

Evelyn Dunlop told me:

"It was very hard on my mom and dad to lose Donald. I was a year and a half younger and was busy dating sailors and skating (ice) and bowling and going to dances at the Castle air base. (It has closed down now (I miss the B-29s going over every day.)"

She wrote me as I was pursuing this investigation: "When Amelia [Clemente] wrote the first letter to us stating ["Eight boys have been around here."]. My parents thought Don was alive. My parents called Castle Air Base— located twenty miles south of Turlock and gave them the letter to read."

Evelyn explains that a picture described by Amelia Clemente as depicting Erickson and his girlfriend was in fact one of Erickson and his sister. She was wearing the black dress, and it was taken in Idaho. "We took the train to Idaho to say goodbye before Don and his crew went overseas."

"Some people must have been down to the crash site and brought stuff of Don's back. Our address must have been in his duffel bag?"

"The thing that has always bothered me—the part in the letter that mentioned Don living three days and nights. That he flashed lights and carved on the tree and was in a sitting position. She said if we would send camera, film, oil for lamps, etc.—they would take donkeys and ropes and go into the ravine and take pictures of the carving on the tree. This was so hard for my mom and dad. I've always wondered if this was true or if she wrote this to other families about their sons."

She did not.

Evelyn Dunlop also wrote me that Bache told her mother "there were gifts boys had bought and money on the plane and this was all taken by people who stole it, that went down [the ravine] after [the] plane was found."

There were rumors I have not been able to confirm that Erickson threw his wallet down from the ravine in the hope of getting help, but that someone made off with it.

What has irked me is the thought that several people in the village reported seeing lights, which were probably flares shot by Erickson, but that no one rescued him. I have tried to think also that in wartime people might not have been anxious to go exploring a snowy mountain ravine, but it is still terrible to think that Erickson might have been saved if he'd been reached by the right people in time.

Evelyn Dunlop also told me this:

"Going through these pictures made me very sad. My mom died in '83 and was almost 83 years old. My dad passed away at 92 years old. Sometimes I wish I still had my brother, being the only one left is lonely."

Erickson is buried in the Sicily-Rome American Military Cemetery, about 38 miles south of Rome, just east of Anzio.

Joe L. Gettys, Jr.

"A better bunch of boys never lived."

Technical Sergeant Joe L. Gettys, Jr. was coming home to marry.

Gettys grew up in Sibley, Iowa. According to his younger brother, Gene, he liked athletics and music. His favorite sports were football and baseball, and he played in the high school band. "I can remember . . . playing catch with him." He was an Eagle Scout, and graduated from Sibley High School at sixteen, going on to study at Coe College in Cedar Rapids, about 240 miles away, for two years.

He entered the Air Force after his sophomore year, on June 8, 1942. He graduated from radio school at Sioux Falls, South Dakota and did his phase training at Boise, Idaho.

He had been fond of building model airplanes. "It was sort of ironic, he would love to build them, but after he had them for a year or so, he would take them and light them on fire and send them up."

During training, Getty's pilot, William Bache, wrote a thank-you note to Getty's mother after the crew had visited with her.

May 26, 1944 Officers' Club Gowen Field, Boise, Idaho:

"Dear Mrs. Gettys:

"I just want to drop you a few lines to tell you how very much the whole crew enjoyed the afternoon we spent with

225

you and Joe's fiancee. It was very thoughtful and gracious of you to ask us to have dinner with you, and I can say for myself, as well as all the other fellows on the crew, that never was an afternoon enjoyed more. In the service, we have had all too little chance to associate with the kind of "women-folk" that we hold so dear, and I know that it was not only to me that you brought pleasant, even if nostalgic, memories of home and of our own mothers and fiancees!

"You asked me, while here, how Joe was doing and I never did get the chance to answer you. Mrs. Gettys, Joe is one of the best men on the crew, bar none, officers and enlisted men. He is a hard-working conscientious, efficient boy, and I have the utmost confidence in him. Please don't think that I am only saying this because I am writing to you, his mother, because that is definitely not the case. If I felt otherwise, I would just not mention it at all, and thus not hurt your feelings, but as it is, I am happy to say, in all sincerity, that Joe is all I could ask for. He knows his job and does it diligently and well.

"And it is not only in an official capacity that I like Joe. He is such a clean-living, likable, fellow that I regret the military custom that makes it impracticable for enlisted men and officers to "fraternize," except on special occasions. He is the kind of a fellow that I would like to consider a real friend of mine.

"So you see, I think quite a lot of that son of yours, both officially and personally.

"Mrs. Gettys, I know that it is natural for a fellow's family to worry, when he goes to combat. As we are just a few weeks removed from combat, it may help you to know that we are flying one of the finest, safest ships that Uncle Sam has, that our crew has all had the very best of training, that we are really ready and able to take care of ourselves in whatever situations may arise, and that the boys who make up the crew are all the type (now that we have managed to replace Sgt. Gould) who will be right there fighting in a pinch. All of these things give us at least an even chance to get the whole crew back safely, and that is all we need, and ask. I am not trying to "cheer you up;" I just want you to feel the confidence that I feel, for whatever help it may be to you in the months to come. They are my crew, and I know of no other men, singly or in a group, that I would rather depend on in combat. I feel a terrific responsibility toward each one of the men, for their safety, but knowing the men, and their abilities has made my job a lot easier.

"Well I guess that's about all. Thanks again for your thoughtfulness and kindness. I am sorry that I couldn't see you before you left, but am looking forward to seeing you again in Topeka or Lincoln."

"Sincerely,
Bill Bache"

Of course Bache's confidence in his crew proved well-placed. They did come through combat, only to die as passengers.

Gettys arrived overseas on July 15, 1944, just a week before my last mission. By the time of this next letter from Bache, Getty's had finished most of his missions.

Nov. 19, 1944
Italy

"My dear Mrs. Gettys:

"It occurred to me that you might like to know how that son of yours has reacted to combat from a third party, so I decided to drop you these few lines. That isn't worded exactly as I intended it to be, for I know that you know Joe far too well to ever have had to wonder how he would react under any and all circumstances, but I thought you might appreciate a "resume."

"Our crew has been through quite a few exciting moments, and I am happy to say that the faith I had in them, while still in the States, has been borne out, here in the thick of things. The team-work and efficiency which we acquired then is paying large dividends now, and has been the means of pulling us out of many a tight spot.

"As for Joe personally I am also happy to say that he has more than lived up to all of the confidence I felt in him. He has done his work in an excellent manner, and, what is equally important, has succeeded in remaining cool and collected in the tight spots. From personal experience, I know just how difficult it is to do that.

"As a man, he has also lived up to what you and his fiancee expect of him. None of the G.I. habit of "seeing Italy, its places and its people" for Joe. His one aim in life has been, and is now, to finish his fifty missions and return to the States the same kind of man he was when he left.

"In all ways you and your husband and Florence can well be proud of your son. No one ever accepted and recognized his responsibilities and discharged them, any better than Joe does, and darned few have done as well.

"As I said, none of this will surprise any of you, for you all know Joe too well, but you might like to know that others, too, recognize his qualities.

"We have just twelve more missions to fly, in order to finish our tour of duty and return home, and I am positive that we will finish these twelve without an unhappy incident. It is said that only a fool is positive, but I guess my confidence in "my boys" makes me somewhat of a fool anyway.

"If so, then I will gladly go on being a fool, for a better bunch of boys never lived. I am terribly proud of them, proud of the work they are doing, and proud of the chance to be their pilot. I am looking forward to renewing our acquaintance some day, and to meeting Mr. Gettys. Until then, keep your fingers crossed for us, and give my best regards to Florence."

"Sincerely,
Bill Bache"

The week after his parents were notified that he was missing, the local newspaper printed an official Air Corps press release about Getty's last mission:

"15th AAF IN ITALY—Technical Sgt. Joe L. Gettys, Jr., 21, son of Mr. and Mrs. Joe L. Gettys, 1206 Baldwin St., Harlan, Iowa, recently flew his 41st mission as a radio operator on a 15th AAF B-24 Liberator based in Italy. His group was recently presented with a second War Department Citation for outstanding performances in the Mediterranean Theater of Operations.

Sgt. Getty's favorite Liberator is "Sleepy Time Gal," a veteran of over 60 combat missions. He has seen action over important targets such as Budapest, Vienna, Ploesti, and many others. During a recent attack on the oil refineries at Ploesti heavy anti-aircraft fire severely damaged "The Gal" and Gettys had a few anxious moments.

"I saw a direct hit under our wing damage one landing gear and I started wondering how our pilot would land her. Then I heard the engineer report that our rudder cables had been severed. Looking out my window I saw one of the engines receive a big burst of flak which put it out of commission. Boy, we were in a bad fix, but "Sleepy Time Gal" came through again and brought us safely home. Our pilot made a beautiful crash landing and we all climbed out uninjured but plenty scared and glad to be on terra firma again!"

Gettys wrote home just three days before the flight of *The Buzzer:*
Wednesday, Dec. 6, 1944
Marked "Returnee"

"Dear Mom, Dad and Gene,

"I received your letter telling of Gene's honors in football and I am plenty proud of it. Keep up the good work, fellow and you'll continue to be up there at the top. The way things look now I should be home so I can see a couple of basketball games. If I am real lucky, I could be home for 'Xmas, but in order to do so I'd have to fly and that's very unlikely. We should leave the base here in a day or so and go to our point of embarkation. Am not sure if I can tell where that will be so I won't. I'm hoping that we will catch a boat right away. Let's wish for a good fast ship.

"We haven't been doing much of anything the last few days. Just getting our flying equipment turned in and our orders through the various channels necessary for us to leave. It is no longer Lt. Bache but it is now Captain Bache. The promotion just came through yesterday and he is feeling pretty happy about it. He really deserved it and am glad to see that he got it. We couldn't have asked for a better man and officer to be our pilot. He is the best there is.

"I'm glad to hear that you had a nice time on Thanksgiving. That was the day we learned that we only had to fly 35 sorties instead of fifty missions. That is one day I'll never forget.

"At present I have most of my things packed and ready to leave. I have only a few odds and ends to put in my B-4 bag and I'll be all set to travel. The faster the better.

"We've got our gas stove red hot and the tent is nice and warm tonight. Everytime I fill the tank up I think "boy wouldn't the people back in the States give a lot to get ahold of this stuff."

"By the way tell Roy that I'll be in to get that malt he promised me before many days have gone by. He is a fine person.

"It's good to hear that work has already begun on the new airport. I hope that they construct a decent one while they are at it. Not some makeshift affair. Imagine that it will be okay though. As to my flying again soon, I want to keep my feet on the ground for awhile until my nerves get back to normal. I'm just like an old hen; if I could wear two chutes I would, every time I go up.

"Guess that I'd better sign off for now.
"So long and
Love,
Joe"

Gettys' pilot, William Bache, wrote to Mrs. Gettys again after her son's plane went missing:

January 8, 1945
New Orleans, La.

"Dear Mrs. Gettys:

Your letter to my sister, Mrs. La Garde, arrived today, and I am taking the liberty of answering it for her.

"This is an awfully hard letter for me to write, Mrs. Gettys. I was going to write you and give you all of the details I had, but I wanted to wait until I was certain that you had been notified through official channels first. Now that you have heard from the Army, I am glad to give you all of the information that I have concerning Joe.

"As Joe told you, I had been recommended for Captain, and when the other boys were ready to leave my promotion had just come through. That meant that I was a few days behind them in being ready to leave the field, as I had to put all of my orders through after the promotion came through. They were all anxious to get home for Christmas, if at all possible, so they decided to go on before me to the Port of Embarkation (Naples, and that if they didn't get out right away, I would catch up with them in just a few days.

"Accordingly, Joe, Erickson, Ballou, Eckerling, and Lt. Doyle hitched a ride to Naples with another crew who were going there, and left, with the understanding that I would probably meet them in just a few days. Naples is the point at which we landed when we reached Italy, and was the point from which we would catch either a plane or a ship for the States."

The letter goes on to describe the search for *The Buzzer*. "I borrowed a co-pilot, engineer, and radioman, and flew twenty-eight hours in three days, looking for some sign of them. Everyone did their utmost to find some trace of them, and we covered every square mile of southern Italy and any part of the country over which they might possibly have flown, even the highly unlikely parts, but without success."

"I believe, Mrs. Gettys, that they had trouble with the weather that day, as I found out later, from the weather office, that it was not very good between our field and Naples, and that they had to make a forced landing in the mountains that lie enroute, and over which they had to fly to get to their destination. That would account for our not being able to find a trace of them, for it would be very easy for a ship to go down in those mountains, ravines, and passes and not be at all visible from the air, no matter how carefully we searched. That is solely my opinion, and not borne out by anything we could learn. "Borne out" isn't exactly what I want to say, because we learned absolutely nothing to bear anything out. It is just my belief as to what happened, and I feel that way because of my knowledge of the terrain and the route they had to fly.

"Well, I guess that is all there is to tell. I left the field and started home after orders came through to discontinue the search, it being impossible to cover any more territory, or to do any more, than had already been done. And you can take my word for it, Mrs. Gettys, the Army spared no effort that could have been helpful in finding my boys. They did everything that was humanly possible to find some trace of the boys and the ship. We can only hope and pray that somehow they will turn up safe, that they will make their way back to one of the fields in the area. I don't have to tell you how I feel about this thing, I'm sure, for you know how I felt about the boys on my crew and about Joe in particular. It will suffice to say that it took most of the pleasure out of my coming home, and I haven't had a moment's peace of mind since it all happened.

"If there is anything I can do for you all or for Florence, please don't hesitate to drop me a line and ask me. I know there must be hundreds of questions that you would like to ask about Joe and I will be only too glad to answer them. I may also be of some help in official matters. Regardless of what it is, just drop me a line, and tell Florence the same thing. I consider Joe a personal friend of mine and anything that I can do to help you all out will be a pleasure. I only wish that I could be writing you more encouraging news [than] is in this letter. However, I think you would want the absolute truth, and that is what I have written.

"I hope you will forgive me for typing this letter. I had so much to tell you that I didn't want to take a chance on skipping any part of it while writing in longhand. I am going to write Ralph Ballou's wife tonite, as you say that she, too, has been notified of the accident.

"I again want to remind you that I will be only too happy to give you whatever other information I have that you may like, if you will only let me know what it is. In return, I would surely appreciate it if you would let me know of any additional news that you receive, as I have no other way of keeping informed. Just address any letters to me here, and my mother will forward them to me, wherever I may be.

"I'll be waiting to hear from you again,"

"Most sincerely,
Bill Bache"

Here is a letter from Gettys' fiancee, Florence Winkler, of Sibley, Iowa, to Mrs. Gettys. The couple were engaged while Gettys was stationed at Salt lake City.

December 5, 1945
Vermillion, S.Dak.

"Dear Mrs. Gettys,

"I am almost ashamed to write to you because it has been too long since I last wrote. Please forgive me.

"Mother said she wrote you not very long ago all the news of what we're doing. Did she tell you I had 9 hours of "A" and six hours of "B" giving me a 91.5 average. I'm really quite proud of that average and I hope to retain it this semester. It has always been my ambition to have about a 90 for at least one semester of my college career.

"It is really quite normal back here at school. Lots of veterans are coming back each week and the fraternities are in full swing again. There is a long line of formals this month so there are lots of things to attend. Although our football and basketball teams weren't and aren't good at least we have them.

"I have started two letters to Gene to congratulate on all the things he has done this year so far. I was so pleased to hear that he was crowned king and made the second all state football team.

"Mother seems really happy here. It is lots of hard work, but it is away from anything too familiar. Now she is busy nursing a group of flu victims. So it is really almost an epidemic.

"One year ago the 9th of December your son and my fiancee was killed. There is no way to tell you how I loved him and how I miss him; but I'm sure you know that. Our big consolation is that he was doing what he thought and believed was right. And, also, he was happy. I hope someday to give someone as much happiness as he gave me. Joe enters into my thoughts so often and I wish he knew how much I really loved him. Maybe he does. I hope so.

"Someday, I hope we know more of the particulars over in Italy but the War Dept. is certainly slow sending out that information. Wars are horrible things, but God must have some purpose in them or they would not be. We'll know the reason someday; till then, we must go on believing.

"I do hope Mother Gettys Estelle is better. Mother and I both speak of you all so often. I hope we can see you sometime after Xmas.

"It is almost twelve o'clock and time for me to go to bed. I'm trying to get seven hours of sleep each night this year. At times it's quite hard.

"Goodnight to you all and the best of everything in the new year. I do think of you so very often."

"Love,
Florence"

Gene Gettys told me: "An ironic twist of fate is that my father's only brother died in France in the First World War and my only brother died in the Second World War. I served in the U.S. Navy 1946–1948. My wife and I feel fortunate that our 4 sons did not have to serve their country during any of the following conflicts around the world."

Gettys is one of the men buried together at Jefferson Barracks National Cemetery in St. Louis.

Ralph G. Ballou

Technical Sergeant Ralph G. Ballou was a nose gunner. He was on his way home to Cedar Rapids, Iowa.

Crewmate Tom Skinas wrote of him: "Of the enlisted crew members, I felt closest to Ralph Ballou. He was the only one who was wounded in combat. He was flying the nose-gunner position when a piece of flak hit him in the head. His steel helmet saved his life." Ballou was awarded a Purple Heart in September, 1944.

However, says Skinas, Ballou became more "worrisome" after being wounded. "He could not stay in the nose-turret when approaching the flak area. This is not to suggest that my regard and admiration for him [were] lessened by the changes brought about by his wound.

Ralph Garfield Ballou was born November 16, 1921, in Center Point, Iowa. The family moved to Cedar Rapids when Ralph was one. His father was Edwin Ballou. His mother, Kathyrn Marie, had once taught Native Americans in the Dakotas. He belonged to a church-run YMCA boy's club, and was a member of the Trinity Methodist Church. He sold magazine subscriptions door to door as a young teenager, and "did pretty good" according to his brother Earl, whom I visited in Cedar Rapids.

Ralph was the oldest of four children. At the time of his death in 1944, his brother Donald Tibbets Ballou was a 21-year-old tail gunner on a B-17 Flying Fortress with the Eighth Air Force. Their sister Audrey Jean was 17, and Earl O. Ballou was 15.

In high school, Ralph set pins in a bowling alley. In 1937 he spent time in the Civilian Conservation Corps, as two other crash victims had. In the summer of 1939, he attended a month-long "Citizen's Military Training Camp" at Camp Harry McHenry, Fort Des Moines. It was a basic course in infantry training.

Earl writes of his brother:

"Ralph was eight years older than I. He would take me rabbit hunting and I would hold them while he skinned them. On my birthday, he would buy me a big bag of peanuts and take me to the Golden Gloves. He left me his bicycle and his car (1937 Pontiac). The car was sold because I was not old enough to get a driver's license."

In his senior year at Roosevelt High School, Ballou was stage manager for the class production of Moliere's *The Merchant Gentleman*. He helped with set building for another play. He graduated in 1940, and went to work at Witwer Wholesale Grocery as a warehouse man. He got his driver's license in June 1941 and his hunting license that September.

He enlisted on May 1, 1942, and was stationed at Camp Shelby, near Hattiesburg, Mississippi for some time. There the climate made a big impression on him. He wrote to his brother, Earl, in August that year.

"I was glad to hear from you again, and I am sending you some coupons.

"I was sorry to hear that you had been sick and that you lack some teeth—are they out in front? If they are I bet you sure look funny.

"No I'm not a General yet, but I expect to be as soon as the President finds out where Mississippi is at - I wish I didn't know where it was. If the Japs ever land here I'm just going to move back one state and let them have this place.

"Did you hear Walter Winchell the other night? He called Camp Shelby the Alcatraz of the Army—I guess he is more than half right.

"Have to close now."

"Love, Ralph."

He wrote to "Mom and all" that September:

I think I will get a chance to take the aptitude test over again so that I can put in for Officer's School. I lacked 1 point of having a high enough score to qualify, as I guess I told you before.

"I am glad Tib got back OK, and I also hope [he] decides to settle down. I guess furloughs start the first of the month, but I don't expect to get one until November. If I get accepted into the Air Corps or should make Officer's School I probably wouldn't get one for quite a while.

"It sure turned cold here all of a sudden - I didn't think it ever got as cold here as it did last night. It was the 1st time I slept under blankets since I've been here and I needed another one.

"They are sure working us hard now I guess they intend to make commandos out of us. Anyway they are really getting us in shape for rough work."

9/26/42 Shelby

"Dear Mom and All,

" . . . I am detached from my company for a week. I am attached to the Division hdq. to act as a chauffeur for the 3rd Army officials, who are inspecting the 85th Division all this week. I am really on the spot and if I should "mess up," they would get a bad impression of the division. I don't know how I got picked for this job, but I did so I guess I'll have to make the best of it, and try to keep my nose clean.

"I heard from Aunt Meta, and also Aunt Del, who sent me a buck. It came just at the right time because I was really broke. I am on duty 24 hours all this week, of course I'm not going to be doing something all the time, but I am subject to call any time they decide to want transportation."

10/8/42 Camp Shelby

"Dear Mom and All,

"Well I guess it's about time I wrote again, but I haven't had very much time lately.

"I didn't get to see the president, because I had to stand by for a call from an officer. They furnished me a "Jeep" to drive while I was there. I am enclosing a paper concerning my accomplishments while on special duty. It isn't much to show, but at least I got a little recognition out of it. You can send this back, as I think I'll have it framed— If I stay here I should get another stripe soon, but I hope I don't stay here. I took the test over, for officer's school, Saturday A.M. and got 123, which is a darn good score. It is 13 points more than I need to qualify. My Air cadet papers are going through too. They are past the regimental commander already. You know they have to go through military channels, and the company commander sent them straight through once; and they came back. He really gave me a good write up concerning my *ability* Etc., and possibilities. I had to sign four copies of his recommend, last night, and I think it will go through O.K. He said I had an excellent chance.

"A lot of the boys have left on furloughs; I guess I'll get mine the first of the month, but it isn't sure yet. We are going to go on two weeks maneuvers the 2nd of Nov. so I hope I'm home.

"I am going on special duty again next week, to take the place of some man on furlough—I guess. Tomorrow I have to practice driving a 2 1/2 ton truck, which I'll be driving. My license says I'm qualified to drive a 2 1/2 ton or larger, but so far the biggest has been a half ton.

10/8/42 Camp Shelby

"Dear Earl,

"I received your letter, and was glad to hear from you again. I am glad you get to work at the games and make a little money.

"I hope I can get home for pheasant hunting too, and I think maybe I will, but I'm not sure yet . . . I suppose that it will really be snowing a lot by the time I get home. I guess you will be shoveling walks pretty soon; you ought to be able to get a lot of jobs, with everyone in the Army."

Well I guess I'll close.
Love Ralph
[PS] Write when you get time.

10/14/42 Camp Shelby

"Dear Mom and all,

"Well we just got back from two weeks maneuvers and I've been in bed for about 24 hours. Boy I was really tired. We were out all night three nights in a row. I had to drive back at night in a convoy and the dust was so thick I couldn't see anything but the tail light in front of me. I'm still sneezing up dust. We had a lot of fun on maneuvers but sure put in long hours.

"I didn't have anytime whatsoever to write. Even if we did get off at night we had a blackout so it was impossible to write.

"I'll be home about the 20th or the 21st. I'm not sure when I'll come or what route; but I'll find out tonight. I sure hope you sent the money I asked for, but if I don't get it in time, I know where I can borrow it."

10/20/42 Camp Shelby

"Dear Mom and all,

"I received your card last night, so will drop you a couple lines this noon before dinner. They are keeping me pretty busy and I don't have much time. I am going to get a book tonight to study up on algebra Etc. because I'll need to know it when I take the Air Cadet test. We are getting in a bunch of new men 8 so far, but there is more coming. I think I will get a transfer O.K. so that will probably gyp me out of a furlough.

"How much, if any, of my money have you available? Or is it all invested in War Bonds? If you have some of *mine* handy, send me about 5.00. If you have to take it out of your money though, don't send it. I should have some money left, but I spent too much on bus fare Etc. when the carnival was here.

"Is Tib coming home to stay or what? I got a letter from Frank he is just 330 miles from home. He says he is in a really nice place and has a good position.

"Must close and get ready for chow."

10/26/42 Camp Shelby

"Dear Mom and all,

"Well I wrote you yesterday, but I have some time on my hands so I'll write again today. I am on a 24 shift all this week and I managed to get the first 24 hours off. That is why I happen to have time on my hands. I am off until 10 o'clock tomorrow morning; then I start working, and am not done again until 10 o'clock Wednesday morning.

"It turned cold again last night and it is really chilly. I am wearing a wool undershirt under my wool shirt. We are wearing our winter outfits now and they really feel good.

"We are still getting in recruits and I look for a lot of changes to be made now. We have already lost several men for Officer's school, and about 10 fellows went down to Louisiana to start a new division. That is where the 18 and 19 year olds will be going after Jan. 1st.

"I guess I told you I had to send my foot locker home? Well anyway in it you will find a camera, which Audrey can have. When we got the orders to send all cameras home, one fellow didn't want to bother mailing his so he put it in my locker to send home. I haven't mailed my locker yet, but when I get it done (today I hope) I'll probably have to send it C.O.D. I'm sorry but I am flat broke; so try to have some money on hand to pay for it.

"I received another card in regard to the allotment. All it was, was a card which I have to fill out in case you change address. There was also another card attached which acknowledged the—I don't know the exact way to say it, but it meant that it was O.K. On it were places which could be checked in case it wasn't going through. There was five reasons, and one of them was worded like this: Quote ("Dependents are not deserving,"—Anyhow, none of the five items were marked; so that means everything was on the up and up. You should be drawing some money any day now. A lot of fellows say their folks have already received 1 or 2 payments. That first payment should be a pretty big one; and the first thing I think you should do is put in as much coal as the coal bin will hold.

"What provisions are made in the two insurance policies that I have; in case I should be missing in action? I suppose they have a clause whereby you would get anything if I should be killed. Let me know about this the next time you write. Of course, I don't expect to turn up missing, but if I should I want you to get the insurance money. The reason I asked this was, because of a notice on all Company Bulletin Boards, to investigate all civilian insurance policies. They mentioned cases in which the policies were valueless if the applicant, was missing in action Etc."

10/28/42 This letter is on USO stationery, with "IDLE GOSSIP SINKS SHIPS" across the bottom of the page.

"Dear Mom and all,

".. I guess I told you I'm on a 24 hour shift this week; driving the camp guard. I drove almost continuously from 10:00 A.M. yesterday, till 6:45 this morning. I stayed in bed till noon but didn't sleep much. I guess I'll have to go to bed early tonight. I guess I also told you that we are going on two weeks maneuvers the rest of the week. I guess that will be some *fun?* because it is really cold at night and awful damp.

"I see Bob is a corporal now? How long ago was it that he signed up? He can't be very old can he?

"I haven't had any encouraging news concerning my transfer yet. If and when I get it I expect to go to New

Mexico or Arizona. However I guess they don't tell you until you get there."

11/16/42 Camp Shelby

"Dear Mom and all,

"Well I'm Twenty-One, and I feel like an old man already. I believe my hair is turning grey already. I should be home sometime Friday. I hope I get some money tomorrow, but if I don't I think I can borrow it someplace.

"I got a nice birthday present this morning: The Company Commander sent for me about 7:30 and gave me a paper authorizing me to appear before the Air Board and take the examination for Air Cadet.

"If I pass O.K. I'll be in the Air Corps before long. I sure hope I pass O.K. I take the test Wednesday the same day I am supposed to leave for home. I might be out on my furlough; so if I'm not home by Friday you know what happened.

"I don't think that I'll lose out on it though, but I won't know until Wednesday; so until then I'll expect the worst. I'm a little worried about the test, but maybe I'll be lucky. I think I'm about due for a break in this man's Army."

12/4/42

"Dear Mom and all,

"Just a line to let you know I arrived O.K. I got the letter with the money in it, and payed off my debts. I'm out in the field again, and it's plenty rough. Awfully damp, and chilly. I arrived in the middle of the night and had to pitch a tent in the dark. I passed my physical exam yesterday so now I guess I'll just have to wait. I'm laying on a blanket by a fire trying to write and it isn't so easy so I guess I'll quit. The wind changes about every 30 seconds and blows smoke in my face."

"Will try to write more Sunday."

1/5/43 Camp Shelby

"Dear Earl,

"I received your *long* letter yesterday and was glad to hear from you again. I also got the salami and it is gone already. I was out all night last night driving in a blackout. It was really tiresome, but plenty exciting too. I just got in at 10:30 this morning I'm awful sleepy, but can't sleep. Boy it was really cold in the "Jeep" last night with the top down. It got down to about 25 above zero and it feels about like it does when it is 10 below at home. I'm glad you got a new coach and I hope you like him better than I liked Wolf. I wrote Tib a letter the other day - I ought to hear from him about Saturday. I don't imagine he will be in Mississippi long, probably a month at the most. I bet it is really cold at home now, but as I've said before, I'd rather walk in snow up to my neck than endure this weather down here. The sardines were really good, and I enjoyed them very much."

2/6/43 Camp Shelby

"Dear Earl,

"I was glad to hear from you again. I hope you get to go with the team. I don't suppose they are winning many games this year. What do you want a fatigue hat for? Only prisoners wear them down here. I can't send you one, but I can bring it with me when I come home again. I'll probably get home around April or May. I'm working in the supply room almost all the time now. I don't do much, and I do hardly anything I don't want to do. I've really got a snap. I went to town last night and didn't get back until late. I had to wait until 3:30 to catch a bus back to camp. Today is Sunday so I guess I'll sleep most of the day. I'm glad the skating is good. I guess it has been cold enough that you should have had plenty of ice. I haven't anything to write about so I guess I'll close."

Then came a transfer to the Army Air Corps and a move in April 1943 to Keesler Field, Mississippi, where Erickson also served.

He wrote Earl from there:

4/29/43

"Dear Earl,

"I guess it's about time I dropped you a line. . . . .This isn't as bad as Camp Shelby, and it's a good place to get a tan . . . My face is burnt almost Black. I don't expect to be down here much more than a month; unless I get hooked as an airplane mechanic. That's what I wanted at first, but they have a school here, and I have no desire to stay here any longer than I absolutely have to. I may be able to get a furlough soon. As soon as Uncle Sam decides to pay off his debts I'm going to try. They owe me about $60.00 for this month, but I won't get it probably until next month; because I didn't sign the payroll this month. I couldn't as I was on shipment, and got redlined. Well guess I'll close.

In August, he went to Sioux Falls, South Dakota.

8/2/43 Army Technical School Sioux Falls, S.Dak.

"Dear Earl,

I received your letter a few days ago and I guess I should have answered sooner. However I thought I'd be home Sunday and Monday. I had things all fixed up so that I could have been home until Tuesday after noon, but I couldn't get in town in time to catch the train. I started hitch hiking and got stranded [in Iowa] about 180 miles from here. I finally grabbed a freight truck going the other way and spent the night in Sioux City. I came into camp on the train this morning. I might try it again next payday, but I don't know - it takes a lot of fixing.

"I got sort of a dirty deal the other day, along with a few other guys. They messed up, and didn't know we were qualified for flying duty. Anyway we were started in the wrong class; so we had to go back about five weeks and start over. I guess I'll graduate in October, and I'll expect a furlough about the same time. Guess I'll close."

He was transferred to Yuma Air Field in Yuma, Arizona in January, 1944, and then to Salt Lake City the following month. From there came a form letter:

2/25/44 Headquarters Army Air Base
Salt Lake City, Utah

"Dear Folks

"This letter will be a little different from most of those you receive from me. It's an arrangement that the Commanding Officer here at the Army Air Base, Salt Lake City, has made to keep our families informed of where we are and what we are doing. Since we will be here only a short time and will have plenty to do and little opportunity to write, this is a fine means of letting you know about this station and what we are doing here.

"Just a short while ago the train pulled into the siding and I found myself on the Army Air Base, Salt Lake City. It's a big place and plenty busy. It's part of the 18th Replacement Wing of Second Air Force. Nearly everyone assigned to Second Air Force passes through this base and after a few days here is assigned to a permanent Second Air Force Bomb Group or Air Base Squadron. The chief reason that everyone comes through this station is to be processed. I have just finished processing; which means simply that I was paid in full, issued what clothing I needed, physically examined, and all my records were brought up to date. Now when I leave here and go to my permanent station I will have everything necessary and there will be nothing to interrupt my training."

After this comes a last paragraph over which Ballou wrote by hand: "Disregard from here on down." As a P.S. he wrote "This does not mean I am going overseas."

Later came stays in Lincoln, Nebraska, and Boise, Idaho. Then Ballou went overseas. From Italy, on August 15, 1944, he sent Earl a V-mail:

"Received your letter and was glad to hear from you. Glad that your eye turned out O.K. too. I'm getting along fine and have quite a few missions in. They keep us pretty busy here, but it's not too bad. As soon as I get back to the States I'm going to quit flying. I've just about had my fill of it. I think the least Tib could do would be to let you know where he is and what he's doing. Myself I don't care what he does or whether I even hear from him again. We went swimming today and I almost decided to swim home, but it was too late and I was afraid I couldn't make it by dark. Guess I'll have to close so take it easy—don't work too hard.—Ralph."

There is another one swearing off flying!

This letter is undated but I presume from the contents it was 1944:

"Dear Earl,

"Guess maybe I should take time to drop you a line and let you know things are O.K. with me. If Dick H. gets home pretty soon and you see him you can probably get all the details about what goes on over here, and it's pretty interesting at times. I wish I had known his squadron before he finished up as I could have probably looked him up. I know he won't be around here someplace. Look Earl (I guess you'll be starting school pretty soon, so I want you to ask Mr. Anderson if he could make a writing desk—or if he has someone around who can make it and wants to make a little money on the deal. If he sounds interested let me know and I'll drop him a line and tell him what I want. Tell him I'll pay him any amount he thinks is reasonable. I want it to be for Xmas for Lorraine so don't say anything about it to her. I want one of those nice big walnut ones, I think he'll know what it is. So find out as soon as you can and let me know the deal right away. Things are O.K. here and I have about one fourth of my missions in. I'll sure be glad when I go on the last one. I had the heck scared out of me a couple of times but it isn't bad. Got some work to do, so I'll close.

As ever,
Ralph

The "Lorraine" referred to in this letter was Ballou's wife, the woman he married just before going overseas.

10/16/44

"Dear Earl -

"I finally heard from you tonight and also got a letter from Mom and Dad. I want one of those desks, but I want the big one they used to make, and not a small one. Hope I hear from you in a couple of days about it. I've been wondering why I haven't heard from home in so long—well one was dated the 4th—the 11th [Sept.] and the 9th. I got one last night dated the 15th which was sent air mail. The rest all had three cent stamps on them. I heard from Aunt Vi and she's griping cause she doesn't hear from Tib. I'm getting by O.K. and have 28 missions in now. I hope to finish up by December.

"If you can find out how much Mr. Anderson wants for the desk and I'll send him the dough payday. I gotta close cause I need some sleep but take it easy."

10/22/44

"Dear Earl,

"Just getting around as close to the stove as I can get. We had a ragged rainstorm tonight, and now it's getting cold. I'm writing letters trying to pass the time. I was going to go to the show but it's raining too hard. Has Tib started flying any missions yet? A lot of the boys are coming here from England. Guess they have a surplus over there. Our missions are coming few and far between now—I don't know why but I have a pretty good idea. Outside of the fact that I'm not flying much everything else is O.K. It gets sorta rough after the first 25 missions because we really sweat them out now. I wrote Andy and told him to send me a bill if and when he was able to get that desk made for me."

In the early days of the Fifteenth Air Force, planners were disappointed that in certain periods, missions were scrubbed by bad weather almost as often as in Northern Europe. They would have been reminded of this as the second winter rolled in.

11/2/44

"Dear Earl,

"Received your letter tonight, and was glad to hear from you. I guess I won't want the desk after all as Lorraine told me her mother bought her one; so if Andy hasn't gotten started on it tell him not to bother. Things are pretty dead around here, and I'm a little afraid I won't get my flying time this month. It's raining now and looks as though we'll have a bad one tonight. I can't tell you any more about my injury except that I was hit by a piece of flak, and was only grounded a short time. It is all O.K. now and doesn't bother me any.

"The hair hasn't grown back yet but it's coming along. I had the Purple Heart and air medal pinned on by the Colonel the other day, and the "Heart" is really a pretty medal. I had to walk out in front of the formation and salute the Colonel and felt like I was a big deal. I couldn't help but think though, all while I was getting the thing, that probably Dick's mother would be getting a Purple Heart soon. I'd sure hate to have Lorraine or Mom get one that way. I sent my medals to Lorraine yesterday so maybe you'll get to see them if they ever get there. Also I sent the piece of flak that hit me. Guess I'll close."

So *The Buzzer* had aboard two men - Arieff and Ballou - who had already suffered combat injuries. Not to mention Erickson's frostbitten hand.

11/14/44

"Dear Earl,

"Received your letter and was glad to hear from you. I worried some about your not writing (I know that my mail is delayed a lot of times, and besides I know how busy you must be with football and all. Things are quiet here and I'm just putting in my time and getting paid for it. I had guard duty until midnight last night, and had to get up for ground school this morning. They are just now - after 34 missions - telling us how to shoot at a fighter. This Army amazes me sometimes with its efficiency. I don't believe I told anyone before but my tail gunner shot down an enemy fighter. He's pretty proud of it too and has reason to be. It's sure getting cold at night and I expect it to snow at anytime, but I guess it never snows in this part of Italy. I know it does in some parts as we've flown over it and it really looks cold."

That tail gunner was probably Tom Skinas. Ballou's comments about only just then getting gunnery training are surprising, given that thousands of gunners, myself included, were graduating from specialized gunnery schools during the war. But his particular path to combat may not have included sufficient gunnery training.

12/1/44

"Dear Folks,

"Not much to write about, but I'll try and scratch a few lines. My crew hasn't finished yet, and we are waiting patiently for the eventful day. I've been spending my time doing some painting in the enlisted men's club. I don't care much for the job, but it helps pass the time and keeps me busy. I got a package from Aunt Emma the other day—not much in it, but it was nice. The weather has been acting up lately—not much rain, but it's cloudy most of the time. I can hardly wait until I get out of here, but I guess I can sweat it out O.K. Guess I'll close."

12/5/44

"Dear Mom,

"Received your letter several days ago and haven't answered mostly because I have nothing to write about. I'm sweating out my orders to go home and hope they come through soon. All the boys on the crew are done now, and I guess we've been pretty lucky . . . "

"Oh yes I made Tech. Sgt. because I wasn't up to the tables of organization, and couldn't ship without being promoted. I was sure glad to get it and hope I don't have any trouble holding it in the States. I'm getting some good recommendations out of this place which should do me quite a bit of good. Well I guess there's no more to say so Merry Xmas—Wish I could make it this year—it was pretty close though and I still have a chance. I haven't gotten your package yet."

His last letter home, dated December 8, the day before the crash, said he would be en route soon. Then, as with the other crewmen's families, there came the Government notifications.

A column in the local paper, "Men and Women in the Service of Their Country" noted that the twenty-three-year-old Ballou had finished his 39 missions—which probably equaled fifty-credits worth - traveling in the *Sleepytime Gal* to targets in Ploesti, Budapest, Munich, Toulon, and Vienna. The article describes Ballou as being "enroute home."

In September 1946, Earl got a letter from a friend of Ballou's. He talks about hearing the news of the crash from another passenger on his troopship ride home. He tells Earl to be sure to get a good education, and remembers Ralph: "Remember the trouble he had in Salt Lake City? Boy! What a fight. I know you are as proud of him as I am. He was one of the best damn soldiers in the U.S. Army."

Researcher Karen Alderson located Ballou's widow, Lorraine, now Lorraine Fowler. Lorraine married Ralph Ballou only six months before he was killed, but they had known one another for some time. When *The Buzzer* crashed, his wife had been making arrangements to go meet him when he was back in the U.S.

Captain Bache contacted her to offer condolences and help, as he did with the other crew families. She corresponded with Getty's parents, who were elderly, until the time of their deaths. She and her family put flowers on his grave every year. Mrs. Fowler's second husband was a survivor of the *Arizona,* sunk at Pearl Harbor.

Ballou's mother was also among those who corresponded with Mrs. Clemente, exchanging gifts for information.

In one of Karen Alderson's reports she described for me how she found Ballou's widow and siblings. After she studied the material I sent her, she called the local genealogy library to see if they had *Cedar Rapids Gazette* obituary clippings for 1944–45. They didn't. She explained to the volunteer what she was looking for and why and he offered to do some checking and call her back. She thinks he may have offered to do this even if they hadn't met and been members of the same genealogical society.

The society has scrapbooks of obituaries donated by local funeral homes, but Ralph's was not among them. The volunteer also tried cemetery indexes and found the listing we were looking for. Fortunately, according to Ms. Alderson, Cedar Memorial, a large private cemetery, has a staff that is "exceedingly kind" to genealogists. A phone call produced the information that Ballou was buried February 26, 1949, and that a marker was placed in 1966.

Ms. Alderson then went to the Cedar Rapids Public Library microfilm newspaper collection and searched all the papers for February 23–28, 1949. She found two funeral notices. Noticing that Ballou's wife was not mentioned in the 1949 notices, she went back to December 1944 and checked the newspaper for the time around the crash. Seeing that news of servicemen killed or missing in action generally appeared on Page One or a news page with continuations of page one stories, she focused her search on those pages.

She also realized that such events typically reached families and the newspapers about a month after they happened. A December 27th article was just published sixteen days after the crash but before Ballou's' family had been notified. Ms. Alderson stopped looking after finding the January 1st, 1945 "Missing" notice.

I had sent her a photocopy of a Cincinnati paper dated August 7, 1945, with a story about the death of one of the other crewmen. This was a clue about the timing of reports; Alderson tried to look in the *Cedar Rapids Gazette* for early August 1945, but the necessary reel of microfilm wasn't where it should be. She decided to continue the search through other sources. I had told her I had not been able to find family members by looking for Ballous in the phone book, so she tried to reach the sister, Audrey Morehead.

She found her in a current Cedar Rapids phone book. She double-checked that it was the right Audrey Morehead by looking in past phone books for 1975, 1945, and 1951. What were the odds of there being someone else with the same name? Ms. Alderson says there was another Ralph Ballou in Cedar Memorial.

As for the parents, she saw that a number of the directories had Edwin O. and Kathryn M. Ballou living at 1107 C Avenue NW, and felt confident in assuming that Edwin was the E.O. named in the newspaper articles. At the local Mormon Family History Center, she looked up the probable parents in the *Social Security Death Index,* finding an Edwin

Ballou born in 1893 and a Kathryn Ballou born in the same year. Edwin died in 1964 and Kathryn in 1983.

Ballou was originally buried in Naples, next to Caldwell's grave. He was brought home in February 1949, and buried in Cedar Memorial Cemetery. He received a posthumous Air Medal with three Oak Leaf Clusters for "meritorious service in aerial flight while participating in sustained operational activities against the enemy from July 30 to Aug. 13, Aug. 17 to Sept. 6, Sept. 8 to October 7, October 17 to Nov. 21."

Alex H. Eckerling

"He hated flying . . ."

Staff Sergeant Alex Herschel Eckerling was another member of Bache's crew on his way home, in his case to the Bronx. He was a waist gunner, exposed like all waist gunners to open air in all weathers, at all altitudes, and a high casualty rate. He was also listed as a radio operator.

His parents were David and Rose Eckerling. They lived on Westchester Avenue. In 1950, his mother's address was shown as care of his sister, Mrs. Hannah E. Zwickel, who also lived in the Bronx, at 931 Faile Street. That address is now the site of an expressway. Mrs. Zwickel died in 1976.

Alex had a relative, Arnie Eckerling, who now lives in Laguna Hills, California halfway between Los Angeles and San Diego. Arnie was sick in a hospital in Bari in southern Italy in November or December 1944, and Alex came to visit him. Grottaglie was close by.

Alex and Arnie's fathers were first cousins, Arnie told me. He said the Eckerlings came to America from a town in Poland. One Eckerling was an obstetrician in Jerusalem. He also said the Eckerlings are related to the Heckerlings, including film director Amy Heckerling, who made *Fast Times at Ridgemont High* and *Clueless*.

It is thought Alex attended Morris High School in the Bronx. Arnie was not well acquainted with Alex before the war. Soon after being shipped to North Africa, he tried to contact him, having heard he was in the same theater. However, they didn't link up until late 1944.

Arnie told me he first heard, in December, that Alex had been recovered from the crash. He thought Alex was alive.

In a 1998 letter to me, Tom Skinas wrote:

"Eckerling was another sort of guy. He hated flying and he was outwardly frightened when we were in flak or under attack. Yet we all tried to get along with him, but none of us could get close to him. He once accused us of not liking him because he was Jewish. He just had problems that I never understood, but none of us really disliked him."

Eckerling is buried with seven of his crewmates in the common grave at Jefferson Barracks National Cemetery.

449th Bomb Group Association

HUMANITARIAN SERVICE AWARD

TO

BENEDICT YEDLIN

As a ball turret gunner on Norm Rogers Crew in the 719th Bomb Squadron, Benedict Yedlin completed 50 missions from April through July 1944. His postwar activities have been many, particularly in research related to 449th aircraft losses and the survivors and families of lost members.

Especially noteworthy were his outstanding humanitarian actions related to the crash and loss of a B-24, "The Buzzer", in Italy in December 1944. Incidentally, "The Buzzer" had been the B-24 on which Ben had flown many of his combat missions. On its final flight, it was ferrying 449th 50-mission combat veterans to Naples for their return home.

After learning of "The Buzzer" crash, over a period of several years, he meticulously researched and pieced together the story of the crash and sixteen men lost in it. On his own initiative, he established contact with families of the crash victims to provide information he had obtained on the crash. His compassionate assistance provided great comfort to the families and helped many of them come to closure on the tragedy.

For this and his many other contributions throughout the history of the 449th, the Association is proud to present Benedict Yedlin this first Humanitarian Service Award.

Richard F. Downey, Lt.Col.

USAF (Ret)

AWARD OF THE SOLDIERS MEDAL

1. Under the provisions of AR 600 45, as amended, and pursuant to authority contained in circular no.26, Headquarters NATOUSA, 6, March 1944 the SOLDIERS MEDAL is awarded to M/Sgt. BARTHOLOMEO PELUSO 32795143, AIR CORPS, United States Army, residence at enlistment, Brooklyn, New York with the following citation;

For heroism at great risk of life at an allied airfield in Italy, on 2 February 1944. Observing a heavy bomber crash on take-off the following named enlisted man rushed to the scene of the burning aircraft, and with complete disregard to his own personal safety, forced his way through the burning debris, amid exploding ammunition rescuing (1) man and bringing him out to safety. Needless of the burning fuel, he again made his way into the wreckage, and carried out another unconscious crew member . . . attempting to rescue other crewmen whom he knew to be trapped, he was knocked to the ground by an explosion in the fuselage on the burning plane. Only when it became obvious that no hope remained for those remaining in the wreckage did he relax his efforts. The heroism and courage displayed by M/Sgt. Peluso in risking his life in an effort to save the lives of others, reflects great credit upon him and the Armed Forces of the United States of America.

BARTHOLOMEO (NMI) PELUSO 32795143 Master Sergeant, 719 Bombardment Squadron, 449 Bombardment Group Residence at enlistment, Brooklyn, New York.

Back To Italy

The actions of Mrs. Amelia Clemente were a source of varying opinions among relatives of the crash victims, as they discussed them in letters to each other after the war and in communications with me fifty years later. Even local people in Oliveto Citra were divided about her passing on the story of Donald Erickson's post-crash ordeal. She had even said that Erickson had carved something into a tree he was propped against, but, maddeningly, this message was never reported or seen.

Even the facts of what she did are not easy to pin down; for instance, some think she got relatives' addresses from letters removed from the bodies and wreckage, while others think she must have had official help in this, once the men were identified, whether it was against the rules or not.

Paul Watson's brother William, who met Mrs. Clemente, thinks she got his mother's address and the others from the American base at Naples, along with the other next of kin addresses. I asked if he thought it was likely that the registration people would give that information about a crashed plane's occupants to an Italian civilian.

"In a time of war . . . it is who is there at the time and what they feel like. Believe me there are a lot of things that go on that are not supposed to go on. And I could write a book about a lot of it."

But what about the idea that she got some addresses from mail found on the plane, on the dead crew and passengers?

"They wouldn't necessarily be carrying a bunch of mail. They were on their way home. You know what I mean?"

Of course, it seems that only seven of those aboard were on their way home.

Mrs. Clemente did receive this letter of thanks from the Allied Force Headquarters:

"30 August 1945

My dear Mrs. Clemente:

"It has been brought to my attention that you have performed splendid service in connection with the location of an American aircraft which crashed last December in the vicinity of Oliveto Citra. Reports received indicated that you personally secured the services of native guides, and at your own expense, investigated the scene of the crash, secured the remaining personal effects and reported the crash to the Allied Military Government authorities in Campagna.

"The Graves Registration Service is presently recovering the bodies of the deceased in order that reinterment in an established United States Military Cemetery may be accomplished. Without your efforts, given so willingly, it is feared that a much longer period of time would have elapsed before the wreckage of the aircraft was discovered.

"I extend my most sincere appreciation for your part in this incident, which again expresses the strong bond of fellowship which exists between the Italian and American people."

"C.W. Christenberry
Colonel, AGD
Adjutant General"

Luckily, I was able to read a pair of letters she sent to Caldwell's mother.

Oliveto Citra Feb. 21 1946

"Dear Mrs. Caldwell:

"I have received your most welcome letter today and quickly I am here to answer you. First of all I will tell you all I know about your son. I did not have your address that is why I could not communicate. Your son Julian has been identified by the identification card and his vaccination card I handed to the government. I found only a tag belonging to Mr. Ralph Ballou and a watch belonging to Lt. Arieff, but I have not his address and I am going to give it to Col. Cristenberry to have him send it to his wife.

"As soon as the plane hit the mountain top it went in flames and the poor boys burned except Sergeant Donald Erickson who remained alive and died after three days. He signaled for three days and nights, but nobody understood so the poor boy suffered because he was also wounded. The place where the accident happened is very dangerous to go. It is like a cleft in the mountain and the plane fell very deep. When I notified the Allies in Campagna, they came to see, but when they saw the place they refused to go down - and if I were not so constant, your sons would have been thought lost and they would have remained where the accident came. The government wanted to reward me for what I had done and for what I had spent for the guides that went down often for me. You see it is about 5 or 6 hundred yards deep and the rocks are slippery. When the Americans came to take out the bodies (all my merit) they had to go down with ropes, masks and all the special equipment. Most everything has been found burned and a very bad smell came from the bodies, who had been buried by the snow and when it melted the sun ray reflected on the wings of the plane. As soon as rumors came to me of the crash I quickly informed myself better and sent a few persons down to investigate. You see they went down for me because my husband has a good reputation in this town and helps many people. Any sum the Americans want to give they always refused, for the arduous travel to get on the spot. I have promised these men something from America and that is why I had asked for something out of use. If you prefer sending some money then let us know how much you want to give and I will pass this money to them even for charity for the dead - and with what you want to send, you can do me the favor of buying a pair of shoes size 4 for my son who is ten years old, and you may include 1 lb. of coffee, some candy some white and black cotton a few needles and a powder puff. Let me know what you spend, and I will pass what you want me to give the men here and the rest I will send to you. You see I want to keep them friendly yet, because as soon as I get some films I am going to have pictures taken of the place and the plane and then I will send a copy to you too. I am to get a fourth baby in May, and now I have been compelled to remain in bed for fifteen days, otherwise I would have been already to Naples where your son Julian has been buried. This is against Army regulations to inform you of the place in fact I have been already advised not to communicate this to you; Mrs. Hazel Cranmers' son, [William Watson] who was station here in Naples came to find me and asked about the former burial place and I told him so I am doing the same with you. I am going next week to the American Military Cemetery and if possible I will take pictures of the grave. I will also put some flowers with your name, as from you. On All Dead's Day Nov. 2 I had special mass celebrated for all the sixteen Boys who lost their lives in the plane accident.

"If you know some other parents of the deceased, I beg you to do as you have received - send a copy of my letter to them. I am very sorry the tag and watch and the rest of Julian's belongings have been burned. His jacket was all burned and the nine bodies that have been identified were one on top of the other. It results that they died immediately. I hope to get those films quickly so that now the snow melted it will be easier to go down.

"Hoping to hear from you soon, I pray you dispose of me in all I can do for you. In my next letter I will send you a copy of the letter the government sent me thanking me for the great part I have taken in the accident.

"May your Dear Son, pray for you and guide you through this thornful life and may He give you the strength to support this great irreparable loss.

"Yours sincerely,
Amelia Rufolo Clemente"

"P.S. You may send the pack directly to Oliveto Citra and please do not send me the stamps anymore. I thank you the same for them and will always be at your disposal for all you want to know."

Oliveto Citra June 15 1946

"Dear Mrs. Caldwell:

"With this morning's post, I have received your gift package which I have appreciated very much. And sincerely I do not find words to express my full thanks to you for your kind thought. I have given a pack of coffee to one of the men that has helped me in my mission. I have promised to take pictures of the place but a little because I could not find the films for my camera and even because we have had election day after twenty-three years here in Italy and the population was all by these different parties so the men that could have went on the place were absorbed and prayed me to wait a little longer. I am in bed now since June fourth, when at three o'clock in the afternoon the faithful stork prized me of a beautiful baby boy, who weighs four pounds and whom I named Londolfo Alfonzo Toby Rufolo, after an antic[sic] descendent of our family Rufolo, who in origin were princes of Ravello near Salerno on the Amalfitan coast and exactly the villa where Greta Garbo came to stay in for her vacation many years back before the war. I am now feeling better and gradually will leave the bed.

"I have received your package in perfect order and am very much content for what you have sent me and am mortified for your extreme kindness. The blue sweater is just cute and fits in color with the sex. We have no refined wool here and what I have are fine wool woven by hand and dyed at home and naturally it is not as soft as machine make kind. The shoes are a little bit big but I will keep them for next year. Everything fits well, and again I repeat my deep and sincere thanks to you. I wish some day, or better as soon as the Italian government permits us to send things to

America, I will not forget you and will send you some embroideries which I am sure you will like and appreciate.

"It is night and in the town there has been some movement for the results of the election. They have voted for the new government and if the population wanted the republic or the King. The northern part of Italy voted for the republic and the south for the King. The truth is that the north that is nearer to Russia and more Communist and they cheated to send the King away. The southern would like revenge and started to strike and parade in favor of the King, who really could have stood at the head of the nation and helped the population. But now the King has left and everybody is very sorry and feel bad for their Highness they have lost. Even the living has become more difficult. They have cut rations. You cannot find sugar anymore. America does not send anymore. Before we could have bought it on the black market but now there are very few Americans and you do not find it. Let us hope that things will change in better soon. Fortunately we produce some wheat so that we will not lack of the main food, especially for my children.

"As soon as I leave the bed I will have some pictures taken. They have promised that the end of the month a photo man is to come here so I will take this chance and send one to you.

"I have received a picture from Mrs. Ganim in which I have learned her lost boy's features. What a beautiful boy! Everytime I think of those boys I feel very badly, sympathizing with their families. I often have masses celebrated in their honor and when I go to Naples again I will return to their graves and put flowers on them. I think your Julian is filed on row seven - but I will get you his exact number. The last time, and that is on April 4, I have been to the Military Ceremony and saw all the graves of the sixteen boys, but I do not remember exactly their graves' numbers. I have spoken to a major about when it was possible for the corpses to go back in the states and he assured me they are to go some day but they had no idea for the moment. He promised to keep me informed about it. Everytime I go to Naples I will believe it my duty to see about it and have you know of every move they intend to do.

"I pray you excuse me as till now I have not gotten any pictures taken yet but it was for the reasons I have written before in this letter. Now that I am feeling better I will again gain full interest and try my best to find the films in Naples.

"Wishing to hear from you soon, I pray you accept my full sympathy and thanks from my husband and my children. May the Soul of your Beloved Julian guide you and your dear ones all your life through."

"Yours sincerely,
Amelia Rufolo Clemente"
Oliveto Citra
Salerno

I asked Paul Watson's brother, William, what his feelings about Mrs. Clemente were: "Well, I thought at the time that she was quite a nice lady. You know that she had gone out of her way to do a lot of things. I know she asked mother and some of them to send them stuff but you have to understand that at that time in Italy, the Germans had overrun Italy and when they were pulling out, and while they were there, they raped the whole country. People would give money and stuff but they didn't have anything. They didn't have clothes, they didn't have anything. Nothing they could buy. In fact they were trying to buy clothes off of us GIs, you know. Paying the exorbitant prices even for dirty socks. And when we first got there, they also didn't have food. You know, very little. And they would do almost anything just for C-rations.

"So I wouldn't put the blame on her [for] wanting something."

I asked if he didn't think she was using the accident to get stuff?

"I never got that impression at all. Some may have. But I never did and . . . what she asked for wasn't anything expensive, you know. She asked for just things that they could use and couldn't get. And I think anybody in that predicament would have done that. She was a very kind and straight forward person."

Watson also helped explain the authorities' letter of thanks to Mrs. Clemente. He told me that after she sent the personal effects that had been gathered to the authorities in Naples, she "tried to get them to go up and get [the bodies.] And they wouldn't even talk to her because of the winter and said that they wouldn't even begin to do anything until the thaw. But then in the spring they [weren't] doing anything either. And my mother started getting on the War Department and I started getting on the authorities down there. I was a tech sergeant at the time, and could get into some circles, you know."

"She didn't just go down there [to Naples] once, she went down there several times trying to find out why they weren't doing anything. And I think that maybe somebody may have given her some names and addresses to get rid of her."

I asked Watson's brother if he thought Mrs. Clemente had worked hard to get things moving. He said "I got that impression. I had that impression all the time. I never once had an impression that she was trying to make something out of it."

"And the pressure was put on and finally they decided to go in. And by that time, the remains were so mangled up and everything that most of them [were] listed as 'one or more of the following.' You know."

Gene Gettys told me, " . . . the folks being concerned and everything they were a little disturbed at the slowness of the government. Of course we never really did get anything out of them and then one of them got this letter and they contacted the Air Force and they said don't have anything to do with her. From what I could gather . . . I guess that's what . . . a few of the people got and not to do anything in regard to this letter, maybe it was a sham; of course the war was still on at that time and they thought, well just to stay away from her. Then looking back in retrospect, I mean, she knew an awful lot more than the government."

Once I got involved in this investigation, I never doubted that I would go to Italy to find out what I could about the crash site and Mrs. Clemente (though I knew she was no longer living (and the surrounding villages of Oliveto Citra and Senerchia. So far I have been there three times since getting interested in *The Buzzer*.

My first visit produced real evidence that *The Buzzer* had gone down nearby. Not that there was any doubt of the general location of the crash; after all, U.S. officials had removed the bodies several months after the crash. Nevertheless it was a very emotional experience to find actual remains of the plane, despite the difficulty of pinning down the precise spot where the bomber came down.

For one thing, a woman named Antonia Di Giorgio had a collection of paper money from Trinidad, Brazil, Senegal, and Tunisia—the typical souvenir money collected by Fifteenth Air Force bomber crews who flew from the States to Italy. For some reason, we all called these little collections "short snorters." She said it had been given to her by a local peddler. I knew it had to have originally come from one of our planes.

In fact, Evelyn Dunlop, Donald Erickson's sister, wrote to me that Captain Bache had told her mother that a quantity of money and gifts had been aboard *The Buzzer*.

Later I found a bucket that had once been part of an oxygen tank, and a section of fuselage. I had help in identifying these by B-24 experts Allan Blue and Roger Criplever.

The oxygen tank is now on my porch. I also discovered that a wedding dress had been fashioned out of the silk of someone's parachute.

I had learned in Romania that it was common to make wedding dresses from parachute silk, and a former Romanian antiaircraft gun operator told me women made hair decorations from "window."

My first two trips were in 1996. I already knew the plane was down in a hard to reach area. That proved right. But I thought it was in Oliveto Citra, and that was the wrong town. The crash site was actually in the municipality of Senerchia, although in real terms it was in rough country between the two towns.

On the first trip, my friend Toni Flint and I flew to Rome, and then drove five or six hours to Oliveto Citra. Like most towns in Italy, Oliveto Citra has remnants of ancient times. There is an Iron Age necropolis nearby, and Etruscan and Greek-influenced objects have been unearthed in the area. It is thought the local people were part of a league that opposed Roman power in the first century B.C. The vicinity was in the news in the 1980s for being one site in a nationwide spate of people claiming to see religious visions. It is a small town; there were fewer than four thousand residents in 1991.

The neighboring town of Senerchia is a town of the Middle Ages, badly damaged in a 1980 earthquake. Both are in the Campagna region.

Despite knowing the plane was in the mountains, I was hopeful, even confident, that I could reach the actual crash site, and find some real remnants of the plane. I knew many portable parts had been scavenged by local people very quickly after the crash, but I thought heavy parts - particularly the four engines - should still be there somewhere.

I was disappointed not to find the actual crash site. But the remnants we found carried as much emotional weight as I would want.

We found warm personal welcomes there, not only among people I met officially but just among passers-by. As we would walk along the main street or sit in the piazza, people would approach us and engage in conversation, many offering whatever they had heard about *The Buzzer.* Of course, most of what people told me was hearsay or double hearsay or beyond.

But one farmer knew very clearly that sixteen men had been aboard the plane. That accuracy was startling after almost fifty years. He was the man who had part of one of the plane's oxygen tanks. His had straw at the bottom and a home-made handle to complete its transformation into a bucket. Then we heard that a farmer was using some part of the plane as the roof of a garden shed.

My interpreter, Serafino Acquaviva, son of a Chicago jeweler who had returned to Italy, was our source for the exciting information that Amelia's husband, Dr. Vito Rufolo, still lived in the area. But it turned that that Dr. Rufolo could tell us nothing, because, amazingly, he knew nothing of his wife's activities in regard to the crash and the letters to and from America.

In addition Serafino's uncle, a restaurateur, drove Toni and me and Serafino around the area. Serafino spoke to two local farm women, and one of them pointed to her husband's garden shed.

The farmer and Serafino and I ripped the decades-old vines from the shed's roof. I took one look at its corrugated metal surface and the hair on the back of my neck stood up.

I was looking at one of *The Buzzer's* bomb bay doors.

It had a huge emotional impact on me. As a ball turret gunner, I had spent a lot of time close to those doors, looking up at them. I knew very well what they looked like. It was one thing to have information that the plane had crashed in this area; it was another to see a piece of it again, after half a century.

At first I didn't feel good about the way the doors had ended up. People have pointed out to me that it was like recycling, just like the wartime use of parachute silk for wedding dresses or the use of aluminum chaff as hair decoration. But I couldn't help feeling it was an ignominious end. Ton later wrote "Serafino was hacking away at 50 years worth of growth, and then to my amazement, the gray metal roof of the barnyard structure came into view. Ben exclaimed, "That looks like bomb bay doors!" I was dumbstruck! I had heard so much about *The Buzzer* from Ben, that the aircraft had become personified to me. And to see portions of it being made use of by a farmer, made me almost want to cry. That brave plane, having survived dangerous combat missions, only to come to an ignominious and tragic end, lived on in parts, still in service."

On my second trip, later that year, I found a complete oxygen tank, and learned that parts of the fuselage were being used as walls in an animal pen. Altogether I have recovered about twelve parts from the airplane, not much when you consider its size and many thousands of parts. I also had help from the men of the local climbing club, whose friendliness and hospitality extended to rappelling down the thickly grown, very steep mountainside in search of a definite wreckage site. They found nothing.

I should add that I wasn't thinking I'd find some part of the wreckage that would be a vital clue, suddenly revealing why the plane crashed. It's possible that some mechanical problem, apart from icing, caused the disaster.

Even though bombers in the line had to undergo progressive inspections of different systems arranged so that complete inspections were accomplished periodically, problems arose and planes went down because of them. Icing remains a strong candidate. Planes could ice up to a dangerous degree in minutes.

It was also on the second visit, on my way back north to Rome and Fiumicino Airport, that I visited the Sicily-Rome American Military Cemetery, just east of Anzio, where three of *The Buzzer* crash victims, Baldwin, Erickson and Marple, are buried. It was late in the afternoon and the trees and grave markers cast long shadows. In the visitor's building I was given a plan of the cemetery and a computer printout showing the three grave locations.

It is hard to fully express how it felt to see and walk among thousands of crosses and Stars of David and read the names. There are 7,862 graves here, and in the chapel are engraved the names of 3,095 missing. I was so angry! And I said to myself, "How could this have been a 'good war?' Here were buried men killed on land, on the sea, in the air, thousands of miles from their homes.

I went back a third time, in 1998, with a film crew, and was given a piece of armor plate by a man in his nineties. Even after three trips to Italy and many trips to our old target, Ploesti, and travel all across the U.S. to meet with relatives of the men killed on *The Buzzer*, I still keep asking myself "Why me?" Why did I survive the war, and why didn't these guys?

Since the war I have found out a lot more about the statistics of my good luck and the bad luck of the men who died on *The Buzzer*. Statistically, the ball turret gunner supposedly had the safest of the gunner's positions, in terms of battle injuries. The waist gunners had it worst.

Of course when a plane was going down, the ball turret gunner was the least likely to get out. I knew that when I was flying missions, and I didn't know that I was statistically safest from getting shot.

As accident victims, the men on *The Buzzer* were, sadly, far from unusual. During the war, more than 35,000 U.S. airmen died in noncombat situations. In 1943 alone, 850 men died in 298 B-24 accidents. According to the AAF Guide published in 1944, there were six accidental deaths per 100 hours flown in the second half of 1943. This was apparently about the same as the decade before the war, and a big improvement on 1942–43.

Back To Ploesti

In 1993, when I was producing *B-24 Bomber Crew*, I decided it would be interesting to get some footage of present-day Ploesti.

I wrote to the Mayor of Ploesti telling him I hoped to visit, that the 2,000-generator smokescreen had been so heavy on my six wartime airborne "visits" that I'd never seen the city or its refineries. I also asked for official permission to do some filming, interviewing, and general information-gathering on the bombings of nearly fifty years earlier.

I drafted the letter in English and it was translated for me by Simona Tata, a Romanian from Constanta, the Black Sea coast city which was the target of my eighteenth mission. She worked as a mother's helper for friends who had adopted four HIV-positive children from Casa Speranta, a home for HIV-infected children in Constanta.

Some of my friends couldn't understand why I wanted to go; they said things like "You'll be lynched!" But I got a very warm and welcoming letter in response and made my first trip in June 1993, flying Tarom nonstop from JFK to Bucharest. I became enchanted with the people. This was only a few years after the fall of the Ceaucescu dictatorship, and Americans were something of a novelty; they were welcomed in Romania, especially outside Bucharest.

I made a second trip in October of that year, bringing eleven cases of baby vitamins, toothbrushes, toothpaste, and Band-Aids donated by Johnson & Johnson and Bristol-Myers Squibb. At my request, Tarom, the Romanian airline, waived freight charges for the supplies, and Mayor Savulescu provided transport from Bucharest to Casa Speranta.

Six months later, I went again, and took part in an international colloquium on the significance of the Ploesti raids, titled "Oil and Bombs in Ploesti." Participants included Romanian academics and local officials, diplomatic representatives from the U.S., the U.K., Canada and Germany, and veterans of the anti-aircraft guns and Romanian fighter defenses.

I spoke on the bombing campaign from information I had and from my own experience, describing the diversity of my crew and the details of the B-24 and its ordnance. POWs were recalled by a Romanian, and we heard the perspective of the former manager of the Romano-Americana Refinery, Acad. Dr. Eng. George Radulescu, who had lived through the campaign on the ground.

I made another trip in December 1994, bringing more children's supplies. In Romania, I met a Doctor "Danny" Anastasiu who had treated a number of downed American airmen during the war. He had me try to get in touch with one of them whose leg he had amputated, John Dudley Palm, of Lower Valley, Texas. Palm was a pilot whose plane was shot down during the famous 1943 raid on Ploesti, undertaken by hundreds of Eighth and Ninth Air Force bombers based in North Africa.

This raid, Operation Tidal Wave, caused a lot of damage but cost us more than fifty planes, and more than 500 crew with them. Palm's exploits feature in several accounts of that famous raid, including *Aerial Gunners: The Unknown Aces of World War II*, by Charles A. Watry and Duane L. Hall. They describe how Palm's plane, *The Brewery Wagon*, part of the 376th Bomb Group, was isolated when it headed for the correct Initial Point while "the" lead group made a wrong turn on the way to target.

According to Watry and Hall, Palm's bomber was hit in the nose by flak, and the navigator and bombardier were both killed. The ship was badly damaged. Palm's leg was wounded so badly he couldn't fully work the controls. The crew unloaded their bombs and turned for home, but a fighter attacked next and the bomber went down. Everyone still alive on the plane survived the crash, and the crew were taken prisoner.

Palm and Dr. Anastasiu had become friends and Dr. Anastasiu wanted to try to get in touch with Palm; but so repressive was the Ceaucescu regime that simply writing a letter to Texas was out of the question. Back in the States, I managed to find a relative of Palm's, but unfortunately Palm himself had died by then.

✈ ✈ ✈ ✈ ✈

Of course, in revisiting Ploesti I was more thoughtful about what it must have been like to be on the receiving end of all those bombs. On my missions there my great concern about getting out alive. As for the people on the ground, they were shooting at us!

Later, when I made my peacetime visits to the oil city and met Romanian antiaircraft gunners at a function at a Romanian Military Museum, I was able to appreciate that they were, after all, defending their own country. I now exchange letters with one of them regularly. I also became more aware of the complexities of Romania's alliance with Hitler - that it wasn't universally popular in Romania.

Yet, I still had different feelings about meeting Romanian fighter pilots. They, too, may have been defending their homeland, but they seemed more like personal enemies than the men firing flak guns four miles below us. When I was first offered an introduction to some Romanian pilots, I wasn't interested. My decision was made easier by the fact that the local man who offered to make the introductions wanted a hundred dollars for it! No, thanks.

Eventually I did meet some Romanian pilots and it wasn't so bad. It was interesting to hear them say that when they were attacking a formation of our bombers, they were scared. There was certainly plenty of fear to go around.

In his unpublished memoir, *The Twenty Weeks of Ploesti,* George A. Radulescu, who was a senior manager at the Romano-Americana Refinery [Standard Oil Company of New Jersey, now Exxon,] detailed the view from the ground during the oil campaign.

He says that the routine of a raid started with an early warning, thanks to German spotters on the Adriatic shore of occupied Yugoslavia; smoke generation and fighter scrambling; the bomber attack itself; and the rapid deployment of German firemen and engineers to get oil flowing again as soon as possible.

When we blew up a big storage tank, the results were spectacular, but it was not as serious a loss to production as damage to processing plants and pumping stations. Many facilities had blast walls around them up to a yard thick.

Ploesti had already been well defended when the big 1943 raid took place, but afterwards there were many drills and practices but no raids until our sustained 1944 campaign started.

However, says Radulescu, on April 4, 1944, there was an alert, and this time, people heard "unusual thuds from the sky and from the ground." It was the noise of the Bucharest raid, the same raid that caused so many casualties in the 449th the day before my crew arrived at Grottaglie. The next day was the first of the many Ploesti raids of that summer, raids that did not end until the Soviets occupied the oilfields in August.

When Radulescu heard, after the Bucharest raid, that Calea Victoriei, the main street of the city, was on fire, he took a train to the city. His wife was at home in their apartment on that street.

With transportation in chaos, he didn't reach his home till two in the morning, "to see big flames coming through the windows of our flat." He tried calling his sister, but no one answered because her house had also been bombed, and he eventually found his wife at 4:00 A.M. staying with friends. Everything they owned had burned. He moved his wife to his parents' home outside the danger area, and continued to stay in bachelor quarters near the refinery.

Amazingly, he says that men stayed in the refinery shelters during the first few raids, to minimize the halt in production. But soon they realized it was safer to get away from the refineries altogether when the alert sounded. There was still a routine, and a place for everyone on some vehicle leaving the plant.

Night raids by the R.A.F. cost him sleep even when his refinery wasn't targeted, adding to the difficulty of daily life. He used a bicycle to make a quick commute to the nearby vineyard where his wife had moved. But the location was still too close; besides the noise of bombs and antiaircraft fire, there was a dangerous hail of flak shell splinters. He recalls seeing storks flying out of their nests in trees when the raids started.

Before one raid, he and his wife went further into the upland vineyards, for a meal of "sheep cheese, home-baked bread, and the famous Romanian wine" with some local people. And they ate as the raid went on not many miles away:

"As the roar of the engines became louder, the oncoming bombers appeared gleaming in the sky, while they dispensed metalized paper strips to confuse the German radar. The suspense was over when the heavy flak guns bellowed out a wild reception. I saw planes being blasted to bits and others turning to balls of fire. While the aerial show grew in cruelty, we saw many parachutes opening, bloating like silvery mushrooms, and small-arms fire was increasing.

"Huge oil storage tanks were exploding, raising solid columns of fire and debris several hundred feet high . . . shells and bombs wove an integrated pattern of annihilation."

I was quite likely in one of the planes up there that day. He returned to the refinery afterward.

"I saw first hand the gruesome spectacle of the roaring burning tanks and bellowing flames from the processing plants. As a German fireman was fighting the fire at one

tank, it got white-hot and buckled, while the ladder col-
lapsed and the man fell inside the burning gasoline."

Radulescu and his wife had a close encounter with our
side the one day we tried dive-bombing targets at Ploesti with
P-38 Lightning fighter-bombers. After the alert, he got to his
wife in the vineyard and was surprised that the bombers were
half an hour "ahead of schedule." The P-38s came in at tree-
top level, and one of the pilots waved at his wife.

It's worth remembering again that Romanians were by
no means all staunch Axis supporters. Pilots on the great
1943 raid reported people on the ground en route to the target waving to them.

On this occasion, Radulescu was not pleased; it was the
first raid to target his refinery, a few miles away from the
rest. His bachelor quarters were destroyed, along with his
books and other belongings.

Still, he says he enjoyed the raids, partly because they
hurt Hitler. He says most people became petrified as the attacks grew in intensity over the weeks, " . . . but I took de-
light in seeing Hitler's gasoline and diesel oil burning and
seeing exploding jerry cans by the thousands. As the days
and weeks wore on, the air raids became a great pleasure for
me. I enjoyed them further as the greatest thrill of my life."

He got more than a thrill one day in early August,
after my own missions were finished. As usual, he was ped-
aling away from the plant after an alert. He was offered
a lift by the refinery manager, so he hid his bike under a
fir tree and the two men drove away. Before long, some of our
fighters zoomed overhead. The manager stopped the car and
the men fled into a cornfield, but were surprised when the
fighters pursued them and seemed to be strafing them. Then
they realized the reason: their hiding place was less than a
hundred yards from an antiaircraft gun. Neither of them
was hit, but "for the first time I was scared to death."

They surveyed the terrific damage to the refinery after
the raid. "Great sheets of liquid were oozing from a big tank,
and everywhere great fires were roaring. The firemen could
no longer fight the blazing heaps of drums and jerry cans

ready for dispatch to the approaching Russian front." The place where he had hidden his bike was now a bomb crater.

Toward the end, though he could still get a lift to the vineyard and dine and drink wine with his wife while the raids took place, morale and conditions deteriorated. He says many soldiers in charge of smoke generators deserted their posts when the alert siren sounded. "They were shot without judgment."

By the end, when King Michael switched sides, "there was almost no plant, storage tank, pumping station, or building" that had not been hit by the bombs.

When visiting Ploesti, I saw an old Jewish cemetery and asked, with foreboding, what had happened to the local Jewish community during the war. I was told that local Jews fared better than in other parts of the country, and that Allied bombers had killed some of the people now in that cemetery. I thought that was ironic, to say the least.

Afterword

I started my search for relatives of men who died on *The Buzzer* with a walk through Manuel Suarez' old neighborhood and will finish this story with comments on Suarez from three men:

> "Citation of Honor
> United States Army Air Forces
> Staff Sergeant Manuel Suarez
> Who gave his life in the Performance of his duty
> December 9, 1944
>
> "He lived to bear his country's arms. He died to save its honor. He was a soldier. . . and he knew a soldier's duty. His sacrifice will help to keep aglow the flaming torch that lights our lives. . . that millions yet unborn may know the priceless joy of liberty. And we who pay him homage, and revere his memory, in solemn pride rededicate ourselves to a complete fulfillment of the task for which he so gallantly has placed his life upon the altar of Man's freedom.
>
> "H.H. Arnold
> General of the Army
> Commanding General, Army Air Forces"

"In Grateful memory of
Staff Sergeant Manuel Suarez
Who died in the service of his country
In the Mediterranean Area, December 9, 1944.
"He stands in the unbroken line of patriots who have
dared to die that freedom might live, and grow, and
increase its blessings.
"Freedom lives, and through it, he lives - in a way
that humbles the undertakings of most men.

Franklin D. Roosevelt"

The last paragraph of a letter Frank Suarez sent me
soon after I contacted him reads:
"We were overwhelmed with grief after receiving notification that Manuel was MIA in 1944 and ultimately, when
The Buzzer was found two years later in 1946 at Olivetto
Citra, Italy and Manuel confirmed dead. Manuel's death
aboard *The Buzzer* on the ill-fated night of December 9,
1944, along with his comrades will never be forgotten. We
were not mistaken that someone, somehow would not forget their sacrifice and the names of the fallen and *The
Buzzer* would again be spoken, written about and brought
to light. Our family never lost hope some illuminating word
would ultimately be received. And so it was."

Appendix

From M. Suarez's manual checklist:

Before Starting Engines: (Outside Airplane)
1. On each landing gear and the nose gear check:
   Tire—Blisters, cuts, inflation, slipping on rim
   Oleo strut for extension (see placard)
   Load & fire valve piston fully extended
   Brake shuttle valve (no play)
   Hydraulic lines for excessive leakage
   Down lock fully engaged - no cracks
2. Ground landing gear locks removed from struts.
3. Check red signal on Lux fire extinguisher
4. With crew member in airplane:
   a. Check ailerons, elevators, rudder and all trim tabs for free and maximum movement.
   b. Extend fully and retract flaps, check for free and even movement and condition of flap chamber.
5. Nose wheel: not turned.
6. Wheel chocks in position.
7. Pitot covers off.
8. Visual check of each engine from in front for any loose wires on connections or loose cowling, DSUZ fasteners, etc.

(Inside airplane)

1. Check pressure—emergency bomb bay air bottle 1800#.
2. Fuel transfer valve: off.

3. Fuel transfer pump: off.
4. Fuel valves on (saftied)
5. Hydraulic tank gauge: full.
6. Emergency brake bottle pressure 1000#: Valve on bottle: open, Air Release Valve: closed.
7. Check loading: All sand bags and other articles in rear tied down (nothing left loose.
8. Check fuel - Complete fuel supply form.
9. Have prop turned by hand two or three revs. (ignition off) If not done within previous hour.
10. Check form No. 1 for completeness and status of airplane.
11. Make out local clearance form.
12. Emergency procedure pamphlet: aboard
13. Radio facility chart and maps of area to be covered in flight: aboard
14. Tools: Pliers, diagonal cutters, 6"screwdriver and crescent wrench: aboard.
15. Brakes set and pressure up.
16. Parachutes available and worn by all members of crew - - life vests available and worn on all over water flights.
17. Check emergency exits for proper security (pilot's hatch release pins in securely)

STARTING ENGINES

Use source other than battery for starting engine[?] in emergency

1. Parking brakes-on.
2. Control flaps-open
3. Landing gear control-down-lock on.
4. Superchargers-low blower
5. Oil shutters-open
6. Carburetor air-cold

7. Nose gear emergency control-normal (up)
8. Main gear emergency control-normal (up)
9. Mixture control-idle cut off
10. Propeller control-high rpm (forward)
11. Throttles-open approximately 2"
12. Propeller switch-automatic
13. Propeller feathering switch-normal (guard down)
14. Main inverter switch-on
15. Spare inverter switch-off
16. All lighting switches and rheostats-off (if not needed)
17. Master ignition switch-on
18. Magneto switches-on
19. Battery switches-on
20. Start auxiliary motor on signal from pilot
21. Start engines
    a. Booster pump-on-for engine being started
    b. Press starter energizing switch (30 seconds)
    c. After engaging switch has been actuated and engine is turning over, press electric priming switch sufficiently to start engine firing, but not over 5 seconds, and then release priming switch
    d. In extremely cold temperatures or if difficulty is encountered in starting engines-prime as in 21c above and after engine is turning over push mixture control to "auto rich" momentarily and then back to "idle cut off" position. Hold for slow count of about 5 and repeat the operation with the mixture control if engine does not fire.
    e. Oil pressure-stop engine if no pressure in 15 seconds
    f. Idle 600 normal and taxiing
    Not under 800 prolonged idling or taxiing
    Not under 1000 for final warm up and awaiting take off at runway
    g. Hydraulic pressure (750 # to 950#)
    h. Booster pump off
    i. Start right engine–(a to h above)

GROUND AND TAKE OFF CHECK

1. M/P: - Set to 25" (oil temp. min. of 40(C)
2. Check magnetos at 2000 rpm (approx. 25"mp) drop of not over 60 rpm
3. Reduce engine speed approx. 200 rpm with prop control handle
4. Return prop control to high rpm-note rpm returns to former speed
5. Repeat item 3 and 4 using manual prop selector switch
6. Increase M/P momentarily to about 40". Rpm should be about 2500
7. Reduce throttles to 1000 rpm
8. Return prop selector switch to automatic
9. Booster pumps-on
10. Battery switches: on auxiliary power unit (putt-putt) off
11. Mixture control "auto rich" for take off
12. Generator-voltmeter-check with both engines at 1900 rpm voltmeter 28.5: if difference in generator readings is greater than 15 amps-investigate
13. Oil temperature–60(C
14. Oil pressure–75 [div by sign] 10lb
15. Fuel pressure–16 div by 1lb
16. Cylinder temperature-do not take off if over 205(C
17. Tabs-as required
18. Wing flaps down (down if necessary to clear obstacle)
19. Hatches-closed and locked
20. Propeller warning lights-not glowing
21. Hydraulic pressure–750# to 950#
22. If idled any length of time while waiting for take off clear engines by running up at 1900 or 2000 temporarily before starting take off run
23. Remove landing gear control lock
24. Check controls for free movement
25. Do not raise landing gear until pilot gives definite signal

AFTER TAKE OFF

1. Raise landing gear on signal from pilot
2. Reduce M/P and then rpm to 38" and 2400 rpm
3. Raise flaps by increments (above 300 feet at between 150–160 mph)
4. Cowl flaps: regulate according to cyl. head temperature
5. Oil coolers: regulate according to oil temperature
6. Adjust m/p and rpm as desired. Synchronize.
7. Booster pumps: off when climb is complete
8. Auto lean not above 30" mp on 2800–41 and 2800–43 engines Side Slip Will Cause Engine To Quit

LANDING

1. Antenna-in
2. Loading: 1 crew member to rear turret area if less than 250 gals. In tanks.
3. Fuel-sufficient in *main tanks*
4. Mixture controls-auto rich
5. Booster pumps on
6. Propeller controls–2400 rpm
7. Landing gear-down (150 mph) *leave control in down position*
8. Check indicators (dial and horn) for gear down
9. Flaps pull down (150 mph)
10. Hydraulic pressure: 750–950

AFTER LANDING

1. Complete landing roll before moving any levers
2. Cowl flaps: open
3. Oil coolers: open
4. Wing flaps: up
5. Propeller control-full forward
6. Booster pumps off

7. *Landing gear control safety lock: on*
   For additional take offs use asterisk items of "Before starting engines" and all of "Ground and take off" checks
8. *Stop with nose wheel straight*
9. Rpm 800 to 1000
10. Mixture control: To idle cut off
11. Throttles: Slowly full forward as engine stops *firing*
12. All switches off-ignition-radio-inverters-generators-battery-lights
13. Parking brakes: off until brakes cool

Barracks cleaning, Fort Belvoir, Virginia

The Buzzer crew officers left to right: Bennett, Rogers, Carlson, Hinds

B-24 crash March Field, California

Sahara Desert enroute to Grottaglie

Roma dirigible hangar Grottaglie base

Wrecked German and Italian Aircraft—Grottaglie Base

Wrecked German aircraft, JU88

The Buzzer crew left to right top row: Simons, Yedlin, Bennett Hinds, Cox
bottom row left to right: Rogers, Carlson, Rizan, Acosta, (stand in for Girton)

Buck Rogers - Pilot

Bobbie Bennett - Co-pilot

Shorty Carlson - Navigator

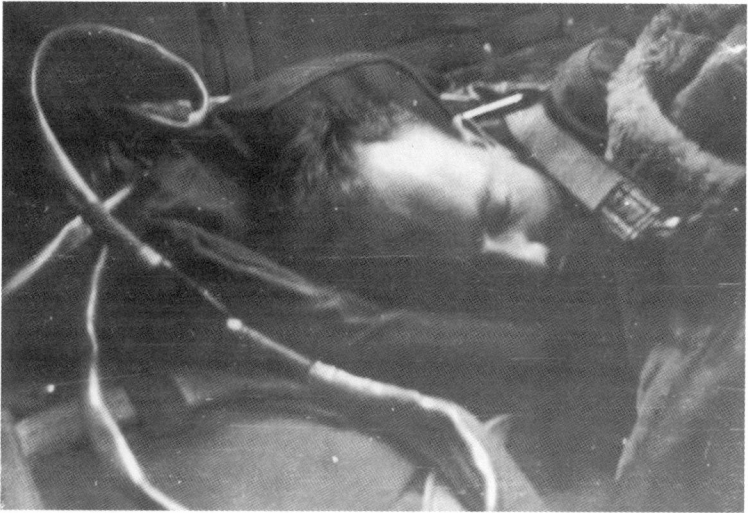

Baldy Hinds - Bombardier

Phil Rizan - flight engineer/top turret
gunner

Rudy Acosta - radio operator/waist gunner

Bob Simons - nose gunner

Jack Cox - tail gunner

Dean Girton - waist gunner

Ben Yedlin Italy 1944, alongside The Buzzer.

Bart Peluso-ground crewchief

The Buzzer ball turret, Ben Yedlin's position

Ball turret B-24

Rest camp at Santa Cesarea Terme

The Buzzer crew at rest camp left to right: Girton, Carlson, Bennett, Italian kid, Hinds, Rogers

Beach at Pulsano - left to right: Yedlin, Rizan, Acosta

The Buzzer

The Buzzer in formation

Ben horsing around with Armando, our errand boy

Ben horsing around on 500# bomb

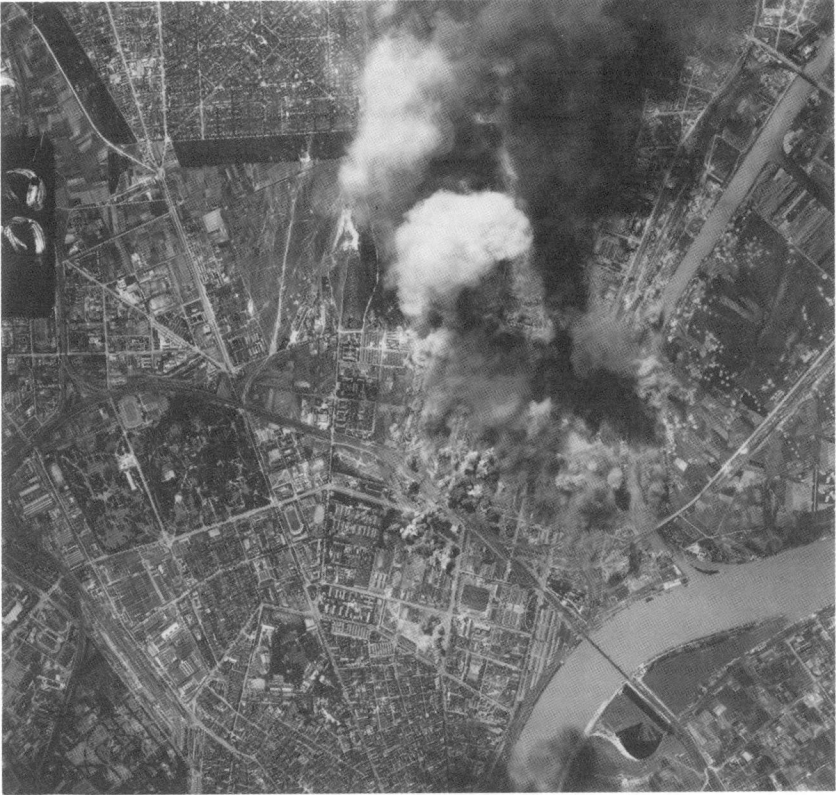

Budapest bombed 1944

Ploesti oil refineries attacked by B-24 on low level August 1, 1943

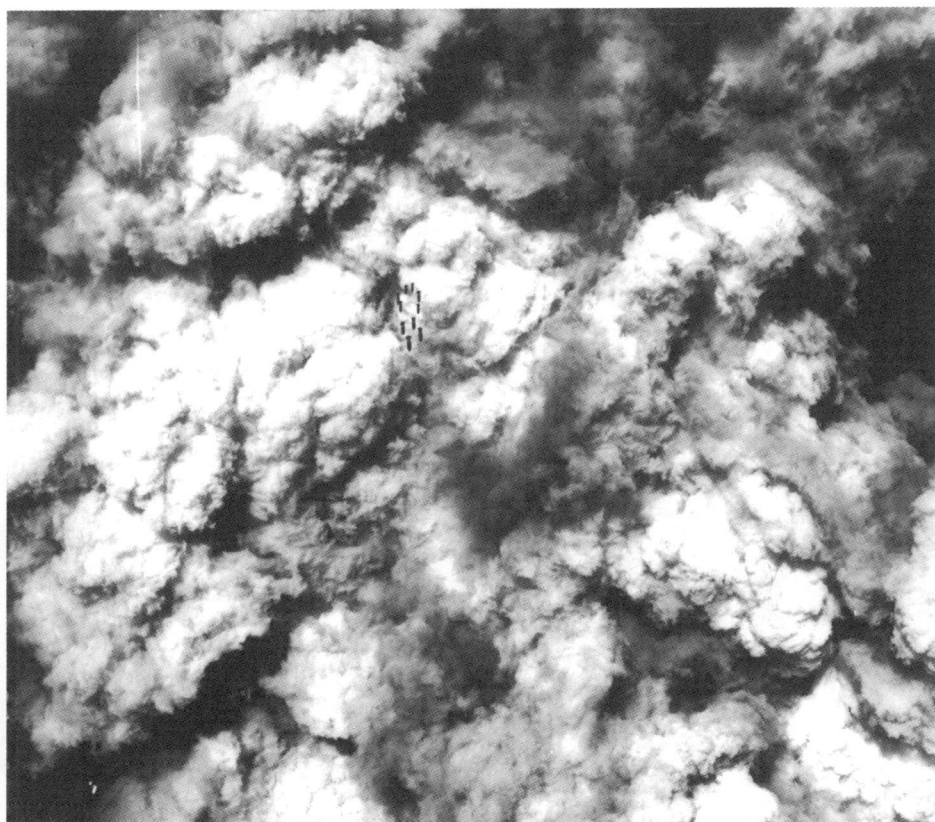
Ploesti being bombed through smoke screen June 1944

Romanian radar ground defense

Ploesti bombing - May 5, 1944 brick factory

Ploesti bombing - May 5, 1944 officers quarters

Fallen B-24 Liberator - Romania

Fallen B-24 Liberator - Romania

Ploesti refinery - today

Romanian fighter aircraft - IAR81

Romanian anti-aircraft defense

Romanian anti-aircraft gunners grave

Index

(page numbers in boldface indicate short biographies)

lege 112; army nickname 10; enlistment 7; m. Rita Cahn 112; Public School 188 7
Yedlin, Nancy 12
Yedlin, Robert 7

Yedlin, Sybil 8, 179
Yuma Air Field 247

Zagreb, Yugoslavia 86, 108
Zartman, William 186